Behavioural Treatment
of
Obsessional States

Behavioural Treatment
of
Obsessional States

H. R. Beech and M. Vaughan

JOHN WILEY & SONS

Chichester · New York · Brisbane · Toronto

Library of Congress Cataloging in Publication Data:

Beech, H. R.
    Behavioural treatment of obsessional states.

    Includes indexes.
    1. Obsessive–compulsive neurosis. 2. Behavior
therapy. I. Vaughan, Margaret, joint author.
II. Title.
RC533.B42   616.8'522'06   78-4552

ISBN 0 471 99646 7

Photosetting by Thomson Press (India) Ltd., New Delhi,
and printed in Great Britain by the Pitman Press Ltd., Bath

Contents

Preface

At worst, the rituals and ruminative thoughts of obsessional patients may be almost completely incapacitating, so that the patient is dependent on others to help him in every aspect of his everyday life. It is not surprising, therefore, that these abnormalities have become the central targets of treatment, the elimination of which has become the yardstick of therapeutic success. But, until quite recently, attempts at treatment have achieved little consistent progress, although reports of behavioural modification in the late 1960s and early 1970s seemed to hold considerable promise and, understandably, were enthusiastically received. Such early accounts have been succeeded by numerous case studies and, less frequently, by controlled treatment trials.

Our aim has been to draw together the published reports of behavioural treatment methods and their theoretical bases, in order to provide a comprehensive reference work which will enable the clinician to rationalize the choice of technique to be used. In doing so we have been critical in our evaluation of many of the papers and, indeed, have sometimes rejected the conclusions which authors have drawn.

Overall, we have concluded that the outcome of behaviour modification in obsessional states has not proved to be as successful as is sometimes claimed in experimental reports and review articles. Undoubtedly, substantial improvement in overt rituals has been shown to occur, but this outcome is by no means certain. Even where there is a reduction in the frequency of major rituals, considerable impairment in other areas of functioning may remain.

We have tried to describe the range of dysfunctions commonly found in these conditions and to indicate how they may best be dealt with in making the point that full treatment of obsessive–compulsive disorders may involve much more than the modification of the rituals or thoughts which have been the focus of behavioural strategies.

In giving emphasis to the need for caution we are not, of course, arguing against the use of behavioural techniques. On the contrary, apotrepic therapy (Meyer, Levy, and Schnurer, 1974) and the closely related combination of modelling and flooding procedures seem to show promise, and are probably the treatments of choice for compulsive rituals. Other techniques, too, seem to be beneficial in some cases and deserve the attention of therapists.

The fact that our conclusion has not been couched in more enthusiastic terms is largely due to the absence of definitive research into both empirical treatment effects and the mechanisms of obsessional disorder. A good deal more careful and systematic work is needed and it is hoped that the encouraging results described in some studies will inspire investigations into both these areas.

December 1977   H. R. Beech
                                                       M. Vaughan

1

Introduction

Our main purpose in compiling this book is that of providing a critical evaluation and overview of the behavioural approach to the treatment of obsessional patients. In part, we are motivated to perform this exercise since, perhaps more than in any other area of treatment, claims have been made for the success of behaviour modification which require detailed and close scrutiny. Another reason for our interest, however, is that our own clinical experience of employing these methods suggests that the problems of treatment in cases of this kind can best be appreciated by a careful, cross-sectional and critical appraisal of relevant experimental work. We should make clear, of course, that our experience of applying behaviour modification to obsessionals has produced a mixed outcome, typical of the substance of published reports; sometimes the results have seemed to be outstandingly good, with patients quickly—perhaps suspiciously so in some cases—being restored to reasonably normal functioning. On other occasions, for reasons which remain unclear, the result has been far from successful, or any benefit conferred has been so speedily lost that the endeavour has been discouraging to both therapist and patient.

However, we would also contend that some bias might exist in published accounts which tend to indicate that favourable and positive outcomes are more, rather than less, typical. Perhaps it is inevitable that the therapist, flushed with success in dealing with his clients, should hasten to inform professional colleagues of such events, rather than to describe any of his *failures* to help. Certainly, there is a receptive and eager readership who are waiting for information on what to do, rather than what is of little value, since the latter is a generally an already familiar experience.

Nevertheless, our own practice of behaviour modification with obsessional patients tends us towards regarding these methods as probably worthwhile and, not infrequently, capable of producing changes which have not come about by other means. We were curious to discover how far this clinical impression could be justified by the published evidence.

1

Naturally, our own research on the mechanisms of obsessional states has had a formative influence upon the explanations we are prepared to advance to account for the vagaries of outcome following behavioural treatment. It seems abundantly clear to us, and we feel that it is now becoming clearer to even those most committed to the orthodoxy of the behavioural position, that these mechanisms must be complex, and that the importance of mood state is apparent (Walker and Beech, 1969; Milner, Walker, and Beech, 1971; Beech, 1971; Beech and Perigault, 1974; Beech and Liddell, 1974).

It is not necessary to present the detailed arguments here, but perhaps the outline of the observations which require explanation and of the kind of model which embraces them, serves a useful purpose.

It is common, among behaviourally oriented therapists, to argue (or simply to adopt the unquestioning assumption) that the maladaptive responses have their origin in traumatic events. Hence, when patients report symptoms and offer themselves for treatment, inquiry 'naturally' focuses upon those events which occurred at about the time the patient identified alterations in behaviour. Thus, it is not difficult for both therapist and patient to attribute environmental influences as causes of change, and often it seems little further inquiry is made. Our own clinical experience, as well as research evidence (Beech and Liddell, 1974; Beech and Perigault, 1974) suggests strongly that it is extremely difficult, without being superficial, to fit this simplistic 'cause and effect' model to the history of the obsessional. Indeed, we would argue that something rather more sophisticated is needed in explaining the appearance of all phobic behaviours, and it is not at all adequate to have recourse to 'modelling' as the key to explaining such behaviours among individuals for whom life's traumas have no obvious connection with the appearance of symptoms.

The question of how and why obsessional symptoms appear remains unanswered; we can only know that it is not likely to be as a result of simple conditioning operations of the kind exemplified in experimental neurosis studies.

We would need to explain, too, the discrepancies between normal subjects and clinical groups in reported trauma (Beech and Liddell, 1974). Apparently obsessionals, mixed neurotics and normals cannot be differentiated in terms of the number of trauma which can be recalled, although clinical groups (especially obsessionals) can recall worrying more when such trauma *did* occur in their lives. Indeed, particularly in respect of punishments and serious disagreements of a painful kind, the clinical groups have significantly fewer incidents to report than have normals, although again the former groups attached greater importance to such events when they did arise.

All this strongly suggests that there is a 'naturally' heightened sensitivity in the clinical groups, and that this extends to their earliest recalled history. Furthermore, this tendency may well occasion avoidance behaviour in a way which minimizes life's unpleasant events. No doubt this mechanism is being tapped in Liddell's experimental observation (Beech and Liddell, 1974; Liddell, 1976) that while obsessionals are not differentiated from others in terms of basal GSR responsivity, they show a significantly raised tendency to reaction when threatened with noxious stimulation.

Certainly the evidence from various experiments (e.g. Walker, 1967; Perigavlt, 1974) suggests that the search for explanatory mechanisms in the trauma themselves may well be misleading. Indeed, it is reasonably obvious that the rather narrow range of environmental stimuli identified by the obsessional (as well as other groups, such as agoraphobics) is hardly consistent with strictly available conditioning opportunities provided by the natural world. Hence, Beech and co-workers have experimented with alternative formulations which basically argue that it is the individual's internal state which determines the reaction to environmental events, and that the primary mechanism in both phobic and obsessional patients is a spontaneously generated state of readiness to respond defensively (Asso and Beech, 1975; Vila and Beech, 1977, 1978). This is not to deny, of course, evidence which shows that the manipulation of the environment may occasion permanent or semi-permanent avoidance reactions and other maladaptive behaviours. We would argue, however, that the noxious events in life are less well documented as causative agents in producing phobias and obsessions and, in any event, such trauma are rarely related so specifically and in such appropriate temporal proximity to symptoms as the behavioural theory tends to demand. From our own viewpoint, there are conditions internal to the organism, generated spontaneously rather than necessarily prompted by noxious external stimulation, which activate defensive systems in a way which parallels reactions to noxious external stimulation. The effect is the same, whether external events or spontaneous internal changes are responsible—the organism has a readiness to respond defensively to relatively innocuous alterations to the environment, and is prompted to acquire habitual (conditioned) avoidance behaviours, and to show increased resistance to extinguishing such behaviours (Vila and Beech, 1977; 1978).

There is evidence, too, that such pathological states of the organism are reflected in mood (Walker, 1967; Walker & Beech, 1969; Beech & Liddell, 1974), although for various reasons one would expect the two to show less than perfect correlation.

We need to question, then, the special role of the organism's state, and that of the prevailing mood if we are to arrive at an adequate formulation of causation and treatment strategy. At the very least one might guess that obsessionals who show marked depressive features, often with considerable fluctuations, might profit from any medication which helps to control mood and thus allows 'habits' to be changed.

It is our impression, on the basis of clinical experience and research findings, that obsessionals showing marked mood impairment as well as extreme alterations in mood state, are less amenable to behavioural treatments. Behavioural treatments tend to neglect the role of mood, and if any attention is given to this variable it is only that accorded to a very secondary consideration.

Such a view is incompatible with the evidence, as we have shown in experiments conducted some years ago (Walker, 1967; Walker and Beech, 1969). These studies show unequivocally that mood is an important—even crucial—determinant of ritualistic behaviour, in respect to both its occurrence and duration.

This being so, how is it possible for behaviour modification to produce the successful results frequently reported in the literature? To some extent we believe such claims, particularly those which have suggested that the rate of success is very high among obsessionals, have often been based upon individual patients who would not ordinarily be regarded as belonging to the diagnostic group in question, e.g. those patients exhibiting 'obsessional' behaviour in the sense simply that they engage repeatedly in fruitless or pointless activities. This matter is dealt with more fully in ensuing chapters.

There is, of course, a great deal of confusion concerning this diagnostic category and it is quite likely that the term applies (reasonably, in the present state of knowledge) to a very varied group of individuals, but who may have certain important features in common. The problems of diagnosis, as well as other related issues, are discussed in Chapter 2.

Returning to the question of the efficacy of behaviour modification, our opinion would be that, since obsessional patients often show considerable fluctuations in mood, it is not inconceivable that there may be a relationship between the value of such treatment and the prevailing mood condition. Our experience certainly leads us to propose that when mood can be controlled by medication, or when this variable 'naturally' returns to a more stable condition, behavioural intervention is not only easier but can be of very considerable value. Nonetheless, such measures may not and do not protect the individual patient from further alterations of internal state which produce renewed outbreaks of symptomatic expression. There is no doubt at all that relapses are very marked among patients belonging to this group, often with the old problems reappearing, but sometimes with new symptoms to take the place of the old.

As an aside, while such a situation is disturbing to the therapist there are therapeutic possibilities which present themselves in respect of mood-control that fall within the ambit of behavioural control. For example, we have for some time made clinical observations on the possibility of containing excrescences of adverse mood using a model deriving from somewhat antiquated notions that a pool of drive may be tapped in socially acceptable ways to produce improvements in state. Briefly, our argument is that there is a relationship between adverse mood and the general drive state characterizing the individual such that a lowering of the latter produces beneficial effects upon the former. In our clinical investigations, we have tried to produce such effects by increasing the frequency of sexual contact, and we believe that this has had the predicted outcome. There is no reason why drive state should not be manipulated in ways other than that which we have chosen, and in any event it may be that the state of sexual tension is not especially easy to deal with in patients who, not infrequently, have problems in sexual functioning.

There is yet another reason why confidence in a behaviour modification approach to obsessional patients may be questioned. We have already indicated that there is some difficulty in identifying critical trauma related to symptom onset and, more often than not, the situation depicted by careful interrogation suggests that patients arrive at the formulation of their feeling state through some cognitive act. It is as if the obsessional, experiencing a state of intense distress, searches for an explanation and attributes these feelings to some probably innocent external cue. There is, in short, no very obvious connection between some identifiable external cause and the discomfort which ensues, but rather, the reverse of this situation.

It remains open to doubt whether this mechanism provides the same kind of practical implications as the model which argues for trauma–anxiety–unadaptive behaviour. In the sense that the adverse feeling is generated by internal, rather than external prompts, the two possibilities are clearly different. Furthermore, to the extent that a continued state of internally generated disturbance of mood may exist, detecting such a state from the 'identified' external cue may not take one very far therapeutically, since the patient will remain disturbed. It is obvious that a cognitive-attribution model at least has the advantage here in explaining the circumscribed nature of obsessional complaints, for example, of dangerous and contaminating contacts, since the vagaries of environmental trauma as causes would undoubtedly have led to a greater variety of cues to anxiety than is in fact found. It is, in short, easier to arrive at a cognitive formulation of 'reasonable' sources of concern than to experience them as being actually afforded by life's circumstances.

Of course, it may be argued that more recent developments in behaviour modification deal with patterns of cognition, and that this helps one to avoid the earlier simplistic behavioural models and their emphasis upon external events. The evidence to be reported in a later section does not encourage us to think that the problem has been resolved in this way.

There are, in addition, the general objections to the adequacy of the behavioural approach of both a theoretical and empirical kind which, it must be conceded, are often cogent and should give cause for concern to the proponents of these treatments. In later chapters we examine some of these objections in reviewing the literature dealing with obsessional states.

Another way of assessing the potential of the behavioural approach to the treatment of obsessionals is to look at factors associated with favourable prognosis. Very little, however, is known about such indices, and we are generally left with only the rather gloomy forecasts made in psychiatric textbooks.

Nevertheless, some evidence of outcome is available, and it is certainly not always that one must expect failure or early relapse. For our part, we have formed clinical impressions that certain factors according to their presence or absence, affect prognosis. Mention has already been made of mood, and we feel confident that the presence of severe mood impairment and substantial fluctuations of mood state point to a poor outcome. No doubt this factor is related to that of the severity of impairment caused by the disorder, either in terms of intensity or of the number of aspects of functioning affected. It is usual to find that these two variables are related.

In our view yet another factor related to outcome is the position which the patient may occupy in relation to psychotic and neurotic types of disturbance.

There is little doubt that some obsessionals are difficult to distinguish from common and mildly disturbed phobics, while others appear to have many features of the psychotic patient. The identification of such features, we feel, is of value in making treatment decisions, but again the point suggests a possible fundamental lack of homogeneity in the group labelled 'obsessional'. It is likely that the presence of a 'psychotic' element is in some ways related to yet another feature which we have noted clinically to be associated with poor prognosis—namely, the strength of 'belief' in the nature of the pathological ideas supporting the symptoms. In our experience many obsessional patients 'know' perfectly well, for example, that their notions of contamination cannot accord with reality, although they may at first appear to be claiming so. On careful probing it will be very clear that these patients are able to concede that the avoidance of certain objects takes place *as if* they were contaminated—the patient acknowledging that while the idea is false he cannot help behaving as if it were true. Such patients are very different in type (and in terms of progress, we believe) from those who are persuaded as to the fundamental validity of ideas which contradict ordinary logic.

Finally, we should mention our interest in personality in the context of determining both outcome of treatment and prognosis. Further mention will be made of this factor in Chapter 2, but here one can say that where these aspects of personality labelled 'obsessional' are markedly present, the outlook generally is less favourable. Especially prominent in our clinical experience, is the oppositional tendency which all therapists can recognize, since it not only affects general motivation for treatment, but also makes it very difficult to secure the patient's co-operation in carrying out certain prescribed exercises. Often allied to this is that aspect of personality which is perhaps best described in homely terms as 'gloomy pessimism', and which effectively interferes with the patient's appreciation and enjoyment of any progress made. In short, those patients showing certain obsessional personality characteristics in addition to their obsessional behaviours, are less amenable to help and more likely to carry an unfavourable prognosis, in our opinion.

Our view, then, is that there are a number of important considerations that would affect and limit the value of a behavioural approach to the treatment of obsessionals. Certainly our experience and research evidence would urge caution in advancing claims as to the efficacy of these techniques, yet the published evidence is often persuasively urging us to accept the opposite conclusion. Naturally, in spite of all the objections raised, both of a theoretical and technical kind, it may still be that the evidence adduced in support of behavioural treatments is incontrovertible. It is our purpose in the following chapters to evaluate critically the published evidence in an attempt to provide greater certainty in relation to the application of such methods to a particular patient population.

2

Obsessive–Compulsive Disorder

Although Esquirol is credited with providing the first case report of obsession, the use of the term is generally attributed to Morel (1866). Westphal (1878) was an early contributor to the description of the condition, stressing the importance of ideas which obtrude into consciousness in spite of efforts to resist them, and which are perceived by the patient to be abnormal. Nevertheless, it was Janet (1903) who provided the first comprehensive description of the syndrome which comprised a number of features thought to be diagnostic of the condition.

Lewis (1936, 1957), however, insisted that the crucial feature enabling the diagnosis to be made was that the patient should be found to struggle against the obsession, although in the experience of the authors this is far from true of many patients so labelled.

Perhaps a key problem in diagnosing the disorder is bound up with the observation that obsessional behaviour can be observed in a number of different diagnostic states, including both so-called functional as well as organic conditions. This being so we tend to find that the diagnosis is often made by exclusion of other disorders or the secondary status of obsessional symptoms rather than by the clear-cut appearance of an obsessional syndrome and, in particular, the presence of a subjectively experienced compulsion overriding an internal resistance (Mayer-Gross, Slater and Roth, 1955). We are left, therefore, with only the provisional heuristic value of the label 'obsessional', and this is important to keep in mind when we consider the studies reporting upon treatment methods.

INCIDENCE AND PREVALENCE

The diagnosis of obsessional neurosis is made relatively infrequently, the incidence in psychiatric patient populations being reported as between 0.1 and 4 per cent. In terms of sheer patient numbers, therefore, this form of disturbance is a relatively minor one, although it is generally thought that the actual figure for

7

the population at large may be greater, since the obsessional is considered to be secretive about his or her problem.

GENETIC CONTRIBUTION

The difficulties usually encountered in establishing genetic influences in psychological disorder tend to increase in an area which generates only limited numbers of sufferers. Twin studies are clearly affected by the small numbers involved and, in any event, are generally insufficiently well documented to inspire confidence. However, as Black (1974) has pointed out, if concordance were entirely random the existence of a co-twin with obsessional disorder would be an extremely unlikely event indeed, and since twenty such Caucasian pairs have been reported in the postwar years, we might suppose that a genetic contribution is possible.

Respecting the incidence of obsessional disorder among first-degree and other relatives of patients diagnosed as suffering from the complaint, one might reasonably conclude that the evidence is consistent with a genetic influence at work (Brown, 1942; Kringlen, 1965; Greer and Cawley, 1966), although other groups of psychiatric patients can also be said to show a similar influence. However, the data are far from convincing on this point and perhaps, at best, tend to suggest an inherited tendency toward emotional instability which may take different forms in related individuals.

PERSONALITY AND SYMPTOMS

There is no doubt that there is a widespread belief in a strong relationship existing between personality and symptoms among those diagnosed as 'obsessional'. Indeed, so strong is this belief that there may well be a tendency to make the diagnosis in the light of premorbid personality traits. It is held, for example, that such traits include exaggerated attitudes towards cleanliness, conscientiousness, orderliness, obstinacy, and doubting (see, for example, Lewis and Mapother, 1941). Black (1974), in reviewing reports from a number of different sources, concludes that these purport to show such a relationship in all but 29 per cent of the 451 patients included. To set against this, however, are those findings which suggest that the incidence of premorbid obsessional personality traits occurs quite frequently in the context of different symptom patterns (Kringlen, 1965), and also that marked 'obsessional' traits may be found in persons who never formally become disturbed in any way.

A very real problem here, of course, is the generally marked absence of any reliable data respecting previous personality, the assessment of which is usually made on the basis of self-report by patients already suffering from the disorder. Some degree of objectivity has been introduced by psychometric studies and the use of statistical techniques, and by these means evidence has been gathered respecting the existence of obsessional symptoms (those things which are distressful to the individual) and the obsessional traits. Both O'Connor (1953) and Lorr, Rubinstein, and Jenkins (1953) have adduced evidence from factorial data for the grouping of obsessional symptoms, while Lorr and Rubinstein (1956) identified a bipolar factor as representing a personality characteristic labelled 'obsessive conscientiousness'. In the latter study an 'obsessive–compulsive reaction' factor was also identified, and the study as a whole lends weight to the notion that the traits and symptoms often associated with obsessionality are to some extent independent. Data analysed by Sandler and Hazari (1960) also resulted in the identification of two independent factors, one being 'obsessional character traits' and the other 'obsessional symptoms'. The former appeared to describe a punctual, meticulous, orderly individual, while the latter described unwelcome thoughts and impulses, and included rituals and doubting.

Cooper (1970) has also provided evidence from the analysis of the Leyton Obsessional Inventory which supports the notion of independence of obsessional symptoms and traits.

COURSE OF DISTURBANCE

There are many who would subscribe to the view that the obsessional state begins with the recognizable clinical symptoms, and would point to the certainty with which patients often refer to the first occasion on which the abnormal idea or activity was experienced. This is particularly the view associated with a behavioural approach, and tends to give emphasis to specific environmental events as 'causes'. We would argue, however, that it is frequently the case that the relevant interrogation stops at a point indicated by the patient as marking the beginning of abnormality, and a false impression is gained of the historical pattern of disturbed behaviour. Indeed, Beech and Liddell (1974) have argued that there is evidence of a predisposition to avoid life's problems—or, at least, to endeavour to do so—which is a lifelong characteristic of both the obsessional and phobic patient. Furthermore, there is evidence which suggests that a relationship may exist between the state of the organism and symptom acquisition (see, for example, Asso and Beech, 1975; Vila and Beech, 1977, 1978) and that a simplistic view of environmental causation is untenable.

It has been frequently found, on the other hand, that alterations in the physical state of the patient, or in his environment, are associated with what is called the 'onset of illness' (Greer and Cawley, 1966; Lo, 1967; Ingram, 1961; Rudin, 1953; Pollitt, 1957; Kringlen, 1965). There is no necessary contradiction between such reports and the view holding that the patient has long been vulnerable to react to life events; our argument is that the condition of the organism reaches a critical state, perhaps on a number of occasions, and is capable of forming quite fortuitous associations with environmental cues at these times. More probable, as we have argued (Beech, 1971; Beech and Perigault, 1974; Asso and Beech, 1975; Vila and Beech, 1977, 1978) is that noxious environmental events—even mildly so—can effectively alter the organism's balance so that a point of critical vulnerability is reached, at which the patient must draw upon past experience as a means of explaining the distress experienced, perhaps incorporating some contemporary critical environmental event. Obviously some mechanism must be postulated which explains the common concerns of obsessional patients, notably with contamination and harm, and the mobilization of defensive reactions at the critical period is certainly often documented in cases which we have examined.

Recently, for example, we have been able to observe a patient whose rituals have only very recently begun, and here an environmental circumstance of concern to her appeared to be superimposed upon an existing state of high arousal. In this case the girl's obsession is associated with ideas of cleanliness which she has held for many years, but the environmental event appeared to produce a major incrementation of emotional arousal leading to a sudden increase in her concern about personal hygiene, and rituals related to this, and incorporating cues available at that time.

In another similar case we have noted the relationship between the 'onset' of formal symptoms of obsessionality and the days immediately prior to menstruation (see Vila and Beech, 1977, 1978), and it is noteworthy that, for this patient, the premenstrual days are still associated with increases in morbid preoccupations and activity.

In formal terms, however, it is generally reported that the first symptoms appear, on average, in the early twenties (Lo, 1967; Ingram, 1961; Pollitt, 1957), although it is interesting to note that a peak of incidence is reported to occur in the early 'teens. Such observations may suggest a relationship with life events which may occur in what is often regarded as a critical period, although it seems equally possible that alterations in physiological states may be responsible. However, as we have just indicated, the onset of formal symptoms may only reflect an association with immediately precipitating factors, and probably have little to do with fundamental causation.

The picture is, however, far from clear, and the differences between published clinical accounts concerning course of illness and mode of onset do little to help. Some authors suggest that the onset is acute in some cases and insidious in others, while other investigators report minor episodes of abnormality occurring before the main onset. Ingram (1961) has suggested that the differences reported reflect four main patterns of development: constant with progressive worsening, constant and static, fluctuating but never symptom-free, and phasic with remissions. Our experience clinically would be consistent with the various possibilities, but we would tend to emphasise the impression that there is, in all cases, a long standing precursory condition which has marked the individual as vulnerable.

PROGNOSIS

So far as the outlook for such patients is concerned most authorities take the view that the condition is both serious in nature and protracted. Kringlen (1965) reported that the illness may remain unchanged, show a gradual improvement, show fluctuations, or may simply become gradually worse. There is, so far as we know, no means by which these varying outcomes can be predicted, but the probability, judging from Kringlen's data, is that for the majority of patients the prognosis is rather poor.

However, it has been argued that certain factors have a favourable influence on the course of the illness. Muller (1953), for example, considered that a normal premorbid personality was advantageous, although Pollitt (1957) has reported that premorbid obsessional traits have a favourable effect. Similarly, while Pollitt (1969) thought an episodic disorder carried a better prognosis, no such association was found by Ingram (1961). It is less surprising, perhaps, to find that the duration of illness prior to treatment has been found more reliably to relate to prognosis, most investigators reporting that the longer the symptoms have gone on, the poorer the outcome. The type of symptoms found in the context of those which are primarily obsessional in character, have sometimes been thought to relate to prognosis, although evidence has been inconsistent on this point, and the same can be said respecting the presence of clear precipitating factors in the clinical onset of the condition, as well as evidence relating to age of onset. In our clinical experience the factors associated with prognosis confirm some of the points raised, but we would particularly stress the doubtful outcome associated with patients in whom the pathological ideas have apparently become fixed beliefs on a delusional scale. Reference has been made to these factors in Chapter 1.

With reference to such delusional ideas, Lewis (1936) has observed that one might express surprise that so few obsessionals succumb to the struggle against repugnant thoughts which are thrust upon them (Gittleson (1966) reported just over 5 per cent of obsessionals as showing 'delusional transition'). However, the issue is very obviously clouded by the problems of diagnosis, and it would be hazardous to assume that there are genuine 'transitional' cases, since these could possibly have been misdiagnosed in the first place. Nonetheless, the incidence of schizophrenia among 'obsessionals' has been noted to be as high as 12 per cent (see Black, 1974).

A similar problem arises in respect of depression which has been so frequently noted in obsessional patients, namely, that of deciding what diagnostic label best applies, with other symptoms being seen as the features of the illness. Certainly depression and obsessional symptoms frequently appear in combination, and depression is more common in relatives of obsessional patients than in the general population. Sakai (1967), for example, reported that 10.8 per cent of a sample of obsessionals had at least one member of the family who was affected by depression, while Gittleson (1966) found that 13 per cent of individuals suffering from a depressive illness had shown clear obsessions before the onset of the depression. Almost one-third of Gittleson's sample had obsessional symptoms as a feature of their depressive illness.

However, Vaughan (1976) has pointed out that in her study obsessions tended to occur almost exclusively in the context of depression marked by agitation, rapid mood changes and, in some cases, by anxiety. Very rarely was retardation found to be a feature of depression in these patients. It is important, then, to qualify the general impression of the relationship by pointing out that only certain aspects of depression are to be found in obsessional patients.

Finally, Walker and Beech (1969) and Beech (1974) have pointed to another important matter relating to mood in obsessional states. This refers to the significance of alterations in mood, particularly depression, in determining ritualistic behaviour, including ruminations. This evidence leaves little room for doubt that the connection between environmental events (such as coming into contact with 'contamination') and pathological behaviour (rituals, ruminations) is profoundly affected by the mood state of the patient. As Beech has indicated, the contaminating event may be ignored, merely noted by the patient, immediately acted upon, deferred, or even *sought out* by the patient; mood, whether adverse or good, seems to have an important part to play in deciding which of these alternatives is adopted.

SUMMARY

Obsessional states are relatively uncommon, although it is probably correct to say that the incidence cannot be adequately estimated from available data, which may well be a significant underestimate of the true figures.

While having certain very obvious features which are easily recognized, and about which there is good agreement, problems of diagnosis arise in mixed conditions. In particular, obsessional features are common in depression, and it is argued that a significant number of obsessionals develop schizophrenia.

The relationship between obsessional symptoms and obsessional personality is not fully understood, but evidence from psychometric studies indicates that symptoms and traits are to a large extent independent. It is likely that formal onset of the illness allows an opportunity for the magnification of premorbid personality characteristics, of whatever kind.

Confusion exists respecting the course which the disturbance pursues. While the course would appear to be different in different individuals, there is at least consensus in that symptom onset usually refers only to formal identification of the disorder. Evidence is generally in favour of the view that there is a precursory period which may well point to a particular vulnerability to breakdown. Prognostic factors are not reliably documented. Clearly the outcome is very different for different individuals, but agreement among authorities about these matters is not substantial save in respect that a lengthy illness before treatment and psychotic features are associated with poor prognosis.

Finally, as complicating features, depression and delusional elements are probably most important. Where the former is concerned it is worthy of note that only certain depressive features appear to be present in obsessionals, and that mood state is an important determinant of ritualistic behaviour and thought.

3

Methods of Assessment

By virtue of their complexity and pervasiveness, a full account of an obsessional patient's symptoms can rarely be obtained by interview alone. Usually, information and hypotheses arising from the interview have to be supplemented by data from formal assessment methods including single subject experiments. The clarification of interactions between variables may be just as important as quantification of relevant variables on their own. When assessment occurs in the context of behaviour modification, most, but not necessarily all, the characteristic features of the disorder have to be taken into consideration. Those which should be assessed routinely are discussed below. The two main areas which may be omitted are cognitive style (see review by Fransella, 1974) and obsessional traits. The lack of concern for traits may seem surprising, but stems from the belief that they are enduring features of personality and thus would not be expected to be altered as a result of treatment. Studies involving some evaluation of traits have tended to confirm this prediction (such as Hodgson, Rachman, and Marks, 1972). The published questionnaire measures of obsessional traits have been discussed by Slade (1974). Neither cognitive style nor traits will be considered further in the present review.

There appear to be two main reasons for conducting a full assessment of an obsessional patient's symptomatology. First, as already mentioned, it is usually necessary to supplement interview material with formal assessment in order to gain a full and accurate account of the maladaptive behaviour and emotions. Following this, the patient's behaviour may be assessed continuously or at regular intervals, as a means of monitoring change during and after treatment. The rationales involved in initial assessment and subsequent monitoring differ in several respects and so will be considered separately. In contrast, there is a great deal of overlap between the assessment measures which are employed in the two, making separate accounts of these redundant. Therefore, general description of both forms of assessment procedure will be given before the assessment tools used in them are discussed.

INITIAL ASSESSMENT

The main aim of the initial assessment is to arrive at a full description of all the salient features of the patient's symptomatology. The view of obsessive–compulsive disorders, given in the foregoing chapters, indicates that there are a number of aspects of the disorder which must be taken into account if the assessment of the problem is to be complete. They may be noted as follows.

1. The number and nature of different obsessions and rituals

It is rare to discover a patient with a mono-symptomatic complaint. Usually patients will be found to have several fears and preoccupations each with associated avoidance and ritualistic responses. Often it will be possible to rank order the fears according to the distress which they cause the patient and the interference in his life; but generally, all will have to be treated at one time or another as there seems to be a tendency for initially subordinate fears to become more prominent as other, more conspicuous ones are eliminated during treatment. In view of this, the remaining aspects of the disorder will have to be defined for each fear individually.

2. The environmental eliciting stimuli

In virtually all cases, the fear will have become associated with environmental stimuli. For example, a patient with a fear of dog's dirt is likely to become apprehensive about parks, the underside of his shoes and gutters. When arranged in order as a hierarchy, these stimuli form an important part of several behavioural treatments (e.g. flooding, systematic desensitization).

3. The emotional response to contact with eliciting stimuli

Patients experience some degree of distress, often characterized by anxiety, depression and hostility on contact with the feared stimuli (Walker and Beech, 1969).

4. Avoidance of eliciting stimuli

5. The frequency and duration of rituals

6. The emotional response associated with the rituals

Execution of the ritual may be accompanied by feelings of anxiety, depression or hostility which change with the execution of the ritual, sometimes improving or alternatively becoming worse (Walker and Beech, 1969; Hodgson, Rachman, and Marks, 1972).

7. The frequency of thoughts associated with the fear

Patients who present with overt rituals as their main symptom are often found to engage in worry concerning their fears almost to the point of rumination. Thus a patient who has a fear of contamination accompanied by washing rituals may spend a great deal of time worrying whether the hem of her skirt touched the toilet seat and, if it did, whether or not she has contaminated herself or her surroundings with it. Such thoughts have been neglected in discussions of obsessional behaviour, but it seems possible that they may play a role in generalization of avoidance and ritualistic responses and may also influence the outcomes of behavioural treatments which involve response prevention during which thought content is left uncontrolled.

8. Mood state

9. Moderating environmental cues

Walker and Beech (1969) observed that an obsessional patient's behaviour is not invariant, in that he does not always respond in the same way to supposedly ritual-evoking stimuli. A given stimulus may evoke rituals of varying length producing differing degrees of distress, and may even fail to elicit a response at all. It is possible that environmental stimuli may be responsible in part for these variations and eventually could be included in the patient's treatment programme.

10. Marital, family, social, and sexual problems

If present, any of these may interfere with rehabilitation.

This list of components of obsessive–compulsive behaviour has been phrased as if it were intended to refer to ritualistic behaviour only. In fact, it may be applied equally well to obsessional thoughts and ruminations. This is not to suggest that all such thoughts are rituals; it is merely that the analysis of the two problems proceeds in the same way.

Although it is improbable that all the necessary information about these aspects of functioning will be obtained from an interview, such a discussion is likely to provide the optimal introduction to the patient's complaints. In many cases the patient's history and presenting symptoms are so complex that he is unable to give a clear account of himself especially if he possesses the verbosity and preoccupation with irrelevant detail which seems to be common amongst obsessionals. Patients of this description have been know to request that the interviewer should ask direct questions and indicate when the required information has been obtained on the grounds that this makes it easier to answer relevantly. Certainly, interviews which are strictly controlled and involve a fairly high proportion of carefully worded closed–ended questions seem to be the easiest way of proceeding with this group.

The information derived from the initial interview may be supplemented by the results from one of the inventories which have been designed to provide information on the range and severity of obsessive–compulsive disorder (Leyton Obsessional Inventory amongst others—see below). From both sources combined, it should be possible to enumerate the nature and number of obsessive fears and rituals possessed, to gain some global estimate of the frequency and duration of the rituals (or obsessive thoughts) and to begin to explore the nature of coexisting marital, social or sexual problems. To some extent the information gained may be verified through interview with a close relative, although not all aspects of the patient's complaint may be apparent to an observer. A hierarchy of eliciting stimuli can be obtained through further discussion with the patient involving rank-ordering procedures such as the fear thermometer ratings described by Wolpe (1958). Apart from this it will probably be necessary to obtain a more exact estimate of the frequency and duration of the patient's rituals by monitoring his behaviour systematically over a number of days or weeks, usually relying on self-report, perhaps backed up by that of an observer, to furnish the data. It would be possible to undertake a more complete analysis of the patient's behaviour by asking him to record eliciting stimuli, feelings and so on as well as ritualistic behaviour, but this may impose excessive demands on his persistence and motivation. It will probably be more rewarding to conduct small-scale investigation experiments with him as a means of assessing these aspects of his functioning.

Walker and Beech's (1969) report of their investigation of a patient's excessive hair-combing provides an example of this kind of work. Their patient feared contamination, feeling that an important source of it was her hair. She had an initial wash and a rest before engaging in hair-combing for several hours and ending with a final wash of up to an hour and a half. The patient was asked to time her progress and to rate her mood state on specially designed scales on initiation or termination of each phase of the ritual. In a second investigation, the patient was instructed to stop her ritual at specified times after its initiation and to record her mood state. Together the results provided detailed information about changes in mood state during the ritual and the effects of terminating it prematurely. The findings were of assistance in understanding both the patient's specific problem and the nature of obsessive compulsive rituals in general. It is likely that investigations such as this will be needed in order to clarify the final details of the disorder for nearly every patient. Such individual-centred investigations, together with interviews and behaviour monitoring, should provide all the information that is required for a full assessment of the patient's symptoms.

ASSESSMENT TO MONITOR PROGRESS DURING TREATMENT

The aim of this form of assessment is to tap those aspects of obsessive –compulsive behaviour which would be likely to be modified during the course of behavioural treatment. In theory, all the features of the disorder covered in the initial assessment fall into that category, although the influence of behavioural intervention of some of them would be indirect. For example, mood and social or marital problems might be expected to improve as a result of a reduction in rituals rather than as a direct effect of behavioural treatment; similarly moderating environmental cues may become less relevant as distress associated with obsessional fears decreases. In practice, it is usual for a subset of the possible components of the disorder to be assessed, its choice reflecting both the prominence of the features in the patient's problem and the symptom focus of the treatment to be used.

The most comprehensive way to determine progress would be to monitor the patient continuously throughout treatment, using daily records provided by the patient, an observer or some automated device (Mills *et al.*, 1973). However, this is cumbersome and time consuming, especially when more than one patient is involved, as in group outcome research. Therefore, the use of daily monitoring appears to have been confined to individual case investigations. Gelfand and Hartmann (1975) provide an excellent chapter on data-collection procedures for this kind of work. They discuss not only optimal strategies of representative sampling but also statistical procedures for data obtained from a single subject which take account of the non-independence of successive observations. Although their book is concerned with child behaviour, the necessary translation to obsessive–compulsive disorders can be made without difficulty.

Work with more than one patient is usually directed toward the evaluation of the effects of treatment. Thus the minimum requirement of monitoring is taken to be assessment before and immediately after treatment with some follow-up appraisal being nearly as essential as the other two. Often additional assessments are performed at strategic points during treatment. Because of the complexity of the design resulting from group comparisons with repeated measures, parametric statistics often have to be adopted. This should place some limitation on the assessment measures which are used, as ideally parametric tests require at least an interval scale of measurement. However, there is no clear consensus of opinion about the robustness of parametric tests to violations of this rule. Contrasting views expressed by Siegel (1956), a proponent of non-parametric tests, and Kerlinger (1964) on the parametric side, give evidence of the differences which may exist but do little to indicate which option should be adopted. In practice parametric tests are used with ordinal data, more it is suspected because of difficulty in ensuring interval measurement and the absence of suitable non-parametric tests than through any firm theoretical considerations.

A further problem in statistical interpretation arises from the fact that the dependent variables, the scores on the measures, are not independent but tend rather to correlate with each other. Often this is disregarded and each dependent variable is analysed separately as if it had no relationship with the others being considered. The significant outcomes are then counted, and the more that there are the greater the therapeutic change is taken to have been. This approach may lead to spurious conclusions if the variables are highly intercorrelated, as the change observed in them may well be attributable to modification of one aspect of functioning that is common to them all. At least the pattern of outcome should be compared with the matrix of intercorrelations between measures to see if the two reflect comparable correspondence between variables. Perhaps it would be better to adopt a multivariate approach as advocated by Kaplan and Litrownik (1977) at the outset, although it is possible that this procedure may prove too complex for researchers without statistical sophistication to use to its best effect.

ASSESSMENT PROCEDURES

The main features of obsessive–compulsive behaviour which may be assessed have been listed already. With two exceptions, all seem to require some other means of assessment other than an interview only. One exception seems to be the determining of environmental-eliciting stimuli which appears to be based on the information gained at interview. It is unlikely that all eliciting stimuli are ever identified but the most important are likely to be mentioned. The other exception is the assessment of moderating environmental cues. This is rarely undertaken although most cues may come to light during extensive treatment. The remaining components of the disorder will be considered in turn with respect to the measures that have been developed to assess them.

1. Number and nature of different obsessions and rituals

The optimal assessment tool would seem to be a questionnaire or similar instrument which may be used to screen for all possible obsessional rituals, fears and thoughts, and which will provide some indication of their nature and frequency. The questionnaire data could be purely descriptive as there is no necessity that it should be used for diagnostic purposes.

(a) Leyton Obsessional Inventory (LOI)

The best-known questionnaire of this nature is the Leyton Obsessional Inventory (LOI) which was developed by Cooper (1970). In fact, the LOI was not designed primarily for work with obsessional patients, but rather as a means of identifying houseproud housewives in a study of mother–child interactions (Cooper and McNeill, 1968). Some of the criticisms to the inventory raised will be concerned solely with its use with obsessional patients; there is no intention to dispute its appropriateness for the purpose for which it was developed.

The LOI comprises 47 items concerning symptoms and 22 relating to traits, of which only the former need to be considered here. Cooper presented the inventory as a card sorting task but this may be adapted easily to a pencil and paper form (Allen and Tune, 1975). The original version may take up to two hours to administer to an obsessional patient. The fact that for all symptom questions the answer 'yes' is indicative of pathology may be a disadvantage because of the possibility of an acquiescent response set. Perhaps the risk of this might not be great with obsessions who value correctness and precision, but nevertheless its influence on patients' scores needs to be investigated.

The symptoms questions cover ten main areas of obsessional functioning and on the whole seem to provide a fairly comprehensive spectrum of common symptomatology. However, there appear to be two major omissions. Firstly,

Cooper (1970) deliberately did not include questions concerning extremely unpleasant or abhorrent thoughts. He did this because he wished to avoid jeopardizing the co-operation of his normal housewives. Although appropriate for his own research, this decision limited the utility of the LOI for use with clinical groups. The second omission may well have arisen from the same sort of consideration. Although there are brief references in several items to personal cleanliness, there is no direct mention of hand-washing, either normal or excessive. The nearest approach to this question is an item referring to fussiness about keeping the hands clean. This is no way reflects the nature of an obsessional's complaint. Thus with both grossly unpleasant thoughts and washing omitted, the picture of obsessional disorder portrayed by the LOI remains incomplete.

The LOI provides details of two other aspects of obsessional functioning which may enhance the overall description. Cooper devised measures of resistance, the degree to which the subject resists performance of the obsessional activity and interference, the extent to which it interferes with her everyday life. All items depicting behaviours or beliefs which the subject indicates that he possesses and which cause interference or are subject to resistance, are presented to her a second time. Each is rated in terms of resistance and interference on four point scales (that for resistance has five categories but two are given equal weight). The totals of the relevant ratings over items constitute resistance and interference scores. One objection to this procedure is that the influence of the rank of the ratings is confounded with the number of items involved in forming the total score. Thus a patient with low resistance ratings on many items may obtain the same score as one with high ratings on a few. This makes interpretation of the total interference and resistance scores extremely difficult; but the problem may be avoided if the totals are abandoned and the ratings of individual items are examined on their own merit.

The reliability of the scale with patients does not seem to have been established, but Cooper (1970) reported some confirmatory evidence arising from Kendell and Discipio's (1970) study of depressed patients with obsessions, before and after recovery, and a small amount of data of his own. The test–retest scores of twenty of Kendell and Discipio's patients, chosen at random from their group of 60, were combined with equivalent results from ten subjects of Cooper's (details not given). The product moment correlation coefficient for the symptom score was 0.87 and for the trait score, 0.91. Although this result is encouraging, a more thorough reliability study needs to be conducted if the LOI is to be taken into routine use.

The validation of the LOI as a screening instrument has not been undertaken. There has been no attempt to establish the correspondence of symptoms acknowledged on the questionnaire and those detected through alternative means of assessment, especially interviews. Nevertheless, Cooper (1970) did demonstrate that obsessional patients, houseproud housewives and normal women differed from each other in terms of symptom, trait, resistance and interference scores, in the predicted directions. At least the LOI seems to be sensitive to large differences in the possession of obsessional complaints. An alternative form of validation lies in the observation that, as might be expected, LOI symptom scores change after behavioural intervention (Hodgson, Rachman, and Marks, 1972). The fact that the symptom scores, and sometimes those for interference and resistance also, do show a decrement following treatment supports the idea and the LOI may be a viable research tool.

(b) Lynfield Obsessional/Compulsive questionnaires

Allen and Tune (1975) have attempted to overcome some of the disadvantages of administration of the card form of the LOI and to rectify its omissions in the development of their shorter Lynfield Obsessional/Compulsive questionnaires. The selection of items for these questionnaires was based on the results of complex principal components' analyses of LOI data performed by Cooper and Kelleher (1973). In this, the scores from all Cooper's (1970) original groups, except the obsessional patients, were combined with those from samples of Irish and English orthopaedic patients obtained by Kelleher (1972). Four separate principal components' analyses were conducted on different subsets of the total group, i.e. Irish (sexes combined), English (sexes combined), men (both nationalities) and women (both nationalities). The results of the analyses were inspected for common components. Occurrence of the same component in most or all analyses was taken as an indication of the generality of the behaviour groupings which were depicted. To some extent this seems to be an erroneous interpretation of the results as the four analyses were not independent, there being considerable overlap between the subjects involved in each; for example, English women would be common to both English and women analyses. Thus some degree of similarity between outcomes might be expected purely on the grounds of the common subject pool.

Nevertheless, Cooper and Kelleher found three components which were identifiable in all four analyses, labelling them 'clean and tidy', 'incompleteness' and 'checking'. These components were defined to a great extent by four, three and four questions respectively.

It was the items from these three components which formed the bases of Allen and Tune's (1975) Lynfield questionnaires. Allen and Tune found that the results from the eleven cardinal questions correlated highly with the score from the entire LOI, indicating that they were tapping the same sort of function as the complete scale. Further items were added to the eleven in order to widen the range of possible responses and to increase the change in score following treatment. The resulting scale consists of twenty items concerned with Cooper and Kelleher's three components and a fourth, previously neglected area—ruminations.

The items are presented as a paper and pencil questionnaire and the patient is given two forms. One requires him to rate each score on a five point scale with respect to resistance, and the other similarly with respect to interference. The patient's ratings are summed for each scale to give his interference and resistance scores. Being scored in this way, the Lynfield questionnaires do not seem to provide a total count of the number of aberrant behaviours which are acknowledged as being possessed by the patient; that is, there is no direct equivalent of the LOI symptom score. Such a total could be obtained from the scale if it is assumed that ratings of 'no, not at all' for both resistance and interference indicate that the patient does not possess the behaviour in question. This clearly is not the case as the patient may, say, be overconscientious or strict with himself without either resisting this or finding that it interferes with his life. It is another issue as to whether such innocuous behaviour should be counted as a symptom or a trait.

Allen and Tune provided no information on reliability, and concerning validity stated merely that the questionnaires correlate highly with the LOI. The size of the coefficients and the number of subjects involved in the correlation study were not given. They suggested that the scores on the Lynfield should be regarded as measures of obsessionals regardless of the main diagnosis of the patient being assessed. In fact the full interpretation of the Lynfield scores seems to depend in part on the acceptance of the rationale of the construction of the scale. Three-fifths of the items came from the main components identified by Cooper and Kelleher (1973) and because of this could be said to represent the most central features of the disorder. However, the interpretation of the components in this way has been questioned already. Further, the subjects for the principal components' analyses were all normal and were not suffering from an obsessive–compulsive disorder. It is not known whether the same components would have emerged if the data had been obtained from obsessional patients. Taking these problems of sampling and interpretation together, it is not clear whether the short Lynfield questionnaires cover all facets of behaviour which are most prominent in obsessive–compulsive disorders. This may be evaluated only through clinical usage and appropriate research.

(c) Hodgson and Rachman's Questionnaire

Hodgson and Rachman (1977) have developed a questionnaire which overcomes most of the shortcomings of the ones which have been mentioned already. From the outset they intended the questionnaire to be used with obsessional patients and used them as subjects in nearly all their preliminary work. A large pool of items was compiled based on clinical experience and published description. From this, 30 items were discovered which would discriminate between obsessionals with overt rituals and other equally introverted neurotics. These items were used to form the questionnaire. In selecting items which were not affirmed by other neurotic patients the range of obsessional behaviour sampled may have been restricted a little by the exclusion of acts shared by other groups. However, the same procedure ensured that the distinguishing features of obsessive–compulsive behaviour were identified. Acquiescent response set was avoided by arranging that half the items were keyed 'true' for pathology and the other half were keyed 'false'.

One hundred adult obsessionals, all with disorders involving rituals which were severe enough to require treatment, were given the questionnaire to fill in. Their responses were subjected to a principal components' analysis with oblique rotations. A five-component solution was apparent. Four of the components were identified as 'checking', 'cleaning', 'slowness' and 'doubting', but the fifth was ignored because it comprised only two items. Both were concerned with unwanted thoughts or ruminations. Inspection of the other questionnaire items reveals that they are the only ones with this content, none of the others having any direct bearing on thoughts. Therefore it seems quite possible that the component comprised only two items because these were the only representations of ruminations in the total pool. The weakness of the component may be merely a function of the paucity of the item sampling rather than indicating that ruminations are of minor importance. It may have been misleading to have ignored the component entirely.

Similarly the interpretation of two of the other components seems to be in some doubt. Although 'cleaning' and 'checking' may be identified easily from their high-loading items, 'slowness' and 'doubting' seem to be defined less readily. For 'slowness' the first and third strongest loading items are the two concerning ruminations (both loaded negatively). The fourth refers to routine and the seventh to counting. Only the second, fifth and sixth make any reference to slowness. It seems questionable whether the component should really be labelled on the basis of these three alone. The 'doubting' component, too, has only two high-loading items, the third and sixth) relating directly to doubt. The two highest items were concerned with honesty. These objections may be open to dispute as it is acknowledged that clinically slowness and doubting may present in the context of a number of correlated traits or behaviours, some of which may be represented in the respective components. However, the definition of the components does not seem to have been sufficiently clear-cut to justify labelling them 'doubting' and 'slowness' without any reference to other associated behaviours. Although this criticism does not modify the validity of the components it does influence their interpretation. This is particularly important if, as Hodgson and Rachman suggest, the scores on the high-loading items of each component are summed to give four subtotals, supposedly reflecting checking, cleaning, slowness and doubting. Until the nature of the last two components is firmly established, it may be safer to consider only the first two, or more conservatively to use only the total score for the questionnaire, described by Hodgson and Rachman as a 'total obsessionality' score.

Hodgson and Rachman established the test–retest reliability of the total score using 50 night-school attenders who were given the questionnaire on two occasions, one month apart. There was agreement in responses for the two occasions in 1341 out of the 1500 (30 items × 50 subjects) response pairs.

The validity of the total score has been evaluated through its correlation with the LOI symptom score. Hodgson and Rachman reported a significant correlation of 0.6 between these two measures for 30 obsessional patients. In fact this seems to be remarkably low considering that the two are ostensibly measuring much the same thing. The only moderate correlation could have arisen through differences in the scope of the questions, reflecting the requirements of the populations for which they were designed (i.e. Cooper's (1970) avoidance of upsetting symptoms). Alternatively, the size of the coefficient may have been determined by a restricted range of scores on both scales as, presumably, obsessional patients would all obtain high scores.

In addition, Hodgson and Rachman's questionnaire was validated by assessing the extent to which it was sensitive to changes in obsessive–compulsive behaviour after treatment. For 40 patients the difference between pretreatment and posttreatment scores was correlated both with patients' and two therapists' ratings of improvement. With pretreatment level eliminated as a covariate, the correlations ranged from 0.53 to 0.74, being lowest for the patient ratings. The therapists had been working daily with the patients during treatment and it was felt that their evaluations were reliable. Hodgson and Rachman conducted a further investigation of the validity of the subtest totals. They considered only 'checking' and 'cleaning' as they were unable to arrive at satisfactory retrospective ratings of 'slowness' and 'doubting'. They rated retrospectively 42 patients on 'checking' and 'cleaning' and found good agreement between these ratings and dichotomized questionnaire subtotal scores.

Although it is clear that more work needs to be done on Hodgson and Rachman's questionnaire, it already possesses several advantages. Not only was it designed specifically for obsessional patients but it is well constructed and quick and easy to administer. In addition, some attempts at establishing reliability and validity have been made. As long as some caution is exercized over the interpretation of the 'slowness' and 'doubting' subscales and the sad omission of ruminations is remembered, this questionnaire seems to possess more merits than the other scales of its kind. Certainly it is much more advanced in terms of construction and description than another recent innovation, a checklist, described by Philpott (1975).

2. Emotional responses associated with eliciting stimuli and rituals

The type of measure that has been used has depended upon whether the aim has been to examine the emotional concomitants of encounter with a stimulus and ensuing ritual on a single occasion, or whether it has been to obtain a global estimate of these responses across occasions, usually to enable monitoring over time. The assessment measures used to fulfil these two aims will be considered separately.

(a) Examination of emotional concomitants on a single occasion

In this context, no distinction seems to have been made between the response evoked by the feared stimulus and that occasioned by the ritual. It seems to have been assumed that they are qualitatively the same. There is a need for investigation as to whether this is really the case. The measures have all involved either subjective rating or psychophysiological measurement.

(i) *Subjective rating.* It seems to have been agreed that patients do not necessarily feel anxiety in the context of eliciting stimuli, but the exact nature of their subjective experience has not been established firmly. This seems to have led to the use of a number of scales in order to ensure that some aspects of their feelings are assessed.

Walker and Beech (1969) required their patient to use a five-point scale of anxiety, the first four scales of the Hildreth Feeling Test concerning depression (Hildreth, 1946) and a specially constructed hostility scale, which was designed along the same lines as the Hildreth test. Similarly, Röper and Rachman (1975) used some parts of the mood scales developed by Spielberger, Gorsuch, and Lushene (1970) in particular sections relating to tension, anxiety and worry. In earlier studies, the same group (Röper, Rachman, and Hodgson, 1973; Hodgson and Rachman, 1972) had used fear thermometer-type ratings (see also Wolpe, 1958) of a global feeling state labelled anxiety/discomfort. In fact, although given this name, the extremes of the scale were called 'complete relaxation' and 'absolute panic', both of which seem to be more reminiscent of anxiety than of discomfort. Subsequently, Rachman, De Silva, and Röper, (1976), attempted to distinguish between the urge to perform the ritual (checking) and the discomfort experienced during response prevention. The distinction may not be a meaningful one as in almost every case the ratings were extremely similar and showed nearly identical changes over time.

All these measures are quick to complete and require little effort on the patient's part. These characteristics are advantageous as assessments often have to be made repeatedly with short intervals between each one. However, the effects of repetition of the patient's responses has not been investigated. It is possible that memory in particular could play an influential part. The fact that in all studies the patient's responses changed in the manner predicted by the therapist goes against this view (assuming that the patients did not know what the therapist had in mind). Indeed, the consistently positive results provide a fair degree of evidence for the validity of the measures. The final choice of the optimal measure must of necessity be postponed until a clearer definition of the mood states and feelings which should be measured is achieved.

(ii) Psychophysiological measurement. There has been extremely little work using psychophysiological measurement as a means of evaluating patients' emotional state aroused by eliciting and stimuli. Marks *et al.* (1969) monitored GSR as a check on their patient's subjective ratings of anxiety in response to imagined contaminated scenes. Spontaneous fluctuations were present during scenes depicting untreated obsessions but not during imagination of treated ones. The GSR record paralleled the reports of subjective anxiety. Similarly, Rabavilas and Boulougouris (1974), studying eight patients, found significant changes in heart rate and skin conductance during imagination of ruminative stimuli as opposed to neutral themes. In contrast, Stern, Lipsedge, and Marks (1973) failed to obtain the same results when the patients (as in Rabavilas and Boulougouris's study) were asked to evoke the ruminative thoughts, but did obtain a very marked skin conductance and heart rate response from one patient

who experienced a rumination spontaneously. Finally, Carr (1970) recorded a decrease of activation following performance of a ritual.

With only this tiny amount of contradictory evidence available, however, the potential usefulness of psychophysiological measurement in this area is yet to be explored. At least the results from the patient of Marks *et al.* (1969) seem to indicate that the pursuit may prove to be worthwhile.

(b) Monitoring emotional concomitants over time

Only Stern, Lipsedge, and Marks (1973) have attempted to use psycho-physiological measurement as an assessment tool in outcome research. They failed to find heart rate and spontaneous fluctuation of skin conductance changes following treatment even in the subgroup of patients who responded well clinically.

All other forms of measures have involved subjective report or the related evaluation of an independent assessor. Of these, two have included some consideration of the emotions accompanying the ritual. Beaumont (1975) and Philpott (1975) have both described rating scales in which this aspect is given recognition. However, neither provided any information about the construction, reliability or validity of the scales; therefore their merits cannot reasonably be discussed. They require systematic evaluation and comparison with scales already in use. The remaining measures appear to have been designed to tap the emotional response to ritual eliciting stimuli. Rachman, Hodgson, and Marks (1971) made use of Wolpe's (1958) fear thermometer to estimate subjective anxiety. They supplemented this with a nine-point rating scale which they have used in all their research (see Chapter 5) and which has been followed with only slight variation by other workers (e.g. Rabavilas, Boulougouris, and Stefanis, 1976). As the scale has been used extensively and data from it has tended to form one of the central features of experimental results, it will be considered in some detail.

Rachman, Hodgson, and Marks (1971) derived their scales and several others described below from ones developed by Gelder and Marks (1966) and Watson and Marks (1971) for use with phobic patients. Parallel forms were constructed to be completed by the patient and an independent assessor. Each had to rate a specified ritual-evoking object or event on a nine-point scale of anxiety, despite the fact that this may not always be the main component of the patient's feeling (Walker and Beech, 1969; Hodgson and Rachman, 1972). The extremes and three additional points of the scale are labelled 'no uneasiness', 'mild uneasiness', 'definite anxiety', 'strong anxiety', and 'panic'. It is difficult to believe that these headings could represent adjacent points on an interval scale, as the equally spaced rating numbers given to them imply. It seems far more likely that the scales yield only ordinal measurement, in which case the results of parametric statistics may be difficult to interpret.

The independent rater is supposed to rate the patient's anxiety in the same way, basing his rating on information obtained at interview. Although the rater may be 'blind' with respect to the treatment which the patient is receiving, he is certainly not independent of the rating which the patient makes himself. The patient has to fill in his scales and be rated several times during the course of the treatment trial. After the first occasion most patients seem to become quite sophisticated and to provide the relevant information at interview before it is requested (M. Vaughan, personal experience). As interview and self-rating often occur in close temporal proximity, it seems highly likely that the response to whichever comes first will influence performance in the other situation. Therefore, it would probably be untrue to maintain that the assessor provides in any way an independent judgment.

Rachman, Hodgson, and Marks (1971) used their scale to rate each of a patient's five main obsessions. Therefore, for either patient or assessor, the patient's anxiety could be evaluated separately for each of the five stimuli, or evaluated globally in terms of the sum of the five separate scores. They did not provide reliability coefficients for these scales, merely citing the favourable correlations obtained for the original phobia scales (Watson and Marks, 1971). It is questionable whether it can be assumed that the scales would be of equivalent reliability with phobic and obsessional patients. Both the characteristics of the eliciting stimuli and the nature of the overall response which they evoke constitute defining differences between phobic and obsessional groups. As the scale has already been used extensively by Rachman and his co-workers (see Chapter 5) it seems inadmissible that a proper reliability study has not been performed.

Little more has been done to establish the validity of the scales. The only evidence at all comes from the fact that the ratings do show predicted changes following treatment (reviewed in Chapter 5). This is certainly encouraging, but does not constitute sufficient evidence on its own.

It is only fair to say that Rachman and his colleagues are well aware of the fact that their scales possess many faults, and would not wish to represent them as entirely adequate tools (Hodgson, 1977, personal communication). It is hoped that this knowledge will encourage them to work towards improvement and refinement of the scales, as in their present form they really do not warrant the extent to which they have been used already.

3. Avoidance of eliciting stimuli

The most obvious way to assess avoidance would be to observe the patient's behaviour. As it is usually not possible to do this whilst the patient pursues his daily routine, the alternative is to evaluate avoidance in a contrived situation. Rachman, Hodgson, and Marks (1971) adopted this approach in developing a behavioural test in which the patient was asked to undertake ten activities which he would usually avoid (touching rubbish, for example). The avoidance score was the percentage of items which the patient could not perform. Rachman, Hodgson, and Marks (1971) did not disclose whether the items were chosen on the basis of their difficulty for the patient. If they were not, comparisons between subjects could be difficult to interpret as there would be no way of telling whether the sets of activities are of comparable difficulty. This might be overcome to some extent by asking the patients to rate their activities in terms of a clearly defined scale.

In addition to a behavioural test, Rachman, Hodgson, and Marks (1971) used the patient's and independent assessor's ratings of avoidance based on scales equivalent to those for anxiety discussed above. The scales for avoidance are subject to the same criticisms as the anxiety ones except perhaps the comment about interval scaling. The five labelled points of the avoidance scale may be abbreviated as 'never avoids', 'hesitates but rarely avoids', 'sometimes avoids', 'usually avoids' and 'invariably avoids'. It is just possible that these headings could refer to points which are evenly spaced. Both assessor's and patient's ratings of avoidance changed in the predicted fashion after treatment (Marks, Hodgson, and Rachman, 1975). In contrast, only assessor's ratings tended to change predictably in Hackmann and McLean's (1975) study, patient's ratings showing no consistent trend. These workers used a seven-point scale of avoidance but gave no further details of its nature.

4. Frequency and duration of rituals and thoughts

The occurrence of overt rituals may be recorded by the patient, an observer, or in special circumstances by a machine (Mills et al., 1973). Observer recording has not been attempted, possibly because of the difficulties in arranging surveillance and the reactive effect of the presence of another person. Mills et al., (1973), however, developed an ingenious means of counting hand-washing sessions automatically. The only available sink was enclosed by a gated pen with a cumulative recorder which was operated when the gate was closed. In this way all visits to the sink were recorded. The use of such apparatus is obviously restricted to situations in which the availability of washing facilities can be controlled and, therefore, would probably not be of much use outside hospital.

In the absence of any versatile alternative, it will be necessary to rely on the patient's report on his rituals. Of course this is the only form of monitoring that is possible for ruminations and thoughts (such as of contamination) associated with rituals. Recording may either take place each day throughout treatment or may be limited to short periods before and after treatment and at follow-up. At the simplest level the patient may be asked merely to provide a global estimate of frequency or average duration for a specified period of time preceding the assessment. A more accurate estimate would probably be to ask the patient to rate relevant aspects of his ritual or thought. Hackmann and McLean (1975) asked their patients to rate time consumed in rituals on a seven-point scale. The scale was completed also by an independent assessor, who must have based his rating on the patient's verbal report. Philpott (1975) has described an elaborate rating measure. Average duration of obsessions over the two weeks prior to assessment has to be rated on a nine-point scale in which all the points are defined in terms of times, ranging from 0 to 5 minutes to eight hours or more per day. The reliability and validity of the scale have yet to be reported.

A more detailed account still may be obtained by asking the patient to recall or report all occurrences of the unwanted ritual, or thoughts either everyday or for a prescribed assessment interval. As already mentioned, Gelfand and Hartmann (1975) provide a comprehensive guide to this form of recording. Leger (1975) investigated the use of patients' reports of spontaneous occurrences of ruminations as a means of assessing treatment effects. He found that in his four patients frequency of ruminations thus obtained changed in a predicted manner in response to experimental manipulation of the patient's state of tension. The other workers to attempt precise monitoring (Hackmann and McLean, 1975) were more ambitious in requiring their patients to keep diaries in which they had to record at half-hourly intervals whether or not a ritual or thought had occurred. It is surprising that this should be the only report of the use of frequency counts in treatment trials, as the occurrence of rituals or thoughts usually constitutes the target for intervention. It seems to be essential that assessment measures concerning frequency and duration of rituals should be developed and refined, for without them the evaluation of treatment effects will be incomplete.

5. Mood state

Quite apart from the emotional changes associated with performing their rituals, many obsessive–compulsive patients experience persistent adverse mood states. Indeed the raised incidence of obsessions in depression is well documented (see, for example, Gittleson, 1966; and Kendell and Discipio, 1970). Vaughan (1976) attempted to determine the nature of depression associated with obsessions and found agitation, rapid mood changes, overactivity and a lack of retardation to be the main features which distinguished it from depression without obsessions. In addition, anxiety was very prominent in patients with obsessions but without obsessional personalities. This picture of a rather anxious, agitated form of depression seems to be consistent with Rachman, Hodgson, and Marks (1971) choice of scales relating to depression and anxiety-type feelings for their research. However, such an analysis of obsessional subjects' mood states may prove to be oversimplified. For instance, the pervasiveness of feelings of hostility of the sort reported by Walker and Beech's (1969) patients has not been investigated. Really, a detailed study of obsessional subjects' mood states should be undertaken. For the present, discussion of measuring instruments will be restricted to roughly the three aspects of mood which have been identified: depression, anxiety and hostility.

There are a number of well-constructed and validated questionnaires rating scales and checklists which have been designed to assess trait anxiety and depression (for example, 'Beck Depression Inventory', Beck et al., 1961; 'State-Trait Anxiety Inventory', Spielberger, Gorsuch, and Lushene, 1970). It is quite possible that a published scale will be found to be suitable for the purpose for which a measure is required. In contrast, there seems to be little available to measure hostility, so that Walker and Beech (1969) had to develop their own scale.

The main drawback with some of the existing measures is that they are too long and time-consuming for frequent use. It may be possible to use only part of the scales as Walker and Beech did with the Hildreth Feeling Scale (Hildreth, 1946); otherwise an alternative form of measurement will have to be devised.

The rating scales developed by Rachman, Hodgson, and Marks, (1971) as pretreatment and posttreatment measures were sufficiently brief for the patient to have filled them in frequently, if that had been wished. Separate nine-point scales were used for rating depression, depersonalization, free-floating anxiety and panics. The scales are subject to all the criticisms of their companion anxiety scale discussed above, except that they all seem to provide an interval scale of measurement. Again the scales were designed to be completed by both patient and independent assessor. The latter was instructed to take note of complaints relating to the symptom rated made by the patient during interview and to base his ratings on these. For example, he had to take note of, amongst other things, loss of interest and early waking when rating depression. Overall, the ratings seem to have been based on standard diagnostic criteria.

As an alternative to defining mood in terms of subjective feeling or psychiatric diagnosis, it may be possible to assess it in terms of psychophysiological response. It has been suggested that obsessional patients may be subject to abnormally high levels of arousal which may fluctuate rather than remain constant (Beech, 1971; Beech and Perigault, 1974). Apart from being consonant with a mood state of agitated depression, support for this hypothesis is provided in some initial evidence reported by Beech and Perigault (1974). They argued that abnormal arousal would be manifested in a failure to habituate to simple stimuli and cited the results from one of the group of obsessionals whom they had tested. The patient failed to show GSR habituation to a tone over twenty trials. This response was said to be typical of other patients tested. Beech and Perigault's report seems to be sufficiently provocative to stimulate more research of a similar kind.

6. Social adjustment

Only Rachman, Hodgson, and Marks (1971) have attempted to assess any aspects of social adjustment. They were comprehensive in their efforts covering areas of work, leisure, sex, family relationships and other relationships. A precisely defined nine-point scale was used for each with two scales for work covering paid occupation and housework. The scales were intended for use for the assessor only, but there seems to be no reason why patients should not complete them. As with their other scales, Rachman, Hodgson, and Marks (1971) did not assess the reliability of these measures. However, had they done so, there is some reason to suspect that it would not have been found to be high.

Gelder and Marks (1966), whose scales formed the bases of the Rachman, Hodgson, and Marks' scale, looked at therapist–assessor reliability for scales tapping the same areas of social adjustment in phobic patients. The correlation coefficient for work was just satisfactory at 0.73; the others ranged from 0.69 to 0.58. These levels are really not adequate for assessment instruments even if they are to be implemented in the context of research. Even though it is not certain that comparable coefficients for obsessional patients would prove to be as low as these, Gelder and Mark's findings do indicate that the reliability of the scales of Rachman *et al.* should be determined before they are used again. Otherwise sound research could be jeopardized by inadequate measures.

CONCLUSION

This review has been restricted to a discussion of assessment procedures which are known to have been designed for or used with obsessional patients. Nearly all, although having advantages, have also been found to be inadequate to some extent, but in most cases the would-be investigator has been left the task of choosing the one which provides the best measure of the area of functioning which he wishes to assess. In many instances, it may not be possible to find a suitable measure, so that a new scale will have to be designed.

In the past, relatively little attention seems to have been paid to the development of assessment tools for obsessionals. Perhaps this has occurred because the emphasis has been on the need to develop treatment procedures for a refractory group. Whatever its cause, neglect of assessment measures may have profound consequences. No treatment, albeit theoretically sound and admirably conducted, can be evaluated meaningfully unless the measures that are employed fit the behaviour to be assessed and are sensitive to subtle changes which may take place. Rather than being a time-consuming sideline, the development of adequate assessment measures is a *sine qua non* of fruitful clinical case investigation and research.

4

Systematic Desensitization

Systematic desensitization was developed by Wolpe (1958, 1969) as a treatment for phobias, but it has also been applied, unadapted, to obsessive–compulsive states. The belief that desensitization could be applied usefully to these latter disorders arose from the assumption that such conditions bear a close resemblance to phobic states. It was considered that specifiable environmental stimuli elicited anxiety in the obsessional and that his rituals served as a form of avoidance response, reducing the anxiety experienced. Hence the patient with fears of contamination would become anxious on seeing or touching a lump of mud and would reduce this anxiety by repeated washing. The combination of stimulus-evoked anxiety followed by avoidance appeared to provide a direct parallel to phobic avoidance behaviour.

As the aim of systematic desensitization is to eliminate the anxiety component, it could as readily be applied to the discomfort experienced by obsessionals as to that felt by phobic patients. In nearly all the published reports of systematic desensitization with obsessional patients, it has been assumed that the anxiety experienced was elicited by the stimulus to which the client attributed it; if the patient said that the mud had made him feel anxious and contaminated, then it was accepted that it is contact with the mud which has elicited the discomfort. Treatment has been directed at relieving the anxiety evoked in this way.

Wolpe (1958) developed the main elements of the procedure of systematic desensitization during his investigations of experimental neuroses in cats. These studies are described fully in his 1958 book and will not be elaborated here. Suffice it to say that his methods of neurosis induction involved shocking the animals whilst they were constrained in a cage, each shock being preceded by a warning noise. He considered that the extreme fear responses which he induced with these procedures were comparable to human neurotic responses.

Wolpe observed that the fear and upset shown by the cats during preparation for a test session seemed to be in direct proportion to the degree of similarity of the animals' present surroundings to the experimental room and cage. Thus,

31

responding was minimal when the animals were in their home cages, increased in a room which resembled the experimental one and became maximal in the test cage with the warning signal being sounded. This observation provided the idea of a hierarchy of fear-eliciting stimuli. In addition, Wolpe noted that the animals would eat only when not afraid, showing no fear when they were eating. This suggested to Wolpe that the two responses were incompatible, the occurrence of one precluding that of the other.

Wolpe went on to treat the induced neuroses using a procedure which later was to be modified to become systematic desensitization. He made use of his observations of a hierarchy of fear-evoking stimuli and of the incompatibility of fear and eating. He arranged a hierarchy of situations ranging from a room unlike the experimental one to the usual test setting, which correspondingly elicited least to most fear. In addition, he argued that in a situation including cues for both eating and fear, but in which those for eating were pre-eminent, the cats should eat and hence not exhibit fear. Such a situation could be arranged by providing the cat with food in surroundings corresponding to the lowest hierarchy item. This Wolpe did, waiting until the hungry cats were eating without distress before progressing gradually in the same way through all the succeeding hierarchy items. Thus the procedure involved both a graded approach and behaviour incompatible with fear and avoidance.

Later, Wolpe was able to combine these two elements in his treatment of phobic patients. His reading of Jacobson's *Progressive Relaxation* (1938) led him to postulate that Jacobson's patients were able to inhibit high levels of anxiety as a result of their lengthy relaxation training. Wolpe, therefore, began to use graded exposure to phobic stimuli with patients who had had intermediate degrees of relaxation training. At first he worked *in vivo*, with the procedure paralleling that used previously with the cats, but later changed to imaginal presentation of the stimuli since this enabled the construction of adequate hierarchies which had considerable advantages over those afforded by the 'real' world.

Wolpe has provided a detailed description of the three components of systematic desensitization; construction of a hierarchy of phobic scenes, training in the incompatible responses of relaxation and presentation of the hierarchy items in the presence of relaxation. His book *The Practice of Behaviour Therapy* (Wolpe, 1969, 1973) is essential reading for anyone without experience of desensitization techniques. As his account is accessible, readable and comprehensive no further description of the procedures will be given here.

Generally these treatment sessions are supplemented with *in vivo* work at home, the patient being required to practise in 'real life' the items which were covered with the therapist. He is usually warned not to go beyond the stage already achieved in imagination. In fact, the *in vivo* procedure may be used without prior imaginal desensitization. The hierarchy has then to be translated directly into a series of *in vivo* approach exercises. Here self-induced muscle relaxation can only be employed to a limited extent since the patient will be moving around, often in very public places. Sometimes it is assumed that the presence of the therapist will be sufficient to create a feeling of calm in the patient. Failing that, a suitable tranquillizer administered prior to the session may produce a state of relaxation which will be incompatible with the experience of anxiety, and this kind of medication may also be used in imaginal sessions when the patient experiences difficulty in learning to relax.

Systematic desensitization has been applied to obsessive–compulsive disorders without modification. The main objects or events feared by the obsessional patients form the basis of hierarchies to be dealt with, either in imagination or *in vivo*. The rituals, which distinguish the obsessional from the phobic patient are usually ignored as it is assumed that they will disappear automatically as a function of anxiety reduction. Numerous examples of systematic desensitization are given in Wolpe's books.

THE THEORETICAL BASIS OF TREATMENT

Wolpe concluded that the success of his treatment of cats occurred because anxiety was inhibited by eating, and this resulted in the development of learned (conditioned) inhibition of the anxiety responses to the eliciting stimuli. In formulating this explanation, Wolpe drew on Hullian learning theory and the investigations of Sherrington (1947). He borrowed the concept of conditioned inhibition from Hull (1943), who had attempted to explain some empirical observations of extinction. Extinction is the name given to the progressive weakening of a conditioned response when it is evoked repeatedly in the absence of reinforcement. Sufficient repetitions of this combination produces cessation of responding. However, after a rest period in which the evoking stimulus is not presented, the response can be elicited by the stimuli once more, although with reduced strength.

Hull suggested that the partial recovery of the response indicated that there are two processes involved in extinction. One, *reactive inhibition*, accounts for the temporary cessation of the response, whilst the other, *conditioned inhibition*, results in some degree of permanent suppression of the response (as evidenced by the fact that it reappears at less than full strength). Hull considered that some form of fatigue-associated state formed the basis of reactive inhibition, and that this state tended to have an inhibitory effect on the response which followed it. This would account for the reduction in the strength of response over unreinforced trials as well as for its cessation. The presence of this 'state' was thought to create a drive which would continue as long as reactive inhibition was operative, in other words, as long as the response was repeated. Drive reduction would, therefore, occur on termination of the response. Because of the reinforcing property of drive reduction, the act of stopping the response would become conditioned to any available stimuli related to the fatigue state. In this way the stimuli associated with the cessation of the response could become conditioned to the inhibition of that response (conditioned inhibition). Thus, repeated acts of response suppression might be expected to lead to permanent extinction. Although the bases of conditioned inhibition had not been determined, Wolpe considered it might be subserved by synaptic processes.

The development of conditioned inhibition was central to Wolpe's explanation of the anxiety reduction which he observed in his cats. By placing the cat in the fear-evoking rooms, the repeated elicitation of the anxiety responses would produce a build-up of both reactive and conditioned inhibition.

It was assumed by Wolpe that conditioned inhibition should eventually result in extinction of the anxiety response without the presence of an incompatible response. His decision to feed his cats in the feared rooms arose from his awareness of Sherrington's (1947) work as well as that of other investigators, but it was Sherrington who had adopted the term 'reciprocal inhibition' to refer to inhibition of one reflex by the elicitation of another, as when stimulation of an ipsolateral afferent nerve produces relaxation of a contracting vastocrureus muscle. Although Sherrington had used the term only in the context of relatively simple muscle reflexes, Wolpe suggested that the same mechanism could apply to any situation in which elicitation of one response inhibited another. The inhibition of anxiety by feeding in the cats' treatment would, therefore, qualify as a case of reciprocal inhibition. Wolpe (1958) did not state whether he was making this generalization on the basis of the observable similarity between the inhibition of reflexes and that of more complex responses, or whether he was assuming an equivalence of underlying processes. Since he does not provide an account of the possible mechanisms subserving reciprocal inhibition in either instance, the level at which he intended his generalization to be made remains undetermined. Nevertheless, the anxiety reduction observed in the cats on feeding, as well as in patients when relaxing, might be considered to be examples of reciprocal inhibition. However, the use of this label does nothing to explain the lasting therapeutic gains, as it is applied only to the immediate observable inhibition.

Wolpe introduced the mechanism of conditioned inhibition in order to account for the permanent reduction of anxiety following repeated trials of reciprocal inhibition. He argued that if conditioned inhibition is developed during extinction because of the juxtaposition of conditioned stimuli traces and reactive inhibition of the conditioned response, then it might also be expected that conditioned inhibition could be developed through some other cause. Specifically, when the inhibition of one response by another incompatible one is followed by major drive reduction, a substantial amount of conditioned inhibition of the first response will be developed. In desensitization, repeated presentation of the same imaginal stimulus to the relaxed patient would produce incrementation of conditioned inhibition with eventual unlearning of the anxiety response. Transfer to the next stimulus in the hierarchy would then occur as a result of stimulus generalization.

Superficially, Wolpe's model appears to fit his treatment well, but it could be argued that crucial weaknesses are evident in the model proposed as exemplified in desensitization. In the first place, it is difficult to conceive of any substantial drive reduction which would serve to reinforce anxiety response cessation. In desensitization, the hierarchy is arranged so that minimal anxiety is aroused on each presentation, in such a way that the amount of reactive inhibition generated must be small and the ensuing drive accordingly weak. It is interesting to note that Wolpe (1958) recognized this when he explained the failure of usual extinction procedures partly in terms of the fact that very little reactive inhibition seems to be generated by anxiety responses. Again, when anxiety is experienced during desensitization the fear-evoking scene is terminated immediately, which would appear to provide little opportunity for reactive inhibition to develop. Thus, it does not seem possible for the drive required to reinforce the development of conditioned inhibition to be a function of reactive inhibition. No acceptable alternative source of drive has been suggested and, indeed, the procedure adopted is specifically designed to reduce all drive states to a minimal level. Such arguments would seem to cast considerable doubt on the validity of Wolpe's theoretical position, but, of course, they do not necessarily affect the assessment of the practical utility of the technique.

Wolpe's model has been challenged several times, but none of the alternative proposals appear to be less free of difficulties than the original (see, for example, the habituation model of Lader and Mathews, 1968). To date, no entirely satisfactory explanation of the effects of systematic desensitization has been put forward, but the technique itself survives, and is used extensively because of its demonstrated efficacy in the treatment of phobic patients.

PUBLISHED CASE REPORTS

There have been no controlled treatment trials to investigate the efficacy of systematic desensitization with obsessive–compulsive patients; all the evidence available is presented in the form of case reports not unlike the example given above. In the majority of cases the stimuli constituting the hierarchy are those which the patient perceives as eliciting his anxiety. Thus, if the patient fears that he will become contaminated by touching the toilet seat when going to the lavatory, scenes depicting varying types and degrees of contact with the seat will be included in the hierarchy. In contrast, Walton and Mather (1967), and subsequently Worsley (1968, 1970) chose stimuli which bore little resemblance to the presenting anxiety situation.

Walton and Mather argued that the anxiety elicited by the feared stimuli was a product of a conditioned autonomic drive, probably developed during child-hood, and cited the case of a 24-year-old teacher who had a six-year history of extensive rituals associated with going to the toilet which were related to her fear of contamination from faeces and urine. In addition, she attempted to avoid having any contact with men and, if such a meeting did occur, she would anxiously wonder whether or not the man had made advances to her and kissed her. Walton and Mather felt that during childhood this girl had overresponded to her very religious Roman Catholic schooling and other social pressures because of her labile autonomic nervous system. This autonomic response, in their view, could have become conditioned to pleasurable sexual stimuli, e.g. masturbation, which were condemned by her religion. In this event, avoidance of stimuli and activities associated with sex would have been rewarded by the consequent reduction of the autonomic drive. The conditioned drive, it was argued, generalized to urination and defecation, and was only reduced by the performance of her elaborate rituals. It appeared to follow that if the strength of the conditioned autonomic drive could be reduced, then the generalized anxiety associated with the ritual-evoking stimuli would diminish and the rituals would cease.

Walton and Mather tested this hypothesis on two male patients with obsessive–compulsive symptoms of recent onset. For one, the conditioned autonomic drive was thought to relate to fear of aggressive feelings, and in the other to concern over his homosexual drives. Both were treated by using reciprocal inhibition by self-assertion. The patients were merely given the instruction to be more assertive with people. There was no direct skills training and no form of hierarchy of social situation. The instructions were aimed solely at interaction with other people and were not concerned with the presenting symptoms of hand-washing and compulsive writing. In both patients, a short course of treatment appeared to be effective in that the major symptoms were alleviated. However, one of these patients failed to reply to attempts at follow-up and the other was readmitted four times in a year having made two suicidal attempts, but, interestingly, had lost his obsessional symptoms.

Considering these two cases at least as limited successes, Walton and Mather went on to investigate the role of conditioned autonomic drive reduction in the treatment of the schoolteacher with chronic sexual inhibitions referred to above. In this case, the prediction was that reduction of the conditioned autonomic drive would not be sufficient as the rituals were of longstanding (six years). Indeed, it was felt that the evocation of anxiety and rituals by present environmental stimuli would have become independent of the conditioned drive and, therefore, not affected by its removal. Here, the conditioned autonomic drive was thought to derive from a learnt fear of sexual contact, although the main presenting symptoms were rituals associated with urination and defecation.

The fear of sexual encounter was treated by systematic desensitization, with sodium amytal-induced relaxation used as the counter-anxiety condition. This patient required 64 sessions over a nine-month period to cover an 82-item hierarchy presented imaginally. The items ranged from seeing a man at a distance on the other side of the road to a tongue kiss and embrace in bed with a man imagined as her husband, and also included items concerned with expressing affection to her parents. The patient showed a marked improvement in behaviour directly related to the hierarchy content, that is, in contact with men and her parents, but her main obsessive–compulsive symptoms remained unmodified.

A similar pattern of outcome was achieved by a 48-year-old woman who spent many hours a day checking and rechecking an excessively detailed account of what was to happen to her body should she be found dead. It appeared that this obsession had developed out of a longstanding claustrophobia which had been exacerbated by reading a newspaper headline—'Man put in Coffin Alive'—about two years prior to receiving treatment. The underlying fear of confined spaces was treated *in vivo*, with increasing amounts of time spent in rooms of decreasing size. Her general claustrophobia improved under this regime, but her fear of being placed in a coffin remained. Part of her instructions concerning the disposal of her body indicated that she wished to prevent any possibility of being pronounced dead before she had died! This was treated directly by systematic desensitization utilizing scenes associated with the confirmation of death and preparation for cremation, but she did not respond to this treatment and her rituals remained unchanged. Although Walton and Mather suspected that there might be some secondary gain associated with illness in this case, they felt that her failure to respond supported the view that removal of the conditioned autonomic drive is not sufficient to ameliorate longstanding obsessive–compulsive behaviour.

Other therapists may also have shared this opinion for, apart from Worsley who successfully helped two patients (Case 3, 1968; Case 2, 1970) with treatments which included some attempt to reduce conditioned drives, there are no further reports of therapy directed at conditioned autonomic drive reduction.

In the remaining reports the attack on the stimuli-evoking rituals is direct, through the use of desensitization in imagination and *in vivo*. The cases reported may be divided roughly into 'successfully treated', 'some improvement' and 'no change', as assessed either from the therapist's published evaluation or from the information provided on the outcome of treatment. The situations and events eliciting rituals are varied but, as far as possible, similar problems have been grouped together in an attempt to impose some arbitrary order on the reports. The review begins on an optimistic note with patients for whom treatment appears to have been successful.

Worsley (1970) reported the case of a 24-year-old housewife, suffering from extreme anxiety associated with sharp instruments such as knives and scissors, of five years' duration. Such anxiety had started when she had woken in the early hours of the morning and thought how frightening it would be if she cut her wrists, and thereafter she avoided sharp instruments. Although there was particularly strong phobic anxiety, Worsley felt that the patient could be considered as obsessional by virtue of the degree of her preoccupation with the thought of cutting her wrist. Desensitization was conducted with relaxation induced by methohexitone, with imaginal and *in vivo* presentation of a series of knives graded for anxiety-evocation. The wrist-cutting thoughts were not treated directly. After 23 sessions, over a period of five months, the patient had lost her fears and preoccupations and was still symptom-free two years later.

Leitenberg *et al.* (1970) also treated a patient who avoided knives. Their *in vivo* treatment approach was graded in terms of the time spent holding a sharp knife. The therapists' praise for holding the knife may have induced responses incompatible with anxiety in the patient. Haslam (1964) treated a patient whose fear of bits of glass had persisted after a leucotomy. The patient felt compelled to check everything in case a small piece of glass might be present. The patient was sedated with chlorpromazine and the treatment was conducted *in vivo* with the presence of the therapist inducing a state incompatible with anxiety. Initially, the patient was asked to eat a grapefruit with sugar on it in the therapist's presence, the sugar arousing anxiety as a result of generalization from glass. In the end, the patient was able to help the therapist clear broken glass off the tennis court. She was still well at a one-year follow-up.

A similar procedure was used by Walton (1960) with a patient who felt compelled to kick stones from his path. In fact he was unable to walk along corridors, pavements and roads because he had to clear all pieces of paper and stones out of his way. If he did not do so, he feared that someone would trip over the offending 'obstacles' and injure himself. A hierarchy of walking situations was devised, in and around the hospital, starting with a clean corridor and increasing progressively in the amount of litter and stones on the route. Chlorpromazine, given before each session, was used to inhibit anxiety, and the patient was asked to follow the therapist along each path in the hierarchy without kicking any stones or picking up paper. The therapist and patient repeated each walk in the hierarchy until it could be undertaken without distress, before proceeding to the next item. In the end, he was able to walk along a road which was still under construction and which had half-bricks as its base. The patient was also treated for excessive hand-washing by other behavioural techniques. Seven months later he returned to the hospital having resumed hand-washing and being excessively slow. However, he remained free from his stone-kicking problem and was reported to have maintained this improvement four months after the end of successful treatment of his other problems.

Two reports by Worsley (1968, 1970) refer to patients who indulged in excessive domestic cleaning and tidying. The first, a housewife, cleaned her home compulsively. The approach adopted here was to train her in relaxation and then desensitize her in imagination, to a hierarchy of scenes in which she refrained, for lengthening periods, from removing increasing amounts of dust. She was discharged after four weeks and was still well two years later. Worsley's other patient (1970, Case 3) had suffered from a severe obsessive–compulsive disorder for 30 years, since the age of seventeen. She spent many hours checking, cleaning, and tidying the shop which she owned and ran. In addition, she feared contamination from urine (perhaps related to bedwetting as a child) and had numerous rituals associated with making sure that the bed was dry each morning, washing her clothes and bathing. She changed her clothes before going into the shop so that she would not carry contamination with her. It seems that this patient was not given any graded exercises with the therapist but, instead, was instructed that she could learn to tolerate feared situations by gradually exposing herself to them, and was encouraged to do this at home. Within two months her activities surrounding the care of the shop were reduced to within reasonable limits and some of her rituals associated with contamination had shown improvement. A few months later she sold the shop for reasons apparently unrelated to her disorder and moved away to live with relatives. At follow-up eighteen months later she reported that improvement had been maintained.

There are several accounts available of formal desensitization for patients with fears of contamination. Wolpe (1964) reported the use of both imaginal and *in vivo* stimuli with a young man whose compulsive washing arose from a fear of contamination from urine, especially his own. He would spend two hours washing following urination and, in addition, took a four-hour morning shower. Initially, desensitization was carried out with imaginal stimuli whilst the patient was relaxed. The lowest hierarchy item was that of someone else dipping a hand into 1 cubic metre of water containing one drop of urine. Five months later the patient was able to imagine himself dipping his hand into pure urine, without anxiety. But, although hand-washing time decreased to 30 minutes, and his shower to just over an hour, there was limited transfer to real life and he was still unable to touch urine. Therefore, an *in vivo* hierarchy was constructed. Initially, he had to approach and handle a bottle containing urine. Then small drops of dilute urine were placed on the back of his hand, and the patient was instructed to relax until his anxiety had disappeared. The concentration of urine was progressively increased until he could tolerate a drop of his own undiluted urine on his hand. He was then required to touch door knobs, other people and other objects with his urine-contaminated hands. Washing and showering were reduced almost to acceptable limits and he returned to school. Eight months later it was found that he had made no further progress and the programme was resumed. Within three months, washing was reduced to three minutes and showering to twenty minutes. He was also treated for sexual and social anxiety.

Worsley (1970, Case 2) encountered an equivalent complaint in a 37-year-old married woman with severe washing rituals associated with menstrual blood. In addition to washing and cleaning herself during her menstrual period, she washed her clothes excessively in between, and at work she was tense and overly tidy. She was treated by desensitization in imagination, having been previously trained in relaxation. Desensitization involved imagining varying degrees of menstrual blood, starting with a trace, and she was instructed to practise the imaginal sessions at home. After two months she experienced no anxiety about her period and, one month later, she became pregnant for the first time. Worsley went on to desensitize her to her father in imagination, as she had reported concern over a mild sexual assault by her father when she was eight.

Not all feared stimuli are so obviously associated with contamination. Walton and Mather's Case 6 (1967) feared contamination from hypercritical people to the extent that he was compelled to wash his hands after touching anything at all. Because of this he routinely took three to five hours to dress. His fears appeared to be associated with his religious father, and to his own homosexual feelings. Treatment was planned in two phases, the first which was designed to eliminate the conditioned autonomic drive, involving two hierarchies concerning religious people and his father. Desensitization was carried out in imagination with relaxation induced by sodium amytal. The patient finished the 'religious people' hierarchy but was still unable to contemplate scenes of his father, nor was there much sign of improvement outside sessions. A leucotomy was carried out to reduce his autonomic lability and, six months later, desensitization was recommended as the patient was still performing his rituals, albeit in a more mechanical way. The 'father' hierarchy was completed without difficulty and the previously refused phase 2 of treatment was begun. This time the desensitization was *in vivo* and was directly related to the ritualistic stimuli. Four hierarchies covered a variety of feared stimuli and actions, including the activities involved in dressing. After five months, he was thought to have made a complete recovery. He was no longer concerned about his father and religious people and his hand-washing and dressing was within normal limits. Since the report was published at the time the patient was discharged, no follow-up data were given.

In this case it is not possible to completely disentangle the effects of desensitization to the conditioned drive stimuli and to the obsessional stimuli. However, it would be consistent with the results from the other treatments based on the reduction of the conditioned autonomic drive, to postulate that the use of 'religious' and 'father' hierarchies resulted in improved relationships with father, and that use of the obsessional stimuli hierarchies was responsible for the elimination of ritualistic behaviour.

The result obtained by Rubin, Merbaum, and Fried (1971, Case 1) provides some support for the view that the reduction of rituals may occur as a result of desensitization to stimuli which evoke them. A 40-year-old housewife had become obsessed with ideas of spreading contamination following a *post-partum* psychosis twenty years previously. She was afraid of poisoning people, for example, after using soap, experienced 'dirty' thoughts which she felt could also poison people, and was compelled to wash after any of these events. She was treated by desensitization in imagination to handling items such as soap, paint and cleanser, and also to 'dirty' thoughts. Her hand-washing in response to handling potential 'poisons' improved, but she continued to wash after experiencing 'dirty' thoughts. This aspect of her washing was finally eliminated by alternative behavioural methods.

Bevan (1960) was successful in treating a patient with ruminative thoughts using desensitization. The young female patient concerned had spoken with a member of the Jehovah's Witnesses and read pamphlets provided by him. Following this she became preoccupied with the 'world crisis' and would think 'awful things'—for example, any man and woman seen together would be thought to be having an affair. After over a year of hospital admissions, ECT and transient relief from symptoms, she was referred for behaviour therapy. Her main preoccupations at that time were with the end of the world, with war, and worry about becoming ill. She was given chlorpromazine before each session and was then asked to read a paper containing headlines relevant to her thoughts. After several weeks, she was able to discuss the Jehovah's Witness pamphlet which had disturbed her initially without feeling upset. However, she relapsed shortly after discharge and was weepy and tense, although her thoughts were not as prominent as previously. After anxiety relief training (Wolpe, 1958) she became symptom-free, but claimed that she now loved another patient and not her husband. It is not clear what role her marital discontent had played in the maintenance of her symptoms and in her relapse.

Bevan's treatment differs from most others described above in that no hierarchy was constructed. However, the use of a reciprocal inhibitor (drug-induced relaxation) provides a greater affinity to desensitization than to any of the other treatments to be described.

The following group of reports to be considered contain many in which treatment has been only partly or equivocally successful. Tanner (1971), for example, treated an obsessional checker who was plagued by the urge to check in response to a great number of stimuli, although only the first ten mentioned at interview were made the focus of treatment. These included the lavatory light, windows, car brake and back door. Following training in relaxation, supplemented by practice at home, desensitization was carried out in imagination with scenes depicting non-performance of the ritual (turning off the gas without checking, for example) and the possible undesired consequences of not checking (a gas explosion, the house burning down). A separate hierarchy was constructed for each of the ten stimuli and all were completed in 26 sessions. The role of desensitization in effecting improvement is far from clear in this report as rituals prompted by all stimuli reduced during relaxation training, although increasing during a break before the desensitization began. For most stimuli there was a decrease in rituals before the relevant hierarchy had been introduced (that is, while other stimuli were being dealt with). In fact, the checking associated with four stimuli ceased before their treatment had started; rituals associated with the other six stimuli reached zero by the end of the therapy. Improvement was not maintained uniformly at ten-month follow-up when reactions to six stimuli were reported to be as severe as before treatment, while one was worse and three were better than before. The patient rated her self-adjustment to be 'somewhat better'. At this stage, she and her husband were referred for marriage counselling, which it appears was one of the main reasons for her referral in the first place.

Agras *et al.* (1971) also obtained only modest success, but in this case the cause might be attributed to the limited experimental treatment given. They were interested in evaluating the role that relaxation played in desensitization, and so conducted several sessions of hierarchy presentation under states of muscle tension between two phases of conventional imaginal desensitization. The patient concerned suffered from the recurrent thought 'I could kill' and, consequently, avoided any situation in which harm to others might be occasioned. At its worst, the thought was said to occur at a frequency of 360 times an hour. Six treatment sessions were given, the first and last two of which were desensitization in imagination to the troublesome thought. In the two middle sessions, the patient was required to sit on a hard chair and deliberately tense herself whilst imagining the scenes. There was a slight reduction in the frequency of thoughts over sessions within each phase, with no discernible difference between the tension and relaxation conditions described. The overall improvement was in fact relatively slight, leaving the patient still handicapped, and there was virtually no change in self-reports of improvement between sessions.

Marks *et al.* (1969) encountered obsessive–compulsive rituals in identical twins, the less severely affected of whom was advised to seek treatment by the other at the age of 24 years. Both suffered extreme fear of contamination by dogs and excrement. The patient was taught to relax and, initially, desensitization was conducted in imagination. As the anxiety had generalized to cats to some extent, a hierarchy of cat stimuli was used. After 12 sessions the patient experienced no discomfort in imagining a cat sitting on his lap. The next twelve sessions involved graded presentation of real stimuli, with the patient relaxing for up to an hour after each session. As he was then able to stroke a cat for half an hour, dog stimuli were introduced, starting with dog hairs. By the end of 24 additional sessions the patient was able to touch the paws, tail and mouth of a stuffed dog and the pelt of another, although there was very little generalization of this progress. It was noted at the end of the imaginal phase that the amount of washing outside sessions had not changed and restrictions were placed on washing from the beginning of *in vivo* treatment. Requests that the amount of washing should be reduced after contamination sessions resulted in a reduction in frequency but an increase in length of each wash. The time taken was then also restricted and, by the end of treatment, the patient was able to eat a meal after 'contamination' but before washing. He was also asked to wear the clothes in which he was contaminated for increasing periods until the point where he could wear the same clothes on two consecutive days. Some sessions of aversion relief training were also given, which had the dual function of increasing his discomfort whilst washing and associating relief with contact with contaminating objects.

Eventually this patient discharged himself against medical advice, but one month later reported that he was only washing his hands two to three times a day and bathing twice a week, although he was not working and still reacted to 'dog' stimuli. After that, contact with the hospital was lost. It is difficult to disentangle the contribution of desensitization from those of response prevention and aversion relief. However, it seems clear that desensitization did increase in session approach to contaminating objects, although this failed to generalize, or it did not seem to affect execution of rituals.

Walton and Mather's Case 5 patient (1967) also feared contamination, this time from dirt. She had a ten-year history of extensive hand-washing after every activity, prolonged baths and contrived avoidance of all 'dirt'. Seven hierarchies were constructed, concerned with contaminating objects and events, for example, touching the doorknob and washing hands without cleaning the wash basin, every hierarchy representing a graded series of exercises which were carried out *in vivo*. She was encouraged to spend longer on touching contaminated items and to practise between sessions. After two months the patient spent less time washing and less avoidance of passing close to other people. The improvement lasted a few weeks, but the patient was unable to contemplate attempting any of the more difficult hierarchy items and so no further progress was made.

Finally, Hodgson and Rachman (1976) noted in passing that their Case 1 showed some slight improvement in his washing rituals after desensitization in imagination, but that he was still considerably disabled.

There are several accounts of patients who failed to respond to desensitization. Walton and Mather's Case 4 (1967) with an extreme fear of being buried alive remained unchanged after extensive desensitization *in vivo* to reading passages about burial alive and in imagination to scenes depicting medical confirmation of death and preparation for cremation prior to burial. Walton and Mather point out that failure to improve could be attributable partly to the fact that there seemed to be some secondary gain accruing from remaining ill. The patient was experiencing considerable domestic difficulties centring on her husband who was an alcoholic.

Secondary gain was not cited as a possible cause of failure in Rubin, Merbaum, and Fried's patients (1971). Case 1 was successfully treated for washing after touching 'contaminated' objects. In contrast, the occurrence of 'dirty' thoughts and consequent washing remained unchanged after systematic desensitization in imagination with relaxation. Their Case 2 was a 45-year-old woman with a five-year history of pathological cleaning of herself and her surroundings associated with ideas concerning contact with dead or dying people. She was treated by desensitization, having to imagine touching 'contaminated' objects without washing, whilst relaxing with the aid of brevital, but her symptoms were not alleviated by this treatment.

Furst and Cooper (1970) also failed in their attempts to help two patients with fears of contamination by insecticide. In both, the fears were manifested in uncertainty about the presence or absence of traces of insecticide, possibly deposited years previously, associated with a wide range of places, objects, and people. Case 1, a 52-year-old housewife, had managed to keep her fears hidden for eighteen years before an increase in her already excessive hand-washing caused her to seek treatment. After several hospitalizations, she was referred for desensitization, her washing having been relieved a little following tofranil and valium medication. However, desensitization in imagination did not bring about any further improvement. Case 2, a young man, suffered from very similar symptoms. Desensitization in imagination enabled him to imagine contact with insecticide without discomfort, but this improvement did not generalize to actual life circumstances.

In addition to the accounts of desensitization conducted following Wolpe's procedure, Worsley (1968, 1970) described three cases in which a graded approach to the feared stimuli was engineered by direct reduction of the ritualistic avoidance behaviour. His 1968 patient was helped to overcome washing and cleaning rituals by gradually reducing the time that she spent washing and the number of sheets of toilet-paper that she used. Similarly, Case 3 (1970) was encouraged to reduce, systematically, the time that was spent on rituals associated with going to the lavatory and praying. In addition, he was instructed to vary the pattern in which his rituals were performed in order to weaken the link between the act and reinforcement of anxiety reduction. This proved too difficult, and so the exercise was rehearsed in imagination under conditions of muscle relaxation. The treatment was successful but no follow-up data were available as treatment had only just been terminated at the time that the report was made. Gradual reduction of rituals was also a part of Case 3's successful programme of treatment for cleaning and tidying rituals. The use of direct ritual reduction is comparable to desensitization in that the graded reduction of rituals exposes the patients to gradually increasing degrees of discomfort (assuming that the rituals are anxiety-reducing). If the anxiety increments are slight, they may be extinguished before each successive step is taken. However, the two procedures are not entirely equivalent and the inclusion of these few reports of graded ritual reduction under the heading systematic desensitization is not made without reservation.

Three follow-up accounts of the outcome of behaviour therapy may be added to the case studies. Wolpe (1958) conducted a follow-up of 88 patients, seven of whom suffered from obsessive–compulsive disorders. One, described as having paranoid obsessions, does not seem to be an obsessional as usually defined, but was rated as cured after systematic desensitization. Two were considered to be much improved after desensitization although in one assertion training was also given. Of the remaining three, all given desensitization, one patient improved, one was unchanged and the third relapsed following an initial improvement which was thought to be due to the therapist's support rather than a treatment effect.

Lazarus (1963) had 22 obsessional patients amongst his series of 126 cases treated for more than six sessions. He considered symptoms, social relationships, tolerance of frustration and gratification of needs. In terms of these criteria, he rated twelve patients as being markedly improved or recovered, and the remaining ten slightly improved, unchanged or deteriorated. Lazarus reported using systematic desensitization, aversion relief training, thought-stopping and drugs in his treatment programme, but did not indicate which techniques were used in any given case. Finally, Cooper, Gelder, and Marks (1965) treated ten obsessional patients in his group of 77 patients who received behaviour therapy. They were thought to be more severely handicapped than those seen by Wolpe (1958), having had their symptoms for a mean of ten years. All received graded practical retraining and systematic desensitization, but seven of the ten failed to improve to any appreciable extent.

EVALUATION

In using the results of the cases which have been reviewed to evaluate the usefulness of desensitization, the studies dealing with the removal of the underlying conditioned autonomic drive (Walton and Mather, 1967, Cases 1, 2 and 3; Worsley, 1968, Case 3) will be excluded. Although their therapists' treatment procedures were firmly based on Wolpe, the choice of stimuli for desensitization was idiosyncratic and was neither in accord with the same workers' treatment of other patients nor that of the other therapists. Similarly, Worsley's (Case 1, 1968; Case 4, 1970) accounts of patients treated by gradual reduction of rituals will not be considered as the procedure did not constitute desensitization as usually defined. Worsley's Case 3 patient (1970) who was asked to reduce rituals will be mentioned as graded approach was also employed. This leaves a total of twenty cases treated by twelve therapists (or groups of therapists). Rubin, Merbaum, and Fried's Case 1 (1971) had suffered from external stimulus-evoked washing and bad thoughts. As the two aspects responded differently to treatment, they were considered separately and will be discussed as if they were two cases, making the total number of 'cases' 21.

It is clear from the reports that the procedures adopted are sufficiently close to Wolpe's original to make them a legitimate basis for evaluation of the efficacy of his technique. Nevertheless, some slight procedural variations are evident. In all but two cases, either a sedative or muscle relaxant were used to reciprocally inhibit anxiety. The drugs appeared to have been administered in adequate doses but the amount of relaxation training often was not stated, so that there was no indication whether the degree of relaxation achieved was sufficient to overcome anxiety. Desensitization in imagination was used in just over 50 per cent (eleven out of twenty) of the cases, the remaining treatments being almost equally divided into entirely *in vivo* and a combination of imaginal and *in vivo* procedures (six and four cases respectively). With all these procedures, the therapists did not always indicate any standard of anxiety reduction for passing on to the next item, but those who did appeared to follow Wolpe's criteria. Failure to visualize clearly was not cited as a reason for discarding imaginal desensitization, but neither were tests of imagery reported as part of the procedure. Although all falling well within the compass of Wolpe's technique, some of these procedural differences may have affected treatment response. Their role in affecting treatment outcome will be discussed below.

The collection of cases reviewed above constitutes the greater proportion of the published material. There was no deliberate or systematic exclusion of cases, so that it is considered that those reviewed form a large and representative sample of the total number of cases. The inclusion of more than one case treated by the same therapist merely reflects the fact that some workers have shown a particular interest in desensitization and have published more frequently than others. However, this clustering of cases with common therapists does make any statistical evaluation of trends over cases unjustified, as each therapist is likely to show consistent preferences in the form of treatment used and may in part determine the outcome that he achieves. Hence, some important treatment factors may be common to all cases seen by the same person.

In the review, the 21 cases were divided into three classes, 'successful', 'slight improvement' and 'no change', depending on the evaluation made by the therapists. On this basis out of the 21 cases there were eleven successful cases, five with slight improvement and five failures. As the improvement made by the intermediate cases was extremely small and was perceived by three out of five sets of therapists as being inadequate (Hodgson and Rachman, 1976; Marks *et al.*, 1969; Walton and Mather (1967), Case 5), it was felt that the slightly improved and no-change groups could be combined. Therefore, overall there appears to be a 52 per cent success rate, with eleven cases doing well and ten showing minimal change. This estimate appears consonant with the results of the three follow-up series. Despite the fact that successful cases are reported to be well at a ten-month to two-year follow-up, this apparent success at chance level cannot be encouraging for the advocates of desensitization, especially as a preponderance of successful outcomes might have been expected amongst reports accepted for publication. However, as there was some variation both amongst the patients and amongst the components of treatment, it is possible that either some types of patient or some variation of procedure, or a particular combination of the two, might have a more successful outcome than the others.

The successful and unchanged patients did not show any marked difference in the length of illness prior to desensitization. Both groups exhibited considerable variation in this respect, with successful cases including Bevan's (1960) case with a one-and-a-half-year history and Worsley's (1970) Case 3 with 30 years of illness, whilst the unchanged group included histories of 35 years (Rubin, Merbaum, and Fried (1971), Case 2) and two years (Walton and Mather's Case 4 (1967) had claustrophobia for 26 years but obsessions for only two). Surprisingly, there seemed to be a slightly higher incidence of concurrent obsessive–compulsive symptoms treated by other behavioural techniques and of marital or sexual problems in the successfully treated cases. They included three cases with other obsessional problems and four with sexual or marital difficulties compared with one and two cases respectively for the failure group. Although this result is provocative, it seems doubtful that it represents anything more than a chance sampling difference. However, even as such, it does indicate clearly that there was no tendency for the presence of other problems to be associated with the no-change group. In this respect, the failures seemed to be no more severely afflicted than their successful peers.

The presenting severity of the symptoms treated was difficult to evaluate as the reports varied greatly in their length and in the detail with which the patients' problems were described. Initial attempts at judging severity were found to be closely related to the fullness of the descriptive account. However, it was felt that one aspect of the presenting symptoms could be evaluated more certainly. It seemed that in a small number of cases, the stimuli-eliciting rituals were clearly defined and would not necessarily be present in the patient's environment all the time. In other words, the patient would not always be confronted with the stimuli which he feared. In the majority of cases the stimuli associated with rituals would nearly always be present, either because they occurred very frequently in the patient's surrounding or because, by their nature, their presence or absence was difficult to discriminate (for example, traces of insecticide), so that there was always the chance that the stimulus might be present. (Meyer and Levy (1973) have made a similar observation.)

In order to divide the cases into these two groups, the main ritual-eliciting stimuli were listed on a small card for each patient. Two clinical psychologists were asked to sort the cards into two categories without consulting each other. They were told to categorize the lists of stimuli either as not present all the time or always (or at least nearly always) present. The raters disagreed over four cases, but both classified three as involving stimuli that are not present all the time and the remainder as having stimuli that are nearly always present. The four cases disagreed upon were discussed but it proved difficult to classify them unequivocally. Therefore, they were left as a third 'undecided' group, probably reflecting an intermediate degree of stimulus presence. The cases in their three categories are listed in Table 1. Each case had also been categorized previously as successful or as showing slight or no improvement after treatment. The relationship between presence of the stimulus and outcome is indicated in Table 1. In view of the less-than-perfect interjudge agreement over categorization and the small numbers, caution must be exercised in interpreting the results. However, there

Table 1 Relationship between degree of presence of ritual eliciting stimuli and outcome

| | | Treatment outcome | |
| | | | Slight improvement |
Presence of stimulus		Success	or no change
Stimulus not always present			
Worsley (1970) Case 1		1	—
Leitenberg et al. (1970)		1	—
Worsley (1970) Case 2		1	—
	Total	3	0
'Undecided'			
Rubin et al. (1971) Case 2		—	1
Haslam (1964)		1	—
Walton (1960)		1	—
Wolpe (1964)		1	—
	Total	3	1
Stimulus (nearly) always present			
Rubin et al. (1971) Case 1 (dirt)		1	—
Rubin et al. (1971) Case 1 (thoughts)		—	1
Worsley (1968) Case 4		1	—
Worsley (1970) Case 3		1	—
Tanner (1971)		—	1
Walton and Mather (1967) Case 6		1	—
Bevan (1960)		1	—
Marks et al. (1969)		—	1
Walton et al. (1967) Case 4		—	1
Agras et al. (1971)		—	1
Hodgson et al. (1976)		—	1
Walton and Mather (1967) Case 5		—	1
Furst and Cooper (1970) Case 1		—	1
Furst and Cooper (1970) Case 2		—	1
	Total	5	9

does appear to be some tendency for cases with stimuli which are not always present to be associated with a good outcome after desensitization (all three cases were successes). On the other hand, the majority of those with always-present stimuli had a poor outcome (nine out of fourteen showed little or no change). It is difficult to know exactly what the dimension of presence represents, although to some extent at least it appears to reflect general severity. The patient who is able to gain some respite from his feared stimuli is likely to spend a little more time free from preoccupation and rituals than one whose encounter with new threats is nearly constant. To the extent that this is so, it appears that desensitization is more effective with less severe cases.

Although extremely tentative, this result is reminiscent of Marks, Boulougouris, and Marset (1971) finding that patients with mono-symptomatic phobias respond well to desensitization whereas agoraphobics do not. In view of this, one might advocate the use of desensitization only with patients whose ritual-eliciting stimuli are circumscribed and not always present. Unfortunately, it appears from the treatment reports reviewed, and from clinical experience, that such cases are relatively rare so that the effective use of desensitization may be limited.

The second way in which the cause of the differing outcomes may be investigated is through consideration of differences in the treatment procedures applied. As all cases were treated by desensitization, these are relatively few in number. The length of treatment given to successful and little or no-change cases is difficult to evaluate as not all the reports of failures indicated how many sessions had been given. However, at least Marks *et al.* (1969), Tanner (1971) and Walton and Mather (1967, Case 4) gave lengthy treatments comparable to the successes, indicating that failure is unlikely to have arisen through lack of persistence. All but two therapists used relaxation training or drugs to reciprocally inhibit anxiety, but the use of either method of inducing relaxation did not appear to be related with outcome. There were examples of relaxation training and drug use in both success and failure groups.

More important, there was some variation between studies in the use of imaginal or *in vivo* desensitization or a combination of the two. The outcome of

Table 2 Relationship between use of imaginal, *in vivo*, and combined procedure and outcome

| Desensitization procedure | Treatment outcome | | |
	Success	Slight improvement or no change	Total
Imaginal	4	6	10
Imaginal and *in vivo*	2	3	5
In vivo	5	1	6
Total	11	10	21

treatment did appear to be related to the form of presentation used. The relationship between use of imaginal or *in vivo* techniques and outcome is given in Table 2. The cases were classified as in the review above. When *in vivo* desensitization is used, the proportion of successes is just over twice as great as that for imaginal treatment or for a combination of the two. It appears therefore that *in vivo* desensitization is more effective. The failure of the combined treatment cases to do as well as those receiving only *in vivo* training may be attributable to the fact that for the combined treatment cases sessions were divided between *in vivo* and imaginal presentations. This meant that the patient received fewer *in vivo* sessions than one treated by *in vivo* methods alone. The apparent superiority of *in vivo* desensitization is consistent with reports of desensitization in phobic cases; for example, Marks (1975 pp. 92–3) has concluded that the *in vivo* practice is the most important part of systematic desensitization for phobic patients.

As the degree of presence of the feared stimuli appeared to influence the outcome of treatment, it seemed possible that this might modify the effects of the variations in procedure. The 'stimuli not always present', 'undecided' and 'nearly always present' groups of cases were considered separately and the outcome for imaginal, *in vivo* and combined treatments were compared within each. Of the three 'not always present' cases, one was treated by each procedure and all were successful. Two undecided cases were treated *in vivo*, one in imagination and one received both. All but the imaginal case were successful. The numbers in these two groups are too small to allow any conclusion about the relative efficacy of the techniques. As regards differences in outcome within the 'stimuli nearly always present' group of cases, three out of four cases treated *in vivo* were successful, whereas both treated with the combined method and six out of eight given imaginal desensitization failed to improve. Thus *in vivo* desensitization seemed to be superior to the other procedures in the treatment of what appear to be seriously afflicted obsessive–compulsive neurotics.

CONCLUSIONS

It is not possible to draw firm or wide-ranging conclusions from any collection of published individual case reports as the nature and degree of bias in selection of cases for publication by the therapist and journal editors is never known. However, in the present series there appear to be several consistent trends over cases which it is difficult to imagine could have occurred merely through the selective influence of authors and editors. This view is reinforced by the fact that the findings appear to parallel the results of group experimental research on systematic desensitization in phobic patients (Marks, Boulougouris, and Marset, 1971; Marks, 1975). Thus it is likely that desensitization is more effective in cases in which the stimuli-eliciting rituals are distinct and not always present in the patient's environment. In addition, it seems almost certain that *in vivo* desensitization is superior to imaginal presentation or to a combination of the two (if this reduces the number of *in vivo* sessions). Overall, the reported success rate of desensitization is only just over 50 per cent which does not provide a strong argument for its continued use.

However, the outcome of cases treated by *in vivo* desensitization appears to be somewhat superior. Five out of six cases treated this way were considered to be successful. As *in vivo* desensitization appeared to maintain its effectiveness even in the more severe cases, it might be hoped that the exclusive use of *in vivo* presentation would improve the success rate in desensitization cases. Despite this positive observation, little interest seems to have been shown in refining desensitization procedures for use with patients with obsessive–compulsive disorders. Instead, many therapists have turned their attention to developing the techniques of flooding, modelling, and response prevention which are reviewed in the next chapter.

5

Modelling, Flooding, Response Prevention, and Apotrepic Therapy

Two related forms of treatment have been developed over a comparable period of time by Meyer and Levy and by Rachman, Hodgson, and Marks. Meyer published the first report in 1966, of a treatment procedure subsequently called *apotrepic therapy*. The development of the treatment appears to have been related to experimental animal work and clinical findings with obsessive–compulsive patients. Meyer (1966) cited Metzner's (1963) review of animal studies of fixated responses which may be considered as an analogue of compulsive behaviour. He suggested that Metzner's conclusion, that an avoidance response may be fixated if it becomes unsuccessful, could be applied usefully to human compulsion if unsuccessful avoidance could be taken to mean that the occurrence of the conditioned stimulus is not under the patient's control. One characteristic of the stimuli associated with phobic conditions is that they are pervasive and difficult to avoid.

Having characterized rituals as avoidance responses, Meyer pointed out that they may serve to reduce not only anxiety elicited by environmental stimuli (contamination, for example) but also fear that harm will come to self or family if the ritual is not performed. As Wolpe (1964) had demonstrated that reduction of anxiety was important in the elimination of avoidance responses, some form of deconditioning procedure seemed to be required. However, the usual desensitization did not seem to meet the special requirements of obsessive–compulsive patients, it was felt to be necessary to keep the avoidance responses under control between sessions and to treat these directly in addition to dealing with the anxiety response (following Walton and Mather, 1963).

In addition the patients' concern about the consequences of non-performance of the rituals required special attention. Meyer considered that if a patient was persuaded to remain in feared situations and was prevented from executing his avoidance rituals, his anxiety would extinguish and he would learn that the feared consequences did not take place. His view was supported by Lomont's (1965) review of animal experimental studies, which indicated that prevention of escape from a feared conditioned stimulus speeds the extinction of the response. The procedure initiated by Meyer (1966) has now been used with at least fifteen published cases (Meyer, Levy, and Schnurer, 1974). In nearly all cases the patient is admitted to hospital, although the procedure may be conducted at home (Meyer, Robertson, and Tatlow, 1975). In hospital, all medication except night sedation is discontinued. Both patient and nurses are instructed in the behavioural principles underlying the treatment. Twenty-four hour supervision is provided by the nurses who prevent the patient from engaging in his rituals, by diversion, persuasion, social and financial reinforcement and occasionally, with consent, mild physical restraint.

Once rituals are eliminated under supervision, the therapist works through a hierarchy of feared objects and situations with the patient. Modelling and manual guidance are used where necessary and reassurance and praise are given. When rituals are suppressed despite the additional stress of hierarchy presentation, nursing supervision is gradually reduced and finally removed. After about a week free from rituals, without supervision, the patient is sent home for increasing periods, and if difficulties arise, receives supervised sessions at home with the therapist. Relatives are taught how to deal with rituals should they occur. The patient is discharged after a satisfactory return home, but is followed up at weekly intervals at first, subsequent interviews being gradually spaced further apart.

Rachman, Hodgson and Marks' treatment procedure (1971) was derived in part from that of Meyer (1966) (see Rachman, Hodgson, and Marzillier (1970), Rachman, Hodgson, and Marks (1971)). However, initially it was also heavily influenced by the work of Bandura (1969) so that the role of modelling was emphasized much more than in Meyer's original. Rachman, Hodgson, and Marks (1971) acknowledged that response prevention was necessary, but found that this could be achieved without 24-hour supervision from the nursing staff, by just asking patients to refrain from their rituals.

Therefore the procedure first used by Rachman, Hodgson, and Marzillier (1970) involved in-patient treatment with minimally supervised response prevention. A hierarchy of feared situations and objects was presented, with participation from the patient after modelling from the therapist. Later, Rachman, Hodgson, and Marks (1971) experimented with flooding rather than modelled graded approach, and finally flooding combined with modelling was tried (Hodgson, Rachman, and Marks, 1972; Rachman, Marks, and Hodgson, 1973). This latter appears to be the procedure which is most commonly used.

The patient is admitted to hospital and a hierarchy of feared objects and situations is elicited. Items at the top end of the hierarchy are tackled straight away, the patient being encouraged to participate in contamination, etc. after modelling by the therapist. In many cases, contamination and contact with the feared objects is carried a little to excess, with, for example, all contents of the patient's room being touched after contact with dirt. The patient is informed of the need to refrain from performing rituals, but is not supervised, although the nursing staff are aware of the treatment in progress. As soon as suitable ritual reduction has been achieved, the patient is discharged after home treatment sessions, where these are found to be necessary.

The procedures developed by Meyer, Levy, and Schnurer (1974) and Rachman *et al.* appear to differ in the emphasis which is placed on formal response prevention and the mode of reduction of anxiety elicited by ritual-evoking stimuli. Meyer, Levy and Schnurer treat the *suppression* of rituals as being of major importance, considering the actual *mode of presentation* of the feared stimuli to be a minor factor. In contrast, Rachman *et al.* concentrate on the optimal manner of presenting the stimuli (flooding versus graded presentation), taking response prevention as being a necessary, but minor, condition. The effect that this differential emphasis may have on outcome has not been investigated but some attempt at clarification has been made in the review below.

THEORETICAL BASES

Modelling, flooding and response prevention procedures all assume the same model of compulsive behaviour. Stimuli such as contamination or evil thoughts which form the centre of the obsessional patient's problems are considered to be conditioned stimuli which elicit strong emotional responses, often anxiety. This leads to two forms of avoidance response: either the patient keeps away from the offending stimuli, or when contact cannot be avoided he indulges in rituals which will rid him of his contamination or nullify his thoughts.

In the initial stages of theorizing about modelling, flooding and response prevention, a two-factor theory of avoidance behaviour was adopted (after Mowrer, 1951). It was considered that the avoidance response was reinforced by emotional drive reduction. This assumption endowed the conditioned emotional response with a controlling function over avoidance behaviour. If avoidance responding is being maintained by drive reduction, then elimination of the drive would render avoidance unnecessary. It would follow from this that treatment should aim at the reduction of the conditioned emotional response. As will be described, this two-factor theory of avoidance has been challenged and the theoretical accounts of the treatment procedures have been modified accordingly.

1. Modelling

Rachman, Hodgson and Marks' (1971) use of modelling in their trials resulted from the work of Bandura (1969). Bandura (in 1969) conceptualized all avoidance responses in terms of a two-factor model, but a few years later he qualified this view a little. He acknowledged that there was considerable experimental evidence, especially from work with animals, which indicated that emotional response and avoidance behaviour are not always related in the way that the two-factor model dictates (Bandura 1971a).

To accommodate these findings he mentioned Rescorla and Solomon's (1967) view that avoidance behaviour is mainly regulated by central mediators which exert control over both autonomic and motor components. Bandura cited laboratory experiments which demonstrated that there may be powerful symbolic control over emotional responses. In particular he described an experiment by Bridger and Mandel (1964) in which emotional responses were conditioned to neutral stimuli by the threat of electric shock and were then abolished by the information that the shocks would be discontinued. In another group in the same experiment it was found that emotional responses conditioned using actual shock were not readily controlled by altered cognitions.

Bandura recognized the similarity between this result and the behaviour of people with phobias outside the laboratory. He noted, for example, that a snake phobic subject would not lose his fear on being told that a snake was harmless. Bandura concluded that conditioned emotional responses vary to the degree to which they are under symbolic control. He seemed to argue that fears for which cognitive control is powerful may be reduced, often immediately, by altering the patient's circumstances or the instructions given to him. In contrast, avoidance responses under autonomic, rather than cognitive control, would not be amenable to cognitive intervention and will require alternative forms of intervention of which modelling is one option.

In declaring that non-mediated avoidance responses are under autonomic control Bandura (1971a) appears to have reverted to the strict two-factor model of avoidance which influenced his work on modelling in 1969. Indeed his 1969 view of modelling effects appears to remain intact. As it follows from the two-factor theory that elimination of the emotional response would make avoidance unnecessary, Bandura concentrated on anxiety reduction. This could be achieved by repeated presentation of the conditioned stimulus in the absence of the unconditioned stimulus, that is Pavlovian extinction. Rather than adopting a direct learning procedure, Bandura (1969) postulated that emotional responses can be extinguished on a vicarious basis.

It would follow that a patient who watched someone else approaching a feared object (say a snake) should repeatedly show improvement, in terms of fear and avoidance, just as he would have done if he had made the approaches himself. He cited results from several studies which upheld this prediction, the most convincing of which was a study by Bandura, Blanchard, and Ritter (1969) with snake phobic subjects. During modelling treatment, subjects were relaxed and then required to watch a film of adults and children engaging in increasingly threatening interaction with a snake. They were instructed to stop the film if anxiety was experienced and to review the scene repeatedly whilst relaxed until no fear was felt. This procedure was found to be as effective as traditional systematic desensitization (without *in vivo* practice) in reducing avoidance behaviour. Although this result is consonant with the views that fear may be eliminated vicariously, it does not indicate whether extinction of anxiety proceeds in a manner comparable to that observed in direct exposure of the patient (imaginal or real life) or whether reduction in avoidance responding is related to decrement in anxiety in the same way in the two conditions. Apart from corroborative findings such as this, Bandura (1969) did not provide any direct evidence for the comparability of vicarious and direct extinction effects.

Bandura's initial discussion was concerned only with observations of a filmed or live model. However, he recognized the potential of active participation by the patient. In the study of Bandura, Blanchard, and Ritter (1969) just mentioned, a third group of subjects received a combination of graduated modelling and guided participation. For each of a graded series of approach responses, the therapist modelled the required behaviour, physically guided the subject through the same act and, finally, withdrew leaving the patient with the snake. This procedure resulted in greater reduction in avoidance behaviour than either modelling without participation or systematic desensitization.

In view of this and other findings, Bandura (1969) seemed to assign an adjunctive, but not a necessary function to participation. He described the probable effects of modelling with participation as two-fold. The repeated modelling reduces the autonomic response evoking potential of the feared stimuli to a level which no longer elicits avoidance behaviour. Approach may then be undertaken and is consolidated during the participation stage, when direct contact with the feared object provides new favourable experiences which extinguish residual anxiety and avoidance tendencies. Despite the lack of any definitive empirical studies and the shortcomings of the theoretical approach, this was the model which was foremost when the work on modelling with obsessionals began.

2. Flooding

Being inspired by the reports of implosion by Hogan and Kirchner (1967) and Stampfl (1967), the early work on flooding with phobic patients emphasized maximization of anxiety as an essential component of treatment (see, for example, Watson and Marks, 1971). The patient had to be exposed for prolonged periods to very high-intensity stimuli until his autonomic responsiveness diminished to a state in which no anxiety could be aroused. In order to ensure continuous exposure, it was necessary to prevent escape by request or social pressure. Thus some degree of response prevention was introduced, but only as a means of attaining the required anxiety conditions and not as a treatment in its own right.

In parallel with the practical procedure, the first theoretical explanation of flooding (Rachman, 1969) was concerned exclusively with the mechanisms involved in the reduction of the autonomic response. The avoidance response was left to take care of itself, as presumably it was assumed that, in accordance with the two-factor theory, avoidance would cease automatically when the anxiety had been eliminated. It was not until it was recognized that this relationship between anxiety and avoidance response does not always hold (see Rachman and Hodgson, 1974) that direct treatment of the avoidance response through response prevention was considered. Several theoretical explanations of response prevention are presented below. The present discussion will be limited to anxiety reduction.

Rachman (1969) has provided the clearest theoretical account of flooding. He attempted to reconcile the seeming necessity for high-anxiety elicitation during treatment with habituation, which was much in vogue as an explanation of desensitization effects at the time. During flooding, he had observed that initially patients tended to become extremely anxious, sometimes for prolonged periods, but that eventually they would achieve a quiescent state. He postulated that by pushing arousal up very high, the patient was put into a paradoxical state in which fear-arousing stimuli failed to evoke a response. This state was thought to reflect a decrease in arousal to below the normal level. The change from high to paradoxically low arousal was taken to be the product of an inherent self-limiting mechanism. Rachman considered that once the state of low arousal had been achieved, very rapid habituation to the feared stimuli might take place. No-one has attempted to discover whether or not habituation is evident during the final phase of exhaustion, and so the hypothesis remains untested.

Although attractive, Rachman's habituation model is essentially unproven and indeed is not the only viable account of the anxiety-reduction component of flooding. Baum (1970), discussing response prevention, suggested that elimination of the autonomic response might represent classical extinction through the repeated presentation of the conditioned stimulus in the absence of the unconditioned stimulus. Again this idea has not been investigated experimentally. Neither Rachman's nor Baum's models can encompass the successful treatment of patients who experience little or no anxiety during flooding (Rachman and Hodgson, 1974). One view which could accommodate such cases is that of Marks (1975). He suggested that the effects of flooding and other behavioural treatments could best be 'explained' in terms of exposure to the feared stimuli. Wolpe (1976) pointed out the lack of explanatory power of this description and indeed gave the idea a sharp, but warranted, dismissal.

Rather than attempting to modify models of autonomic responding to fit situations in which no such response is evident, it would seem to be more fruitful to seek explanations in terms of direct modification of the avoidance response, for which no autonomic response is required. It seems likely that the change in patients who do not experience anxiety may be accounted for most easily in terms of response prevention effects.

3. Response prevention

Baum (1970) has suggested three alternative explanations for the ameliorative effects of prevention of escape from feared stimuli on subsequent avoidance, based on work with animals, mostly rats. The first, which has been mentioned already, was the possibility of classical extinction of the autonomic response. The other two explanations were directly concerned with respondent behaviour.

One, named the *competing response* theory, was first described by Page (1955). It was contended that Pavlovian extinction does not occur during response prevention, but rather, new responses (for example crouching and freezing in rats) are developed to cope with the fear. Therefore the fear may remain, but be dealt with through new coping responses, not by avoidance. Franchina, Hauser, and Agee (1975) cast doubt on the validity of this competing-responses interpretation of response prevention effects. They argued that if competing responses are developed during response prevention, then subsequent retraining of the original avoidance response should be impeded as the competing responses would have to be extinguished or inhibited. This was not found to be the case as rats given response prevention differed from others receiving control, neutral restraint only on the first two trials of retraining. Subsequently there was no difference between the groups. Findings such as this support Baum's (1970) conclusion that the competing response theory is unlikely to be a viable explanation of response prevention effects.

The third theory mentioned by Baum seems to represent no real advance on the other two. He suggested that rather than either extinction or competing responses occurring during response prevention, the subject learns, specifically, to relax. He felt that the behaviour exhibited by rats during response prevention was consistent with this interpretation. It seems likely that this relaxation 'theory' would be subject to at least the same criticisms as that concerned with competing responses and possibly more.

Rachman and Hodgson (1974) have cited a further possible reason for response prevention effects. They pointed out that Gray (1971) stated that an avoidance response may not be reinforced by anxiety reduction, but rather by approach to 'safety signals' which have secondary rewarding properties. This being so, response prevention would serve to break the connection between execution of the avoidance response and presentation of the safety signals. This description is too general to be taken as any form of explanation of response-prevention effects and awaits refinement and empirical support. So far it appears to have been neglected by those working with flooding techniques.

4. Conclusions

Modelling, flooding, and response prevention have been shown to be based on only shaky theoretical foundations. In no case has a really adequate explanation of their effectiveness been provided. Correspondingly there has been a worrying lack of carefully designed experiments using human subjects to test the few theoretical assumptions which do exist.

These observations may reflect a more general retrograde step in behaviour therapy from rigorous scientific method, as illustrated many times in Eysenck's *Behaviour Therapy and the Neuroses*, (1960) to thoughtless empirical pursuit. It does not reflect well on behaviour therapy to have to conclude that the treatments in the studies to be reviewed have no sound theoretical bases.

PUBLISHED TREATMENT REPORTS

1. Meyer and Levy's apotrepic therapy

Meyer, Levy, and Schnurer (1974) reported the outcome of an apotrepic treatment in fifteen obsessive–compulsive patients. The first eight cases had been described previously in a cumulative series of reports (Meyer, 1966; Levy and Meyer, 1971; and Meyer and Levy, 1973) and a single case study (Meyer and Levy, 1970). The descriptions of the patients' complaints and the treatment methods were given in most detail by Meyer (1966). His Case 1, a 33-year old schoolmistress with a six-year history of obsessive compulsive symptoms will be taken as an example.

The patient had experienced some compulsive checking for three years prior to the main illness. However, after the birth of her child she began to overwash the nappies and to worry about anything which might be contaminated by dirt. She felt that the baby or herself might contract disease through contamination. She became housebound and washed and cleaned excessively, using vast amounts of cleansing agents. She was not helped by ECT supportive psychotherapy or drugs. Whilst in hospital, she had responded to systematic desensitization and tranquilizers, but relapsed on return home.

At the start of apotrepic therapy she was taken off all medication and was put under the constant supervision of the nursing staff. Reassurance and encouragement were used to persuade her not to perform her rituals. Sessions with the therapist involved making her perform activities associated with avoidance, for example, touching door knobs and shopping. Initially she was unco-operative, but became more settled so that by the end of four weeks her excessive washing was almost eliminated. Supervision was withdrawn gradually over the next five weeks, and she was allowed home at weekends for three further weeks before discharge. Initially her rituals increased a little when supervision was lifted, but they eventually reduced again and stabilized at about four ritualistic washes and three avoidances a day, although she seemed mildly depressed. Fourteen months after discharge her ritual remained at the same frequency, although their duration and thoroughness had increased. She still tended to avoid contamination, but could refrain from washing if in contact with it. She was able to go out, had increased her leisure and social activities and had resumed teaching. Her relationship with her husband and child had improved greatly and sexual intercourse had been resumed, although she was still frigid.

All fifteen patients listed by Meyer, Levy, and Schnurer (1974) were treated in an equivalent manner with home treatment sessions at the time of discharge in most cases. These patients exhibited washing, cleaning, repetition and checking compulsions alone or in combination as the main complaint, although associated psychological difficulties were always present. Nearly all were felt to be severely affected and this was reflected in their failure to respond to a wide range of treatments in the past. There were eleven women and four men with a mean age of 34 and mean duration of symptoms of 15.6 years (range 4 to 36). With one exception, patients were admitted to hospital for treatment.

The patients and a non-independent observer rated rituals, anxiety, depression, work adjustment, social adjustment, sexual adjustment and leisure activities on a visual analogue scale. Ratings were made before and after treatment and at follow-up intervals varying from eighteen months to six years. Outcome was evaluated from the percentage change in observer rating of rituals from before to after treatment. Patients with a fall of 75 per cent or more were classified as 'much improved', those with a 50 to 75 per cent change as 'improved', a 25 to 50 per cent drop indicated 'slight improvement' and anything below that 'no change'.

At the end of treatment, ten patients were 'much improved', three having no symptoms; four were 'improved' and one showed 'slight improvement'. Follow-up information was available for all but the last three patients seen as these had only recently completed treatment (all 'much improved'). Two who were improved at the end of treatment continued to improve, the seven with the most favourable immediate outcome maintained their change, and the remaining two showed a slight return to their compulsive behaviour. To these successes may be added one further case, reported by Meyer, Robertson, and Tatlow (1975). Their female patient was given brief home treatment for her washing and cleaning rituals resulting from contact with objects associated with death. Eight months after treatment she reported no return of rituals. The results from the series of fifteen patients also indicated that where there were problems with depression, anxiety, work, leisure and sexual life at the outset of treatment, these tended to improve a great deal during treatment or the follow-up period. Only sexual adjustment remained unchanged and very impaired in most cases.

Meyer, Levy, and Schnurer (1974) were aware that it is difficult to draw firm conclusions about the efficacy of their treatment as their trial included no control procedures. However, they pointed out that many of their patients had failed to respond to other treatments including other behaviour therapy techniques. In addition their success rate seemed to compare favourably with studies of prognosis (Kringlen, 1965) and behavioural treatment outcome (Cooper, Gelder, and Marks, 1965) in obsessive–compulsive states. Overall they were justified in concluding that the results obtained with apotrepic treatment were relatively good.

Meyer, Levy, and Schnurer (1974) considered that several factors might have been operative in producing improvement in symptoms. As the therapist frequently demonstrated contaminating actions when persuading the patient to co-operate, some degree of modelling took place and in addition the therapist would manually guide the patient to the stimulus in a manner reminiscent of Maier (1949). The total response prevention was felt to be of crucial importance. As long as this was enforced, the exact way in which the stimuli were presented was felt to be a minor influence. The apparent similarity of the procedure to implosion or flooding was noted, but Meyer, Levy, and Schnurer (1974) pointed out that no deliberate attempt was made to induce or maximize anxiety. On the contrary, very little change in anxiety level during sessions was recorded in their patients. In addition treatment sessions may have helped relatives to become less involved in the rituals and to learn the treatment techniques for future use. Apart from providing the information for identification of these contributory factors, Meyer and Levy's series of case studies do not allow any real assessment of the relative importance of each. The promise of their initial results provide good grounds for further investigation.

2. Modelling, flooding, and response prevention (after Rachman, Hodgson, and Marks, 1971)

(a) Case Reports

Rachman, Hodgson, and Marzillier (1970) presented an elaborate description of the treatment of a single case which seemed to provide the stimulus for their own later group experimental work as well as for investigations by other teams of therapists. Their patient had developed some obsessive–compulsive difficulties during adolescence, but did not seek treatment until the age of twenty. After four hospital admissions, a modified leucotomy was performed, reducing the patient's feelings of tension, but leaving his rituals unchanged. Six months later he was referred for behavioural treatment. Supportive therapy and imaginal de-sensitization produced only slight improvement. At this stage he was spending four-and-a-half hours a day on compulsive washing activities especially related to going to the lavatory. Prior to full treatment, the effects of possible behavioural interventions were investigated experimentally. For this purpose, a behavioural avoidance test was constructed comprising five items ranging from a small dish of marmalade to a smear of dog excrement. First, the patient was given eleven sessions of flooding in imagination with tape-recorded descriptions of anxiety-evoking scenes. The first nine sessions each lasted 40 minutes; three were concerned with excrement, three with horror scenes (accidents, etc.) and three with neutral scenes. The remaining two lasted two hours and covered con-tamination with excrement. None of the three kinds of flooding content produced any appreciable change in the patient's avoidance behaviour.

Flooding was succeeded by eleven sessions of modelling, involving graded approach to contaminating stimuli, first modelled by the therapist. Inevitably some response prevention was involved. This procedure brought rapid improve-ment in avoidance so that by the ninth session the patient reported considerable improvement outside sessions. For example his washing after urination was reduced from twenty to six minutes.

The third phase of the investigation centred on response prevention (five sessions). The patient was required to touch a smear of excrement and had to refrain from washing for increasing lengths of time. The improvement noted after modelling was maintained. As the rituals had not quite been eliminated, two months of modelling and response prevention were given. After modelling, the patient touched contaminated objects, refraining from washing for several hours, during which time he pursued his usual occupational therapy activities. In the last week of treatment he washed his hands on average only twice a day, although taking about fifteen minutes over each wash, and he spent about eight minutes on each visit to the toilet. During treatment he had spent sixteen days at home without upset, but was not given home treatment.

He was reassessed three months after discharge, when his washing frequency was found to have increased as had his times spent going to the toilet and to a lesser extent washing. However, he was holding down a job satisfactorily and was not avoiding contaminated places. By the six-month follow-up his frequencies and times had returned to their level at discharge. Hodgson and Rachman (1976, Case A) ended their almost identical account of the same patient with a note that two years after the six-month follow-up, the patient was married and was enjoying domestic life, including gardening.

Rainey (1972) reported dramatic success with an extremely incapacitated patient, using a rather idiosyncratic form of flooding procedure. The patient had a twelve-year history of fears of contamination starting in 1957 when he learnt that one of his classmates had fleas. Over the twelve years he had several forms of treatment including psychotherapy and ECT. On being referred for behavioural treatment, he was restricted to his apartment and was taking elaborate precautions to keep contamination brought in on letters and so on out of the house. The floor was almost completely covered with newspaper placed on areas which had been ritualistically washed. He had given up showering as it took him many hours to clean the shower afterwards.

At the beginning of treatment the patient was asked to acquire a 1957 coin and a magazine of the same year and to carry them around with him. It was felt that these items would strongly signify 1957, the dreaded year when his fears began, and that his contact with them would contaminate him and hence he would be flooded. He was also told not to perform his rituals. He acquired the magazine, but instead of finding an ordinary coin he purchased a gold sovereign of the appropriate year, which he valued greatly. Although experiencing great anxiety initially, he refrained from his rituals and by the end of the third day could handle objects without discomfort. During the rest of the week he was able to start putting his apartment in order. He received this treatment for six more weeks and then received aid with establishing social relationships. Eighteen months later he was symptom-free and fully employed.

Rainey pointed out that the therapeutic effect may not have been attributable entirely to flooding. The gold coin proved to be extremely reinforcing both through pride in ownership and through the positive attention from the other patients which it evoked. This may have helped to counteract the anxiety elicited by the fact that it was minted in 1957.

A further account by Lambley (1974) deals with compulsive praying rather than washing, in response to contamination. The patient was a female student who had become distressed and tearful, constantly repeating lines of prayer to herself, shortly after attempting sexual intercourse with her boyfriend for the first time. She had a deeply religious background and felt sinful. The praying seemed to act as a means of avoiding the fears of losing control which she was experiencing and so flooding had to involve non-performance of the avoidance praying ritual. The patient was encouraged to stop praying and to experience the discomfort, in the presence of the therapist. She only persisted for ten minutes and then indicated that she wished to stop as the procedure was making her feel worse. Eventually she was treated successfully using covert reinforcement techniques. This case cannot be taken as a failure for flooding, as some discomfort would be expected in the early stages of treatment, but had the patient been persuaded to persist, the ensuing decrease in anxiety might have resulted in some symptomatic relief.

Finally, Catts and McConaghy (1975) reported the results of treatment in a series of six patients using modelling and flooding with patient-controlled response prevention, backed up with nurse supervision on the few occasions where this was indicated. Home treatment, retraining of relatives and drug therapy were all implemented when it was felt that this was necessary. Treatment sessions were given three times a week for three-and-a-half months and the patients were followed up after 9 to 24 months. At discharge, ritualistic behaviour was absent in one patient, 'much improved' in a second and 'improved' in the remaining four. Subjective anxiety showed slightly less change with three patients 'much improved', two 'improved' and one showing 'no change'. The social adjustment of two patients was rated as 'adequate', one as 'much improved' and one as 'improved'. Catts and McConaghy felt that most of the improvement had occurred in the first few weeks of treatment. However, the patients continued to change in the follow-up period so that their final improvement ratings tended to be more favourable than at discharge. As Catts and McConaghy gave very little detail of the chronicity of symptoms, it is not possible to compare these results with those of other studies.

Several other case studies could be outlined as Hodgson, Rachman, and Marks present illustrative accounts of individual patients who were involved in their group research (Rachman et al., 1971, 1973; Hodgson et al., 1972; Marks et al., 1975). However, the treatment procedures and outcomes for such patients will be described in the context of controlled experimental work below.

(b) Controlled treatment trials

The experimental investigations of flooding, modelling and response prevention have been conducted with three distinct aims: to demonstrate the efficacy of the composite treatment and separately of the three components and also to look at procedural manipulations within each component. The studies associated with each aim will be discussed in turn. However, the central body of findings has come from a succession of related papers by Rachman et al. (1971), Hodgson et al. (1972), Rachman et al. (1973), and Marks et al. (1975). The main focus of this work is on the efficacy of the total treatment and component parts. Because the comparisons for the two are based on the same patients, it would be redundant to discuss the two separately. Therefore the Rachman et al. series will be presented in detail, before a more general review is undertaken.

In their first investigation, Rachman et al. (1971) compared two groups of five patients who were all given relaxation as a control treatment prior to receiving either modelling or flooding. Hodgson et al. (1972) treated five more patients with relaxation followed by flooding and modelling combined and compared them directly with the two previous groups. Rachman et al. (1973) replicated the modelling and flooding combined procedure without the relaxation phase with five patients and compared the outcome with those of the previous studies. In this way five patients receiving modelling and five receiving flooding were compared both with each other and with ten patients given flooding and modelling.

All twenty patients were followed up and their state was reported after six months and two years (Marks et al., 1975). The researchers acknowledged that their procedure of adding groups after considerable lapses of time could lead to accidental bias in sampling. However, they were not aware of any such bias, and the similarity between their various groups of patients reduced the possibility that such had occurred. Therefore no further notice will be taken of the time lapses between groups and for clarity, the studies will be discussed as if all patients had been treated at the same time. The two combined treatment groups will be distinguished from each other by referring to them as modelling and flooding groups 1 and 2 where necessary.

The patients' sex ratio of seventeen women to three men is not typical of that for patients with obsessive–compulsive disorder in general and was thought to be unexplained quirks of sampling. However, recently Dowson (1977) has found cleaning rituals at least occur more frequently in women than in men, so that Marks et al.'s sample of twenty may not be so atypical as was at first considered.

All twenty patients were considered to be in the chronic stage of illness having exhibited compulsive rituals for a minimum of one year, with a mean duration of ten years. Nearly all had received previous psychiatric care which had had little effect, but with the exception of three who had been taking antidepressants over long periods and who continued to take them, the patients were not on medication during the treatment trial. Twelve patients experienced fears of contamination from various sources and engaged in washing and cleaning rituals. Seven checked excessively and one constantly had to straighten and tidy herself and her home. The frequency of patients with washing and checking rituals was more or less comparable in the four treatment groups.

Patients in the modelling (M), flooding (F) and modelling and flooding 1 (MF1) groups were admitted to hospital for seven weeks. One week of observation and recording was succeeded by three weeks control relaxation training and three weeks of modelling and/or flooding. The hospital stay for modelling and flooding 2 (MF2) patients was shorter as the relaxation training phase was omitted. Assessments were made before and after treatment.

Relaxation treatment consisted of fifteen 40 to 60 minute sessions in which the patient relaxed to tape-recorded instructions. During the last ten minutes of each session, she was asked to think of one of her obsessive worries whilst relaxing. All subjects were given fifteen 40 to 60 minute sessions of modelling, flooding or combined treatments over three weeks. In the M group, the patient and therapist compiled a hierarchical list of situations evoking distress, avoidance and rituals and the therapist modelled an approach to each item, starting with the least feared. The patient had to follow the therapist's example at each step. As Rachman points out, the treatment resulted in 'in vivo desensitization, with modelling added. The F group patients also constructed a hierarchy, but they were required to go into the most feared situation immediately, without prior modelling from the therapist, although the latter stayed calm and reassuring throughout. Patients in both combined groups (MF1 and 2) followed the flooding procedure of entering the most-feared situations, but after observing the therapist doing so. After each session, all patients, regardless of group, were asked to remain contaminated and/or refrain from rituals for increasing periods of time. This restraint was voluntary, as there was no direct supervision. Nevertheless, this request (from a high-prestige therapist) does represent one form of response prevention, which contributes a component part of all three treatment procedures. In addition all patients were denied reassurance for their obsessional worries. Any patient who needed extra treatment received as many sessions as necessary during the follow-up period.

The results are scattered and to some extent replicated in the four papers. The order of presentation here does not always follow that in the originals, but it is hoped that the present approach will provide some structure for the complex series of results. The results relating to the efficacy of the treatments will be given first. These will be followed by those comparing components of treatment, with a comment on procedural variations and finally by follow-up results. The question 'is the treatment more effective than the relaxation control?' may be asked of modelling, flooding and combined treatments separately. Rachman, Hodgson, and Marks (1971) compared modelling (M) and flooding (F) individually with relaxation control. For each group, improvement during the relaxation phase was compared with improvement during treatment proper on a number of outcome measures. The five M group patients showed greater improvement after modelling than after relaxation on the assessor's ratings of phobic anxiety and of phobic avoidance (concerning the main obsessions), the patient's self-ratings on the same two dimensions, fear thermometer ratings and the patients' ratings of anxiety. The assessor's rating of depression also shows relating improvement. However, as Rachman *et al.* (1971) state that four M group patients showed mild to moderate depression during modelling treatment, it seems questionable whether the stated direction of change is correct. The results from the avoidance test were not given, indicating that they were not significant. However, appropriate avoidance tests could not be constructed for two patients in this group. Any comparison based on $N = 3$ would have very limited meaning.

The F group patients showed relatively more improvement after flooding than after relaxation on assessor's ratings of phobic anxiety and phobic avoidance concerning obsessions and for the patient's equivalent rating of anxiety. When assessor's and patient's ratings on both scales were all combined, the improvement remained significant; but this seems to add very little to the information achieved from the separate analyses and is not independent of them. Improvement on fear thermometer ratings and avoidance test scores was also significantly greater during the flooding stage. For some unspecified reason, Rachman *et al.* also analysed the results for the two groups pooled, and not surprisingly obtained much the same findings as for the separate analyses. Both forms of treatment failed to yield improvement on a number of scales, but with the exception of Leyton Obsessional Inventory scores, these tended to be much less closely related to the ritualistic behaviour than the ones showing positive changes, being mostly semantic differential and PEN (Eysenck and Eysenck, 1969) scores.

Overall, therefore, it appears that both modelling and flooding may have some effect in the treatment of obsessive–compulsive disorders. The effect is made more marked by the fact that the patients showed only minimal change during the relaxation phase, despite the fact that the introduction of the first and novel treatment might be expected to have some 'placebo' effect (Boulougouris, Marset, and Marks, 1971).

The effectiveness of modelling and flooding combined was assessed by Rachman, Marks, and Hodgson (1973). Their five MF2 group patients were not given relaxation themselves, but their treatment improvement was compared with that for the relaxation phase of the fifteen patients treated previously, (Rachman et al., 1971; Hodgson et al., 1972). The results were analysed using a multivariate analyses of variance, so that related variables were considered together. MF2 group patients showed significantly greater improvement than relaxation controls on all four groups of measures: clinical ratings (self and assessor ratings of symptoms avoidance and anxiety), Leyton Obsessional Inventory scores, avoidance test, and semantic differential scores. This affirmed the relative efficacy of modelling and flooding combined, but again there was no real indication of the extent of the change.

One objective of the research appeared to be to determine whether flooding and modelling differed in their effectiveness and further whether there was any advantage to be gained from combining them. The initial study of Rachman et al. (1971) was designed to investigate the first of these problems. The M and F groups were compared in terms of the response to the treatment phase. The only significant difference was that M group patients rated themselves significantly less anxious in general after treatment than patients who received flooding.

Modelling and flooding combined has been compared with modelling and flooding alone twice. The results of Hodgson et al. (1972) were reanalysed, with the addition of the second combined group, by Rachman et al. (1973). Hodgson et al. (1972) compared the M group results with those of the MF1 group and found significantly greater improvement for the MF1 group in the patient's ratings of anxiety and of avoidance concerning the obsession and in interference and resistance scores on the Leyton Obsessional Inventory. These findings seemed to indicate that the combined treatment might be slightly superior to modelling alone, at least in some areas of change. However, this effect disappeared with reanalysis on the addition of the second combined treatment group (Rachman et al., 1973). A multivariate analysis of variance was used, comparing F, M and MF1 and MF2 groups. There was no indication of the superiority of the modelling and flooding treatment on any measure. It is by no means clear why the previously significant differences failed to emerge, especially as the composition of the samples remained unchanged except for the addition of the MF2 group patients. However, Rachman et al. appeared to accept the result of the more recent analysis, in concluding that there was no difference between the effectiveness of modelling and flooding and modelling alone.

The 1973 study was also favoured in their parallel conclusion that flooding and the combined treatment did not differ in their effectiveness. Hodgson *et al.* (1972) had found that the modelling and flooding patients showed significantly greater improvement on patients' ratings of anxiety to do with obsessions, the avoidance test and Leyton Obsessional Inventory interference scores. Again, these differences were not apparent in the later analysis.

All patients were followed up after six months and again after two years from the beginning of treatment. As many patients had received further treatment and booster sessions, the findings represent the results of rather more than three weeks treatment. Rachman *et al.* (1973) compared states at the end of treatment with that at the six-month stage. There was no significant change over this period on any measure. Further, the effects of modelling, flooding and combined treatments did not differ in this respect. Marks, Hodgson, and Rachman (1975) contacted the patients after two years and found that improvement had been at least maintained, and in some cases seemed to have continued a little.

Having described the general nature of the Maudsley studies, relevant aspects of them will be reintroduced in the more general discussion of outcome, components of treatment and procedural variations.

(i) Outcome of treatment by modelling and flooding combined. Hackmann and McLean (1975) found some indication of improvement after four sessions of modelling and flooding in an experimental comparison of this technique with thought-stopping. Ten obessive-compulsive patients given modelling and flooding first showed significant improvement on only four to fourteen self-report and assessor ratings, whereas ten given the same treatment after thought-stopping improved on only two. As this was an experimental trial, treatment was incomplete at this stage and no follow-up information was given.

The main evidence for the efficacy of modelling and flooding comes from the series of studies by Rachman, Hodgson and Marks described above. At the end of treatment, the two modelling and flooding groups had shown substantial change on many of the outcome measures. However, the improvement was not equally marked in all cases. Rachman *et al.* (1973) used the pooled self and assessor ratings on anxiety and avoidance on obsession as a global index of change. Patients changing four or more points on an eight-point scale between the beginning and end of treatment were said to be 'much improved', those changing two to 3.9 points, 'improved' and the remainder were considered to have shown 'no improvement'. On these criteria, four of the patients in the first modelling and flooding group were 'much improved' and one showed 'no change'. For the second group the corresponding figures were one and two, with two patients being 'improved'.

Marks *et al.* (1975) reported that patients were given extra sessions as necessary before discharge and that home treatment and booster sessions were given when need arose between discharge and two-year follow-up. The rate of additional sessions was not given separately for the modelling, flooding and combined groups. Overall, the mean number of treatment sessions given after the treatment trial was 7.7 (no SD cited) including both booster and domiciliary sessions. A mean of three home visits were made to eleven patients. Nine patients needed antidepressants during follow-up, two were given marital therapy and one assertive training. Unfortunately, Marks *et al.* give no indication which patients required further treatment, making interpretation of the seemingly impressive follow-up results impossible.

The ten variously boosted modelling and flooding patients maintained their improvement at six months and two years (compared with before treatment) but there was little indication of improvement continuing beyond the end of the three-week treatment stage as there were no differences between post-treatment and six month follow-up scores. This finding appears to contradict the notion that patients were given further treatment until ready for discharge. If that was the case, the follow-up results should be more favourable than post-treatment, reflecting the effects of the additional sessions. If the additional sessions had no effect then the patients should never have been discharged, as the reason for the extra treatment was that they could not be discharged in their existing state. It seems more likely that the sessions were effective, but that after discharge the patients tended to move back towards their end-of-treatment level so that the follow-up comparisons indicated no change. Some relapse after additional treatment has very different implications for further investigation to the contention of Marks *et al.* (1975) that treatment beyond the three-week stage had very little effect. Nevertheless the six-month follow-up results with modelling and flooding with extra treatment appeared encouraging.

The two-year findings were even more notable. A pooled self-rating of anxiety and avoidance concerning obsessions was used as an index with the same criteria for improvement (since the beginning of treatment) as before. Again all four treatment groups were considered together only; at two years fourteen patients were 'much improved', one 'improved' and five showed 'no improvement'. The outcome for each patient at two years was very strongly associated with her outcome at six months and after treatment and there was a slight tendency for outcome to improve during the longer follow-up period.

(ii) Components of treatment: modelling, flooding, and response prevention.
Modelling. Hodgson, Rachman, and Marks (1972) demonstrated that their modelling procedure could be effective an bringing about both short-term and long-term improvement. A comparable degree of change was reported by Röper (1977) in two groups of five patients treated by the Rachman *et al.* (1971) modelling procedure following observation of the therapist practising re-laxation, or modelling by the therapist without patient participation. However, neither of these demonstrations can be said to have tested the efficacy of modelling (Bandura, 1969) per se, as both involved graded approach to the feared situation in addition to modelling by the therapist. As Rachman *et al.* (1971) pointed out, the procedure resembled *in vivo* desensitization plus modelling. As *in vivo* desensitization on its own has been shown to be effective in some case of obsessive-compulsive disorder (see Chapter 4), it is unclear whether

the improvement in the Hodgson *et al.* (1972) and Röper (1977) groups was due to desensitization or whether modelling had an additional effect.

In order to clarify the influence of modelling, the modelling procedure should be compared with *in vivo* desensitization on its own. To some extent this has been undertaken by Boersma *et al.* (1976). Four patients given flooding and response prevention and three patients given gradual exposure and response prevention were compared with six patients whose treatment included modelling, two of whom had received flooding and four, gradual exposure. Each patient had fifteen two-hour sessions, held on average three times a week. For all patients together there was significant improvement at the end of treatment on measures equivalent to those used by Rachman *et al.* (1973). However, the addition of modelling seemed to add very little to the flooding and graded exposure effects as the modelling patients showed significantly greater improvement only on 'avoidance–other compulsions', rated by the therapist.

In addition, the effect of modelling may be assessed from the Rachman *et al.* (1973) comparisons of flooding and modelling and flooding groups. Hodgson *et al.* (1972) report indicated that the combined treatment group seemed to do rather better than patients receiving flooding alone on several measures. At the end of treatment four combined-treatment patients, but only one from the flooding group were considered 'much improved' on the usual pooled measure of change. One combined patient and two flooding ones showed no improvement whereas the remaining two flooding patients were classified as improved. The outcome at six-month follow-up was the same for the combined patients, but two flooding patients were now classified as 'much improved' and the rest as 'not improved'. Paradoxically, the second group of patients given modelling and flooding (Rachman *et al.*, 1973) behaved more like the flooding group than their combined-treatment predecessors. Their immediate improvement rate was the same as that of the flooding group, although by six-months follow-up, three were much improved, one improved and only one showed no change. Although Rachman *et al.* (1973) do not report any statistical appraisal of the difference (or lack of it) between the outcome for their two modelling plus flooding groups, they obviously assumed that the two did not differ as they combined the results for comparison with those for the flooding group. On this basis it was concluded that flooding, and modelling and flooding did not differ in their effectiveness. It would follow from this that modelling failed to add anything to the flooding procedure.

However, the assumption that the outcome for the two modelling plus flooding groups was equivalent may be questioned, especially as the second group seemed to have less favourable results. There was an important procedural difference between the two, in that patients in the first had been in hospital for three or four weeks receiving relaxation training whilst those in the second had been in hospital only for a short assessment period before treatment started. Hodgson *et al.* (1972) have demonstrated that relaxation training on its own did not influence the compulsive behaviour. However, it is still possible that it may have had some indirect influence on treatment outcome. Although not specifically instructed to do so, some patients may have relaxed themselves during flooding or combined treatment and thus facilitated contact with the feared stimuli allowing treatment to progress more smoothly. The published reports give no indication whether this may have been the case.

In addition, one consequence of being in hospital would be that the patient would become very familiar with her surroundings, enabling her to establish her ritual routines before treatment proper began. Thus it might be possible to treat a wider range of her habitual rituals than if her arrival at the hospital was more recent.

With these two possibilities in mind, it seems reasonable to argue that the two modelling and flooding groups experienced differing treatment. As the prior relaxation training would be expected to enhance results, this factor might account for the observed differences in outcome. In this case the most appropriate test of the effectiveness of modelling would be the comparison of flooding, and modelling plus flooding conducted by Hodgson *et al.* (1972). From this it appeared that the introduction of modelling by the therapist may add something to the effects of flooding. This finding needs to be replicated in a more convincing manner.

Flooding. It has been indicated already that flooding may be no more effective than graded modelling procedures (Rachman *et al.*, 1971; Hodgson *et al.*, 1972). The results obtained by Boersma *et al.* (1976) in the study described previously, are consistent with this as the outcomes of the two treatments differed significantly on only one of a number of measures. However, it has been suggested tentatively that a combination of modelling and flooding may be slightly better than flooding on its own.

A further account of flooding in obsessive–compulsive patients comes from Boulougouris and Bassiakos (1973). They reported on the outcome of an uncontrolled trial of flooding with three patients; but their careful monitoring of progress and outcome make their observations more informative than in many case reports. Two of the patients washed excessively in association with fears of contamination and the other had to touch certain objects and to dress in a stereotyped manner. Their symptoms had persisted for nine to 25 years. They received fantasy sessions of 40 to 50 minutes in which feelings of insecurity as a result of contamination were stressed and when reduction of anxiety during these was experienced, *in vivo* sessions of 90 to 150 minutes were instituted. During these, modelling was kept to a minimum and the patient was cajoled (sometimes with physical pressure) into the most avoided situations. As treatment was carried out on an outpatient basis, response prevention was conducted with the help of the families. The patients received three to five sessions in fantasy, and one to seven in fantasy and *in vivo* combined.

Patients' and therapists' ratings of obsessions, anxiety and depression decreased after treatment and improvement was maintained at follow-up. Independent assessor ratings showed a similar change from before to after treatment. Measures of heart rate, spontaneous fluctuation of skin conductance and maximal deflection of skin conductance were taken before and after treatment. All were less responsive to ritual-evoking scenes after treatment.

Following the work of Boulougouris and Bassiakos, Rabavilas, Boulougouris, and Stefanis (1976) compared long and short fantasy and *in vivo* sessions in an attempt, primarily, to assess the contributions of these factors to outcome. The study is discussed fully in the context of procedural variations below. In essence, twelve obsessive–compulsive patients received two sessions of each of the four possible combinations of long versus short duration, and fantasy versus *in vivo* presentation. After these eight sessions the patients showed significant improvement on self, assessor and therapist ratings of main obsession and untreated obsession. Patient and assessor ratings of anxiety were also significant, but no raters indicated significant change in depression (which was not much in evidence before treatment). Leyton Obsessional Inventory symptom, interference and resistance scores all improved. Semantic differential scores showed an increase in favourable attitude towards the treated and untreated obsessions.

It is apparent that these results and Boulougouris and Bassiakos' case study findings are consistent with the view that flooding is effective in the treatment of obsessive–compulsive patients. However, there is as yet little evidence about the relative effectiveness of flooding compared with other procedures.

Response Prevention. All the reported modelling and flooding treatments involved an element of response prevention. The patients were usually asked to refrain from indulging in their rituals during or after treatment for as long as possible. No direct supervision was given, but it was explained that indulgence in rituals would interfere with the progress of treatment. As such instructions were always given, and therefore presumably thought to be important, it is surprising that the effects of response prevention were not investigated in the protracted series of studies issuing from Rachman, Hodgson and Marks.

Mills *et al.* (1973) seem to have been the only ones to have attempted to disentangle the effects of response prevention from exposure to feared stimuli. They presented an elegant series of five single-case investigations, one of which will be described in some detail here. The remaining four followed the same general procedure so that only the main results will be given. Mills *et al.* started their investigation with hand-washers. They were able to count the number of times that the patient went to wash by allowing him to do so only at one particular sink; a pen was placed round the sink and a cumulative recorder was operated each time the patient opened the gate to wash. Further, the handles of the sink taps were removable so that response prevention could be imposed automatically. Their first experiment was to establish that response prevention was necessary for reduction in washing to occur. The 31-year-old patient had a two-year history of hand-washing associated with fears of contamination. She had received a number of other treatments including flooding and desensitization, all of which had failed. At the time of treatment, she was washing her hands ten to twenty times a day with elaborate routines associated with each wash. Treatment was conducted following an ABA design. Throughout all phases that patient was brought into contact with objects known to elicit washing. Each day for ten hours on the hour the patient was presented with a ritual-eliciting object. In the first and third phase of treatment, she was allowed ten minutes for washing afterwards if she wished, but in the second phase this was denied. In all phases she was required to go and socialize for five minutes afterwards, otherwise she tended to withdraw. The baseline, phase 1, comprised seven days of exposure during which the patient could wash as often as she wished. She averaged, per day, 7.7 washes and eight reports of the urge to wash. Phase 2, response prevention, lasted fourteen days. The taps were removed from the sink and ward showers and the patient was allowed only one supervised shower a day. The staff gave no praise or feedback. The patient reported an average of 6.5 urges to wash each day. Finally for fourteen days there was a return to baseline conditions with the patient given free access to the sink. She washed her hands once at the end of each day and reported on average only 3.6 urges to wash. Because she continued to be distressed by a few special items (for example, camphor), the patient was exposed to these for a further five days before discharge.

This case demonstrated that exposure to stimuli-eliciting rituals without restriction on washing did not bring about improvement. It was only when response prevention was introduced that reduction in rituals occurred. Three of the other four single-case studies replicated this finding and further indicated that the response prevention effect is not merely either a function of the general instruction to cut down on washing or a placebo effect. The fourth study demonstrated the effectiveness of response prevention in a boy with elaborate rituals associated with going to bed and getting up.

Altogether, Mills *et al.* (1973) appear to have confirmed the importance of response prevention in producing change. It is to be hoped that their ingenious investigations will encourage others to engage in group experimental work on the effects of response prevention. Even as things stand, it is clear that it would be unwise to conclude that either flooding or modelling or a combination of the two are necessarily the main contributors to the promising treatment outcomes which have been observed. It is not impossible that the way in which the stimuli are introduced to the patient has but a minor influence, the more important factor being the completeness of the response prevention which ensues.

Variations in treatment procedures. Only two studies have been concerned primarily with procedural variations within the basic treatments. Rabavilas, Boulougouris, and Stefanis (1976) investigated the length of flooding sessions and the mode of presentation, and Röper, Rachman, and Marks (1975) studied the role of active participation by the patient in modelling.

Rabavilas, Boulougouris, and Stefanis (1976) used a latin-square design, giving two sessions of each of four treatments to each of twelve patients. The treatments comprised all possible combinations of fantasy or *in vivo* practice (without modelling) and long or short exposure. Each session lasted two hours; in the short-exposure condition this was spent in alternating ten-minute presentations of obsessional stimuli and five minutes of neutral material, whilst for long exposure 80 minutes of continued presentation of feared stimuli was followed by 40 minutes of neutral material.

Although the study was designed specifically to look at the influence of duration and mode of presentation, no main effect results were reported for those factors. However, inspection of their rather gross outcome histograms indicates that it is unlikely that either of these variables had any significant effect overall. There did not seem to be any appreciable difference between long and short exposure (fantasy and *in vivo* practice combined) or between fantasy and *in vivo* practice (long and short presentation combined). However significant differences between short and long presentation in the *in vivo* condition were reported. Long practice was superior to short practice on patients, therapists' and assessors' ratings of improvement on the main obsession and total obsessions and on the therapists' ratings of the untreated obsession. Leyton Obsessional Inventory scores also showed more improvement for the long-practice and there was a change in evaluating attitudes towards the main obsessions, favouring the same procedure. The remaining ten outcome measures did not differentiate between the two procedures. There were no parallel differences between long and short presentation within the fantasy condition. There were one or two further differences between other pairs of conditions, but these might well have occurred by chance in the numerous comparisons that appear to have been made.

Thus it seems that whilst the outcome of fantasy was not influenced by the length of exposure, long *in vivo* presentations were superior to short ones. Rabavilas *et al.*'s more general claim that long practice was superior to all other procedures appears to be entirely groundless as no statistical analyses of the comparison of the four treatment conditions were presented. Further, as far as could be gathered from the unacceptably small histograms, there was very little difference between any of the groups, the difference between short and long *in vivo* presentation being as much due to the fact that the former tended to be less effective than the other conditions as to the slight superiority of the latter.

Röper *et al.* (1975) investigated one aspect of modelling which was seen to be of theoretical, if not practical, importance. They wished to know whether patients who merely watched the therapist enter contaminating situations (symbolic modelling) would show as much improvement as patients who copied the therapist's actions.

Two groups of five obsessional patients, of comparable severity to those in Rachman, Hodgson and Marks's earlier studies were given six weeks' treatment. Patients in one group received fifteen sessions of control relaxation training in which the patient copied the therapist's modelled relaxation exercises, followed by fifteen sessions of participant modelling in which the patient was actively engaged, following Rachman *et al.* (1971). The other group of patients had fifteen sessions of passive modelling in which they observed the therapist working through the hierarchy of feared situations, followed by fifteen sessions of participant modelling. The assessment measures were the same as in the previous study. Passive modelling produced significantly greater improvement than relaxation training on self-ratings of avoidance, the avoidance test and the Leyton Obsessional Inventory interference score. Self- and assessor-ratings of total obsessions almost reached significance. The changes after participant modelling were reported as being more marked and covering a wider range of behaviour. The fear and avoidance ratings made by the patients and independent assessor were presented graphically. The superiority of participant modelling was most evident when the change after passive modelling was compared with that after participant modelling preceded by relaxation. The participant scores showed a much steeper drop than passive scores. However, within the group of subjects receiving both passive and participant modelling the decrease in scores after participant modelling was no different from that after passive training. Rather than being reactive to the preceding treatments, this apparent discrepancy between the effects of participant modelling in the two groups may reflect a floor effect as both groups attained approximately the same level after treatment.

These results appear to indicate that whilst watching a therapist engage in ritual-evoking activities without apprehension or dire consequences may produce some improvement, active participation by the patient will enhance the treatment effect. These observations seem to parallel those obtained from desensitization studies, in which desensitization in imagination was found to be much enhanced by *in vivo* graded practice. In so far as the patient perceives the therapist as being similar to herself, the therapist's modelling activities may not be dissimilar to the patient's rehearsal in imagination of a comparable performance by herself. Quite apart from their main aim of comparing treatment techniques, Röper, Rachman, and Marks (1975) were reassured to find that the outcome for both groups was consistent with that in the other Rachman, Hodgson and Marks studies. Overall, five patients were 'much improved', three 'improved' and 'not improved'. After six months' follow-up including additional treatment for a proportion of patients, the position was almost the same with only one 'much improved' patient slipping back into the 'improved' category.

(c) Conclusions

The findings from the controlled treatment studies and from the work of Meyer, Levy, and Schnurer (1974) provide information on three important aspects of clinical practice. They give guides to optimal treatment procedures, indicate the success in outcome which is to be expected and provide a general view of the patient population to which the treatment may be applied. These three areas will be considered in turn, with the studies following Meyer (1966) and Rachman *et al.* (1971) being discussed together except where differences between them exist.

(i) Patient characteristics. All the studies except that by Rabavilas, Boulougouris, and Stefanis (1976) provide sufficient information about the patients to allow several general conclusions to be drawn. Apart from the preponderance of females in the studies by Rachman, Hodgson, and Marks (Marks *et al.* 1975) and Meyer *et al.* (1974), the sexes were about equally represented in the other reports. The majority of patients had one to ten-year histories of disorder with the remainder having been ill for considerably longer periods (20 to 50 years). Meyer *et al.*'s cohort included a slightly greater

proportion of patients with very long histories than did other studies. Very many patients had received previous psychiatric treatment, usually without effect.

Virtually all the patients exhibited overt rituals and avoidance, which in some cases were accompanied by ruminative thoughts. The universality of rituals arose through selection in most studies as the treatments were not designed to deal with obsessional thoughts and ruminations. About two-thirds of the patients had rituals involving cleansing and washing associated with fears of contamination and avoidance. The remaining third were divided between pervasive checking, repetition and other miscellaneous complaints including straightening and rigidity in behaviour patterns, for example, dressing. The occurrence of these forms of symptom was independent of sex. The proportions of cases suffering from each were similar for male and female patients (considering all studies combined). Taking these observations together, it appears that these patients were likely to be comparable to those who attend most psychiatric clinics. Therefore, findings from the studies may be applied meaningfully to obsessive–compulsive patients with overt rituals.

As the patients within as well as between studies varied in their response to treatment, it is possible that some types of client are more likely to respond than others. Very few studies indicated which of the patients whose symptoms had been described improved and which did not, so that a search for relevant patient variables over all studies combined, was not possible. Although there were no definite reports of patient attributes affecting outcome, it seems to be agreed that length of history, age at onset, severity, age and sex are unlikely to be found to be influential (Meyer *et al.* 1974).

On the other hand, several positive observations, based on experience with patients have been made. Marks *et al.* (1975) considered that the patient's ability to reduce rituals between sessions on the first few days was a good predictive index and Meyer *et al.* (1974) believed that the degree of subjective resistance experienced may prove to be of predictive value. Rachman *et al.* (1973) felt that the most difficult patients to treat were those with pervasive checking rituals, involving up to 50 to 100 checks a day in a wide variety of situations. Rachman *et al.* (1971) had already intimated that patients with extensive rituals might not be worth treating unless treatment could be carried out at home as well as in hospital.

In contrast, Rachman *et al.* (1973) considered that the patients with the best prognosis seemed to be those with fairly circumscribed contamination fears and washing rituals. These two observations seem to be consistent with Meyer *et al.*'s (1974) comment that the type of symptom and the degree to which it is situation dependent may be of importance. Moreover, they appear to bear more than a passing resemblance to the tentative conclusions given in the previous chapter about the relative efficacy of desensitization with circumscribed and pervasive disorders. All these observations require validation as they have far-reaching implications for patient selection and for the need for alternative treatment techniques.

The one patient in Meyer *et al.*'s (1974) series who failed to exhibit any marked improvement was found to show little resistance to her rituals (as judged from Leyton Obsessional Inventory score) and there was an almost delusional-like quality in her belief about contamination. Similarly, of the five patients who showed no improvement in the Rachman, Hodgson, and Marks series only the failure of one patient, who co-operated in all ways, was inexplicable. The remaining four were unco-operative and did not obey the instruction not to perform rituals between sessions. It is not clear why these patients failed to co-operate. It seems equally possible either that they lacked the motivation to endure the discomfort required of them, or that they found the treatment exceptionally upsetting and were unable to control their rituals. It would be possible to devise measures of both motivation and discomfort and to determine which, if either, of these factors predicted treatment outcome.

As it has been shown that patients respond differently to treatment, there is a need for further clarification of the patient variables which are likely to influence outcome. Although purpose-designed group studies of outcome might provide the most definitive information, the difficulty in collecting and treating a large group of relatively uncommon and demanding patients at one time places such an approach beyond the reach of many clinicians. However, there seems to be no reason why meaningful information cannot be collected by careful assessment and monitoring of individual patients as they are referred for treatment. Although such an approach is complicated by heterogeneity of treatment circumstances and procedures, any predictive variables consistently identified in this situation could be generalized with some confidence to future routine clinical work.

(ii) Outcome of treatment. The results of all the studies are in agreement in demonstrating that modelling, flooding, response prevention, and apotrepic treatments bring about improvement in the majority of patients. The results reported by Marks (1977) support this view. However, it is equally apparent that very few patients lose their symptoms or are functioning well in all areas of life at follow-up. In evaluating the overall efficacy of treatment it is necessary to consider the range and extent of improvement, the prospects of further change and the need for additional treatment and for booster sessions after relapse. The findings relating to these areas of change will be reviewed.

Range of improvement. The studies were unanimous in finding improvement at the end of treatment and at follow-up on measures directly related to the treated obsessive–compulsive symptoms. Although change was not always found on all such measures, the overall consistency of the results make them appear conclusive. In addition, Rabavilas, Boulougouris, and Stefenis (1976) found that improvement in treated rituals generalized to those which had not been dealt with directly.

On the whole, there was no clear tendency for associated psychiatric symptoms to show a similar reduction. Depression, free floating anxiety, panics and depersonalization showed no consistent changes in the group of studies associated with Rachman *et al.* (1971). In contrast, Meyer *et al.*'s (1974) patients tended to show improvement in anxiety and depression, paralleling changes in their ritual behaviour.

Apart from the possibility of real differences in outcome or in the patients used, there are several alternative explanations for the discrepancy between the two sets of findings. The possible effects of rater differences seems to be reduced by the use of patient ratings in several analyses, as it seems unlikely that there would be consistent differences between studies in the patients' response bias. However, the scales used differed not only in the form of the rating required (point versus visual analogue), but also perhaps, in the definition of anxiety, depression, etc. that were adopted. It seems unlikely that these relatively minor technical details would have accounted for markedly different trends in the results. The latter are more likely to be a function of some aspect of the treatment used, but the operative factor is not apparent from the published account.

Meyer, Levy and Schnurer's (1974) patients also tended to show improvement on ratings of work and social adjustments and leisure activities. No consistent comparable changes were noted in the other studies. Again this discrepancy seems unlikely to be attributable to differences in the scales alone.

Finally, all the studies were in agreement in finding that sexual adjustment usually remained unimproved.

These findings are based on ratings from scales either devised for another patient group (Rachman *et al.* 1971) or of unknown reliability (Meyer *et al.* 1974). However, the results obtained from them have been found to agree with the reports of relatives (Marks *et al.* 1975) so that they appear to be of relevance despite their limitations.

The comparisons between the Rachman *et al.* and Meyer *et al.* studies are made more difficult by the fact that the results of the latter were not subjected to statistical analyses. It is not possible to determine whether the more subtle changes which were observed are sufficient to constitute a real trend. With these difficulties in mind, it seems remarkable that the trends in outcome already described should have been observed.

Despite everything it does seem that treatment will be likely to bring about improvement in rituals and phobic anxiety directly related to the feared situation. Depression and anxiety may improve in some cases, but by no means all, and similarly, work, social and leisure activities will not be certain to change (these latter only improved in Meyer *et al.*'s patients). Sexual adjustment will be almost sure to remain poor. In short, the patient may be relieved of his rituals, but may continue to experience difficulty with many other aspects of his life.

Degree of improvement in symptoms. Only improvement in rituals and anxiety associated with them are reviewed as there is insufficient information in the published reports to allow an adequate appraisal of other areas of functioning. Omission of details of non-significant results and of means and standard deviations (as in the accounts of Rachman *et al.* and their followers) may facilitate succinct presentation, but it also distorts the full picture of the findings and prevents future researchers from gaining full benefit from the work.

Out of all the patients treated, only nine were reported to be totally free from rituals at the end of treatment (three by Meyer *et al.* 1974; two by Rachman *et al.*, 1971; three by Boersma *et al.*, 1976; and one by Mills *et al.*, 1973). Of these the severity of disorder in Boersma *et al.*'s patients may be questioned as some of their sample came to treatment in response to a newspaper advertisement rather than through medical referral. It is not clear whether the successful cases were amongst these volunteers. Incomplete reporting makes it impossible to tell whether these were the only patients to be 'cured', but as total remission is a remarkable event, it seems likely that others would have been reported had they occurred.

About one-quarter to one-fifth of the patients in Rachman, Hodgson, and Marks' studies failed to improve (Röper, Rachman, and Marks, 1975). Judging from change graphs (mostly based on group means) most of the other patients managed to achieve a low level of anxiety and avoidance by the end of the treatment phase. For example, Rachman *et al.*'s (1973) patients averaged about two on a scale ranging from zero to eight. This failure to eliminate rituals entirely does not seem to be a consequence of premature termination of treatment as most of Meyer *et al.*'s (1974) patients who received a longer programme still retained some vestige of symptoms.

This consistent stabilization at a low level of ritual behaviour resembles the traditional smoking-reduction minimum of about four cigarettes a day which is achieved in most smoking elimination studies (McFall and Hammen, 1971). When likened to smoking, the failure to abandon obsessive–compulsive behaviour entirely may be seen as reflecting the general difficulty with which longstanding heavily reinforced habits are eliminated.

The 'success' rates of three-quarters to four-fifths showing some improvement and far fewer being relieved completely, indicates that modelling, flooding, and response prevention can by no means be considered as a 'cure'. Indeed the efficacy of this procedure compared with alternative available methods may be brought into question.

Behavioural techniques characteristically require more therapist time and effort than most physical methods and therefore need to show correspondingly greater gains if their use is to be recommended. Only one experimental comparison between the two forms of treatment has been made.

Marks (1977) reported an attempt to compare the effects of clomipramine (thought to have an anti-depressant effect—see Chapter 9) with modelling and flooding treatment. At the time of writing the full results were still being analysed so that no firm statement of the outcome could be made. However it looked as if, at least, both forms of treatment will prove to have had some effect.

In the absence of the necessary controlled trials, the best that may be done is to compare the published outcomes of behavioural procedures with those obtained by other workers using alternative treatment methods and different criteria of improvement. Obviously, such comparisons on their own are not sufficient to confirm or to refute the relative efficacy of flooding, modelling, and response prevention and physical methods. Nevertheless, they may provide some indication of the seriousness of the need for further research.

One of the best-documented follow-ups of obsessive–compulsive patients was conducted by Pollitt (1960). He collected 72 male and 87 female patients, following them up after three months up to fifteen years. The patients had been ill for an average of 4.3 years before first seeking treatment and can therefore be considered chronic. They were treated by a variety of (non-behavioural) methods. At follow-up it was found that one-third had been free from symptoms or had achieved an adequate social adaptation at least for a period of time. Overall, two-thirds of those who could be contacted could be said to have improved.

More recently, Sternberg (1974) reviewed the status of physical treatments, including leucotomy, in obsessive–compulsive disorder. He concluded that a fair estimate of the proportion of patients who would obtain no help from any physical treatment would be about 5 per cent. It may be inferred from this that the other 95 per cent would be expected to derive at least some benefit from treatment by physical methods.

The reports of improvement rates claimed for modelling, flooding, and response prevention on the one hand, and physical methods on the other, are sufficiently close to make the need for further properly controlled comparisons of the two approaches clear. It could be that such a trial would fail to confirm the superiority of modelling, flooding, and response prevention that tends to have been assumed.

Need for further treatment. Meyer, Levy, and Schnurer (1974) designed their treatment programmes to progress from stage to stage as the individual patient improved so that the question of treatment in addition to that in the initial course did not arise. The original programme continued until the patient was discharged.

In contrast, Rachman *et al.* (1971) and their followers gave a standard three-week package and then additional treatment when required. An unspecified number of patients did require this additional care (Röper *et al.* 1975). For example, Rachman *et al.* (1971) reported that two patients received more than twenty additional sessions in hospital and at home. Home treatment sessions were an integral part of Meyer *et al.*'s procedure and were given to most patients as additional sessions at the end of Rachman *et al.*'s three-week inpatient stage. They are considered of such importance by all the workers that Rachman *et al.* (1971) felt patients with extensive rituals may not be worth treating unless home treatments could be guaranteed.

Therefore it seems that three weeks is the absolute minimum estimate for treatment length and that home treatment sessions may be essential if the maximum improvement is to be achieved.

Booster sessions and change during follow-up. Meyer *et al.* (1974) arranged frequent follow-up interviews with their patients after discharge, only gradually spacing them out as they became more accustomed to being at home. They do not report having given any further booster treatment sessions in addition to these interviews. Rachman, Hodgson, and Marks did not maintain such frequent contact with their patients, but instead gave booster sessions when this was found to be necessary. Eleven of their twenty patients required help at some stage during the two-year follow-up (Marks *et al.*, 1975). Often a simple *in vivo* home treatment was sufficient on any one occasion that the patient became distressed. In addition some patients required antidepressants, as had been the case before treatment and further behavioural treatment for marital, social skills, and sexual problems.

With or without the aid of booster sessions, the patients tended to maintain their progress during the follow-up period (two years for Rachman *et al.*, one to ten years for Meyer *et al.*). In several cases, rituals and avoidance continued to improve during follow-up whilst a few deteriorated a little, but the majority stayed more or less the same as they had been at the end of the treatment stage. Meyer *et al.*'s (1974) patients also tended to maintain the progress which they had made in work and social adjustment and leisure activities at the time of discharge. It appears that the patients who improve during treatment (three-quarters to four-fifths of those treated) may maintain their improvement for two or more years with only infrequent therapist contact.

(iii) Recommended treatment procedure. Although some aspects of treatment have been investigated experimentally, many others have been dropped on what appears to be a fairly arbitrary basis. Aspects of treatment which appear to have been accepted by the major groups of workers as being convenient, if not optimal, have been combined with those of demonstrated effectiveness in the following list of treatment procedures.

Place of treatment. Some period of inpatient treatment at the outset is considered to be highly desirable (Meyer *et al.*, 1974; Rachman *et al.*, 1971), but is not essential (Boersma *et al.*, 1976; Meyer *et al.*, 1976). After that, home treatment sessions are necessary in nearly all cases.

Duration of treatment. Marks *et al.* (1975) considered that little further gains were made after three weeks of daily sessions at the inpatient stage. However, this period did not include a phase of response prevention prior to exposure to stimuli as exercized by Meyer *et al.* (1974) and further sessions were found to be necessary for some patients. Therefore it seems that three weeks should be taken as the very minimum estimate of treatment length. It is possible that frequent follow-up appointments after discharge (Meyer *et al.*, 1974) will facilitate the patient's return home. However, the use of such contacts has yet to be compared with Rachman *et al.*'s (1973) longer interval before follow-up. Booster sessions have been found to be essential.

Treatment components. There is general agreement that *response prevention* is a necessary part of treatment. Meyer *et al.* (1974) and Mills *et al.* (1973) emphasize its central importance although Rachman *et al.* consider its role to be secondary to that of exposure. Rachman *et al.* (1971) have shown that the total supervision by nurses advocated by Meyer *et al.* (1974) is not usually necessary as most patients can control their own rituals if requested. It is possible that nurse supervision may aid patients who cannot control themselves, but Marks *et al.* (1975) feel that such patients may find ways to avoid the nurse's surveillance. It seems that instructing the patients not to perform their rituals will be sufficient in most cases.

Boersma *et al.* (1976) found no meaningful difference in efficacy between *graded exposure* and *flooding*. In addition Rachman *et al.* (1971) found that flooding was no more effective than modelling (with graded exposure), but was if anything more distressing to the patients. In view of this, there seems to be little reason to use the more upsetting flooding approach. Meyer *et al.* (1974) have also used graded exposure with effect.

Modelling. Although as yet there has been no unequivocal demonstration that modelling by the therapist adds anything to the effectiveness, at least some patients seem to find it helpful (Rachman *et al.*, 1973). Others do not, as Rachman *et al.* (1973) observed with one patient who explained that he knew that other people did not have the same trouble as he did, and so was not convinced by the therapist's fearless performance. In view of this, the possibility of using already treated patients as models might be investigated as coping models may be more effective than competent ones (Bandura, 1969).

In practice, this treatment package would be combined with drugs and counselling of relatives and the treatment of other problems as felt necessary. These additional approaches are described in Chapter 9.

This prescription of recommended treatment procedures has assumed that the behavioural interventions were responsible for the improvements in symptomatology which have been observed. The failure to find any appreciable effects of varying the behavioural components of treatment must weaken this argument considerably. In fact, the evidence in support of this assumption rests mainly in the favourable comparison made by Rachman, Hodgson, and Marks of the behavioural treatments with placebo relaxation training.

The possibility that relaxation training does not represent an adequate control for non-behavioural treatment effects in modelling, flooding and response prevention regimes has not been explored. In many respects relaxation training does represent a suitable placebo treatment. The procedure involves a protracted interaction between patient and therapist, designed to eliminate symptoms which are distressing through the execution of a set of especially learnt responses. These attributes mirror those of modelling, flooding, and response prevention and therefore control for potentially influential non-behavioural effects. On the other hand, several aspects of modelling, flooding, and response prevention are not shared by relaxation training or by other treatment techniques such as drugs. These include several incidental effects of the treatment procedures, patient expectations and some aspects of the special patient–therapist relationship which may develop.* Before describing these, however, the dramatic nature of the modelling, flooding, and response prevention treatment must be considered. It must come as a great surprise to well-seasoned psychiatric patients who have

---

* The second author (M. Vaughan) has discussed some of these aspects of treatment on several occasions with R. J. Hodgson and G. Röper. Inevitably, their ideas have intermingled with her own.

long experience of drugs, psychotherapy and ECT to find that the therapist is prepared to run his hand round the inside of the toilet, eat biscuits laced with dust or, even more extraordinarily, to prance round the ward with a dustbin lid on his head (Rachman *et al.*, 1973). Such capers depart quite widely from the more usual staid consultations in the doctor's office. The very close involvement of therapist and patient as a working team in a series of therapeutic tasks of an unusual and sometimes slightly bizarre nature, may well have an impact on the patient's motivation and performance which cannot easily be described in terms of modelling or reciprocal inhibition accruing from the therapist's presence.

In addition, the therapist's instructions to the patient may have consequences over and above those dictated by the strict behavioural model. In telling the patient what to do—for example, not to wash her hands—the therapist may be seen as assuming responsibility for all the patient's conduct. It has been observed that some patients reduce or lose their rituals spontaneously for a while after admission to hospital only regaining them when they become used to their surroundings and begin to feel responsible for the care of their room and possessions. Patients have also commented that the therapist's presence during sessions reduces the discomfort which would normally be experienced as they do not feel responsible, say, for checking that the door is closed. It is possible that this perceived transfer of responsibility plays some part in the rapid improvement which is sometimes witnessed during the early stages of treatment. It is unlikely to be instrumental in the longer term as the patient has to resume full responsibility on discharge from hospital.

The therapist's instructions may have another beneficial non-behavioural effect by eliminating any doubt in the patient's mind about the need to continue with ritualistic activity. Walker and Beech (1969) have indicated that obsessional patients may experience impairment of decision-making, which might result in a prolongation of their rituals arising from difficulty in deciding when to stop. In a related interpretation of obsessive–compulsive behaviour, Mather (1970) suggested that these patients were unable to discriminate between clean and contaminated materials and so were compelled to continue with their rituals excessively.

If either discrimination or decision-making was faulty, the therapist's authoritative instruction not to perform rituals would eliminate the patient's uncertainty about whether to continue and would enable her to stop. Again, this effect would be apparent during treatment, but would not be maintained at home unless the therapist's clear judgment had enabled the patient to improve her decision-making skills.

A third effect of the therapist's instructions has not yet been explained adequately. Most therapists will have experienced the occurrence of 'miraculous cures' which cannot be attributed to any real behavioural intervention. One of the authors (M. Vaughan) inadvertently engineered a spectacular remission in a 48-year-old housewife with a 25-year history of checking, repetition, ruminations and preoccupation with all aspects of opening her bowels. She identified difficulty in using the lavatory as her main problem (although there were many others). She would have to inspect the toilet before and after use to make sure that there were no traces of faeces or urine, use about twenty sheets of toilet-paper, folded and applied in a special way and strain violently and repeatedly to make sure that she was not going to pass a motion. She took about two-and-a-half hours in the toilet to pass a motion and half-an-hour to urinate. This must have been particularly taxing in the winter as the lavatory was outside and unheated. She had experienced these difficulties for about twenty years, although they had become worse in the past twelve months when she had been taken off amphetamines which had been maintaining her. Half way through the first interview the patient mentioned that she would like to go to the toilet to urinate, but was afraid to do so because of her 'problem'. The patient was instructed to go and to be back within five minutes. This she achieved, much to her own surprise, and has never spent an excessive time in the toilet since then (a period of three-and-a-half years). She consistently spends five to ten minutes to pass urine and twenty minutes to open her bowels. Although these times may be a little longer than average, the patient does not find her social or family life inconvenienced by them. Despite several temporary relapses in some of her other symptoms, she has never needed formal treatment for this aspect of her behaviour.

This form of sudden remission or cure is not rare, but cannot really be attributed to any definite therapeutic intervention. As modelling, flooding, and response prevention involve a good deal of direct instruction of the patient, it is possible that such remissions occur more frequently during their course than they would with other therapeutic approaches. In so doing they would contribute to the apparent efficacy of the behavioural techniques.

Whilst the patient is involved in the response-prevention phase of treatment, she may develop and experiment with new ways of controlling her own behaviour. For example, one male patient used the image of his therapist topped with the dustbin lid as a coping response which he felt helped to reduce avoidance of dirty objects (Rachman et al., 1973). In addition, the patient, aided by nursing staff, may learn to use conversation and occupation as distractions from the discomfort being experienced and as activities incompatible with performance of the rituals. Any self-control procedures which the patient developed would aid her progress during treatment and facilitate transfer to the home.

Another fortuitous effect of response prevention may be that the patient learns both that abstaining from the rituals is not followed by an uncontrollable escalation in anxiety and that the expected disastrous consequences of non-performance do not occur (Meyer, 1966). This cognitive change in expectations would substantially reduce or eliminate the need to engage in the rituals which were designed to guard against untoward consequences. The attitude change achieved during treatment would be expected to generalize to the non-occurrence of rituals at home and hence would enable the patient to refrain from her compulsive acts.

Quite apart from the effects of the treatment procedure, the patient's interactions with the therapist could bring about some behavioural and attitudinal change. There are some grounds for arguing that the relationships achieved between patient and therapist during flooding, modelling, and response prevention differ from those accruing from other forms of psychotherapy and the administration of drugs. The therapist spends a great deal of time with the patient in hospital and more importantly at her home. The seemingly silly exercises such as practising *not* checking doors, sitting on the floor and doing everything in fours instead of threes, which are engaged in equally by both parties, often lead to the development of a humorous and slightly joking interaction which is appreciated by the patient as well as by her mentor. In close and prolonged contact with the patient at home it very often becomes almost impossible to retain the remaining vestiges of a conventional patient–client relationship. For example, it was necessary for one of the authors (M. Vaughan) to spend several successive evenings and nights at a patient's home in order to deal with rituals associated with dressing and preparing for work. As the therapist was the same age and sex as patient and shared several of her interests, it would have jeopardized rapport to have attempted to retain the usual degree of professional restraint in the divulgence of personal information and attitudes. Instead conversations ranged generally over housekeeping, work, interests, education, etc., much as it would in the development of an ordinary friendship.

This is far from being the only instance in which fairly informal friendships have arisen between therapist and patient during treatment. From discussion with four or five colleagues involved in the treatment of obsessionals, it seems that it occurs quite frequently.

At the very least, the development of such friendships would be expected to enhance the reciprocally inhibiting effect of the therapist's presence during treatment. In some cases it may achieve more than this. As many patients are socially isolated or alienated, often because of their incapacitating rituals, the development of a new friendship may be particularly significant.

The ensuing change in the patient's self-esteem and self-evaluation have not been determined so far and the effect of such a change on subsequent behaviour has yet to be investigated. However, it seems possible that one friendly encounter would encourage the patient to make more effort to establish new social relationships. This would probably be more likely to be a consequence of friendships developed during modelling, flooding, and response prevention than of relationships developed during psychotherapy, as the two-day nature of the former give them a closer resemblance to friendships occurring in 'real life'.

The development of a friendship between patient and therapist seems to facilitate requests for and advice about trivial and major problems not being dealt with in the formal behavioural treatment programme. It is not uncommon for patients to wish to discuss sexual, marital, domestic and social skills problems. In some cases, the problems prove to be severe enough to warrant formal treatment. For the remainder some relief may be obtained from merely disclosing the worry to somebody else, or the problem may be eliminated by discussion, clarification and advice. It is not known how much these subsidiary interventions affect the outcome of the behavioural programme.

Quite apart from the formal and informal counselling which may take place, the patient is likely to learn some other important information from the therapist. Patients whose rituals have been present for many years often complain that they are unable to remember how everyday tasks should be performed. One patient treated by the authors used to vacuum-clean her carpets excessively as she felt compelled to repeat most acts which she performed. She said that she no longer knew how much vacuum-cleaning would be sufficient to clean the carpet. Demonstration by the therapist combined with verbal explanation, enabled her to set new standards for her performance. Having done this, she was able to restrict her cleaning without experiencing undue discomfort.

Other patients have asked about 'normal' standards of washing, dressing and checking. By answering such questions directly or by giving unsolicited cues through modelling and instruction during treatment, the therapist will provide the patient with new standards against which to evaluate her behaviour. The introduction of a new standard of behaviour will help the patient to regulate her own behaviour and thereby to control her rituals (see Chapter 9). Like the effects of instruction from the therapist, the answers to the patient's questions will also help to eliminate any decision-making problems which may exist.

It is not being suggested that these incidental treatment factors, rather than modelling, flooding, and response prevention, are responsible for the reductions in rituals which have been observed. However, the extent to which they add to the overall treatment effectiveness has not been evaluated.

Until this has been determined, there would be no justification in saying that the specified behavioural elements in treatment are responsible for the clinical improvements which have been obtained. This may only be concluded when modelling, flooding and response prevention have been favourably compared with a control treatment incorporating all the incidental factors described. This work would best be undertaken before the search for optimal behavioural intervention has been pursued at any length.

6

Satiation Training

Rachman (1971a, 1976), described a form of treatment which he named 'satiation training' and which he felt, could be used to ameliorate obsessional ruminations. As such, it constituted an important addition to the range of behavioural techniques as almost all others had been directed towards the modification of overt rituals rather than thoughts.

Rachman (1971a) defined obsessional ruminations as being unacceptable thoughts which are both repetitive and intensive and which may be distasteful, worrying or abhorrent. He considered that their content was generally concerned with thoughts of causing accidents or harm to others, obscenities and other unpleasant ideas. In fact, Rachman appears to be describing only a subset of obsessional thought aberrations, the obsessional ideas, images and phobias and impulses identified by Lewis and Mapother (1941) and Henderson and Gillespie (1962). Despite his use of the term, true obsessional ruminations do not feature in his account.

Ruminations are characterized by prolonged and often fruitless attempts to solve a self-set problem to which there is no real or acceptable solution. They involve recurrent internal doubt and debate and may engage the patient's attention for hours at a time. The rumination may be initiated by a sudden thought or fear such as that of harming others as noted by Rachman, but then continues to be elaborated in the way described. One patient with severe ruminations feared (groundlessly) that she had caused a road accident some years previously. Each time she thought of this possibility, she would earnestly attempt to recall minute details of the events preceding and succeeding the supposed disaster in an effort to determine whether any action on her part could have caused an accident. She was seldom satisfied with negative evidence, believing that her memory could have been at fault or that vital evidence had been withheld, unwittingly, by other people. She would spend several hours a day in this pursuit only stopping when she was satisfied that she had not caused the accident. But such relief was only temporary and soon fresh doubt would arise and she would begin again.

The distinction between ruminations such as this, and the thoughts and impulses enumerated by Rachman, is not being raised as a pedantic issue, but is considered to be important as Rachman made some additions to his treatment to meet the requirements of the forms of disorder which were involved. Specifically he observed, correctly, that many obsessional thoughts, particularly those of harm or accident, are accompanied by what appear to be 'putting right' rituals. The patient may have to conjure up a 'good' thought in order to counteract a 'bad' one or undo the effects of a 'bad' thought by repetitive counting, checking or cleaning. Repetitive requests for reassurance seem to serve a similar function. Part of Rachman's treatment procedure, described below, is designed to control these 'putting right' rituals (Freud's name for this being 'undoing').

Patients who ruminate also frequently exhibit 'putting right' rituals, particularly reassurance-seeking, and so may be amenable to Rachman's methods of control. However, in addition to the usual undoing rituals, some parts of the rumination seem to be attempts to redress the initial disturbing idea. The patient who feared she had caused a road accident embarked on her rumination apparently with the sole purpose of allaying her fear. When asked, she said that although her attempts to recall her possible involvement were upsetting, she would have found it far more distressing to tolerate the fear and doubt occasioned by the initial thought which she felt would persist if she made no effort to find a solution. The doubt and not knowing were worse for her than the rumination itself.

Her prolonged rumination appeared to be serving a similar function to an anxiety-arousing overt ritual (Walker and Beech, 1969). Teasdale (1974) has suggested that the reinforcement maintaining avoidance behaviour of this nature may be described in terms of the idea, put forward by Herrnstein (1969), that the extent of noxious stimulation is reduced following execution of the avoidance response (here the ruminative ritual) than following the non-performance of it. It is felt that the lengthy ruminations following the occurrence of an unpleasant thought could be added to Rachman's group of undoing rituals. Therefore these ruminations may be responsive to the same form of treatments as the other thoughts which he described.

SATIATION TREATMENT

The bases of satiation treatment appear to have been described by Rachman (1971), although he did not adopt that label for his procedure until he presented a second description in 1976. In this he recommended satiation training to deal with all forms of obsessional thoughts and added a response-prevention procedure for those which are normally followed by a 'putting right' ritual. Therefore the total treatment is in two parts; satiation training for all cases plus response prevention if associated covert or overt rituals are evident.

Rachman's (1976) description of both phases was extremely brief and provided barely sufficient information to enable other therapists to adopt his method. He stated that after the patient has been given full therapeutic instruction and explanation, baseline records of ruminations are collected. Following this 'the most troublesome' obsessions are treated by satiation training. The patient is asked to evoke and maintain the obsession for sustained periods of up to fifteen minutes. It was not indicated whether this excercise should be overt or covert and in the presence or absence of prompts from the therapist. In his 1971 report it was suggested that the patient should be in a calm state for optimal effect, perhaps indicating that relaxation might be used. There was no mention of any optimal state for training in the later account (although adverse mood states in general were discussed as is mentioned below).

Further, Rachman did not give any indication as to what should determine trial or session length. In 1971 he remarked that the degree of subjective and psychophysiological disturbance in response to a thought could be used to assess change. However in 1976 he remarked that good progress would be indicated by an increase in latency in obtaining the obsession and growing tendency for it to fade during the trial period. He gave no hint as to whether it was necessary to wait for signs such as these to occur before a session is ended. He also failed to mention when treatment itself should end, other than saying that control should be transferred to the patient to practise at home. Probably it may be assumed that termination is determined by the disappearance of the obsessions between sessions, although this leaves the difficulty of what should happen if less than adequate increases in latency and fading occur before this stage is reached.

Essentially, this is all that constitutes satiation training. If the patient shows no 'putting right' rituals, including asking for reassurance, it is thought to be sufficient to rid him of his ruminations. It is likely that those without ancillary rituals are in a minority, and that most patients will be in need of Rachman's additional treatment to deal with their 'putting right' responses. Rachman (1976) stated that response-prevention procedures are introduced once satiation treatment is under way although no guidelines were given as to when this should take place. It seems that all that is involved in these procedures is to urge the patient to avoid carrying out any 'neutralizing' ('putting right') activities. This may be sufficient to control some overt rituals since Beech and his colleagues have found that washing and checking may be inhibited at the therapist's request. Response prevention in their flooding and modelling trials was carried out without supervision from therapists or nursing staff (see, for example, Rachman, Marks, and Hodgson, 1973).

But what about thoughts? Many patients neutralize ruminations with special thoughts and images. Often their reports indicate that the neutralizing thoughts could be controlled since they spend time and effort deliberately conjuring them up. However it may be questionable whether this is always the case with neutralizing simple letter or number sequences or even simple words. If the patient has repeatedly followed a rumination with a single 'putting right' thought and been reinforced by the ensuing anxiety reduction, it seems quite likely that this neutralizing thought will tend to be evoked by the rumination without the patient's deliberate intent. To ask the patient to stop the 'putting right' response in this event would be nearly as fruitless as to demand that he should stop the rumination on his own. This objection to simple response prevention has yet to be verified, as no information about patients' control over neutralizing thoughts has been collected. It is mentioned merely as a caution that the procedure may not always be as straightforward as reports may suggest.

Rachman did not state how long response prevention should be continued after a treatment session although it may be assumed that he intended it to be operative until the urge to perform the neutralizing ritual has been dissipated. He suggested also that the patient should response prevent himself at home every time an unwanted thought occurs.

Rachman (1971a, 1976) noted the strong association which has been observed between obsessions and depression (Beech, 1974) and the fact that in many patients, ruminations occurring in the context of a depressive illness disappear when a normal mood has been restored (Kendell and Discipio, 1970). He recommended that the patient's mood should be given careful attention and anti-depressants or tranquillizers should be prescribed as required. In addition to the general ameliorative effect of medication, he felt that a reasonably calm mood state is necessary for satiation training to succeed, an observation which has been made by Beech (1971, 1974, 1976) in the general context of behavioural approaches.

CASE STUDIES

Despite their apparent relevance, Rachman's accounts of satiation treatment have not precipitated the expected rash of case reports. Three cases of his own, mentioned in his 1976 paper and five reported by Emmelkamp and Kwee (1977) seem to be the only published accounts of the use of satiation training.

One patient was an attorney who suffered from obsessional doubts about whether he had written or might write a compromising letter to a criminal whom he had prosecuted. This led to a great deal of checking to put matters right and to the deliberate formation of images of clean paper which served the same function. All that Rachman reported about treatment was that the patient was asked to hold the ruminations for five to fifteen minutes per trial without neutralizing images and to refrain from carrying out overt checking rituals. The clinical outcome was described briefly as successful, the frequency of ruminations and associated rituals having declined steeply.

The treatments of the other two patients was not described at all, although both were said to yield significantly reduced ruminations and rituals. One concerned a woman with ruminations about harm coming to her close relatives, and ritualistic neutralizing actions and thoughts. The other involved a patient who experienced unpleasant images including one of four people, dead, in a grave. She had to 'rectify' matters by imagining the people walking about and healthy. Neither of these cases are described in sufficient detail to allow any inferences to be made about the effectiveness of the technique.

Emmelkamp and Kwee (1977) attempted to compare prolonged exposure in imagination, based on Rachman (1971a), with thought-stopping in five patients with ruminations but no rituals. Their thought-stopping procedure was a modified version of that used by Hackmann and McLean (1975) (see Chapter 7). During exposure treatment the patients had to imagine their obsessional thoughts, as described by the therapist, repeatedly without avoiding them in any way. There was no attempt to increase feelings of anxiety. Five one-hour sessions were given for each treatment. Each patient received both treatments, three having exposure first and the other two starting with thought-stopping.

There was a tendency for the patients to show improvement after the completion of both treatments (ten sessions) but the significance of this is difficult to determine as the results were analysed using t–tests which do not seem to be appropriate when $n = 5$. Despite the stated aim of the investigation, no formal comparison of thought-stopping and exposure was made. Instead, for each patient a histogram showing the mean daily frequency of obsessions before, between and after the treatments was given and the results were appraised by eye. The only two patients who improved also responded to thought-stopping as did one of the exposure failures. It is not possible to evaluate the effects of prolonged exposure in imagination from results presented in this way.

Broadhurst (1976) provided a more substantial account of a patient whom she treated by a method which seems tantamount to satiation training. Her patient was aged 70 and had a 35-year history of ruminations without rituals relating to worry over a love affair. The ruminations took the form of jingles incorporating the names of places associated with the affair and reference to menstrual blood. The patient claimed never to be free of these thoughts although he was able to work and converse despite them.

Because the repetition of all the main phrases was found to be too cumbersome, it was decided to concentrate on the initial phrase in the series, on the assumption that the elimination of this would weaken the tendency to initiate the remaining part of the chain. During the first six sessions, the patient was required to repeat the phrase continuously for five-minute periods, which were alternated with one-minute rest intervals. From the seventh session onwards the repetition periods were extended to ten minutes and the breaks to three minutes. Conversation on non-ruminative topics was permitted during the rest intervals as the patient felt uncomfortable with silence. In all, the patient received eighteen sessions, eight with the therapist at the clinic and ten which he carried out on his own at home.

Improvement was evidenced by slight reductions in the number of thoughts per minute from first to last practice-period within each session and overall between the second and the eighteenth sessions. At the end he was averaging about 21 per minute (an estimate, as the results were presented as histograms). As his rate was only about 27 per minute at the outset, this represents only a modest improvement, as Broadhurst readily acknowledged.

The patient continued to practise at home and attended the clinic for brief periods approximately fortnightly for the next two years, to give progress reports. He continued to improve, showing the most dramatic change during the second year when, instead of experiencing all bad thoughts, he reported that his thoughts were mixed—some good and some bad. It was not stated whether he was still practising at that time. He showed further improvement two years later. As no information was given about practice during the lengthy follow-up period, the relationship between treatment and change is difficult to evaluate. Certainly the regular and enjoyable follow-up visits may have contributed a non-specific influence on the overall outcome. Therefore, although encouraging, this account does little to establish whether a satiation training-type procedure has any real effect.

As these nine cases appear to constitute all the published work involving satiation training, it is clear that its efficacy has not been evaluated. At first sight, it appears that some confirmatory evidence might be gleaned from the work on paradoxical intention (Solyom *et al.* 1972) as this procedure seems to have elements in common with satiation training. However, Rachman (1976) has pointed out that there are also important differences, particularly in the set with which the patient approaches training. In paradoxical intention the patient has to dwell on the thoughts and elaborate and exaggerate them whereas in satiation training the patient is taught to regard his thoughts as alien and useless. Although the importance of differences such as this are not known, their possible relevance makes it unwise to generalize from one treatment to the other. Thus the need for controlled investigation of satiation training remains imperative.

THEORETICAL BASES

The two parts of treatment, satiation training, and response prevention were developed from different theoretical considerations and so will be considered separately here. Rachman (1976) took response prevention directly from his work on the modification of overt rituals (see, for example, Rachman, Hodgson, and Marks, 1971). The theoretical underpinnings of the technique, such as they are, have been discussed in Chapter 5 and so need not be restated here. Satiation training was developed on the basis of an habituation model, but an alternative in terms of conditioned inhibition may also be applied. Both will be considered in more detail.

1. Habituation

Rachman's use of the concept of habituation in developing his treatment procedure arose from his theoretical evaluation of the nature of ruminations. He suggested that ruminations are unacceptable thoughts, the content of which is seen as disturbing because of the upbringing of the patient. They may be considered to be noxious conditioned stimuli which resemble phobic stimuli in so far as they evoke subjective distress, psychophysiological disturbance and avoidance behaviour. Rachman (1971a) considered that the main differences between the two forms of stimuli were that ruminations are more likely to have a large endogenous element and to be associated with depression rather than anxiety. These differences did not seem sufficient to prevent useful extrapolation from knowledge of the nature of phobic stimuli to ruminations.

On a parallel with phobic stimuli, Rachman suggested that ruminations may be seen as noxious stimuli to which the patient has difficulty in habituating. Following Groves and Thompson (1970), he argued that independent hypothetical constructs of habituation and sensitization interact to produce the overall response to repeated stimulation. An increase in responsiveness (sensitization) can occur when the stimulus is of high intensity and is of significance to the patient. It follows that personally significant ruminations would be likely to produce sensitization. In so far as sensitization is incompatible with habituation, such ruminations should take longer to habituate and thus should continue for prolonged periods. The relationship between sensitization potency and duration of rumination has not been investigated empirically, but needs to be confirmed if the theoretical account is to hold.

Rachman also argued that disturbed mood states such as agitated depression (involving heightened excitability) will facilitate sensitization. Because of this, sensitization to ruminations and adverse mood may interact to become an upwards spiral, producing a continuation of the thoughts. This idea is based on only indirect psychophysiological evidence and is badly in need of evaluation. Some support may arise from the similarity between Rachman's views and the more general model of obsessional behaviour, developed previously by Beech (1971), and Beech and Perigault (1974); although still not fully verified, the latter has a considerable amount of evidence to support it.

The posited interaction between rumination and mood state does not account for the persistence of the unwanted thoughts after the mood state has returned to normal, or the occurrence of ruminations in the context of what appears to be only mildly upsetting mood. Rachman (1976) suggested that the occurrence of the rumination may be maintained by the temporary reduction in distress resulting from the use of neutralizing rituals. This argument seems to possess a central logical flaw in that if the discomfort reduction is sufficient to reinforce the rumination, it should also reinforce the ritual. Thus, the neutralizing ritual should become increasingly likely to be performed over a series of reinforced trials. Eventually, each unwanted thought should be followed promptly by a ritual so that the ruminative sequence would be attenuated rather than maintained.

In addition, a weak part of Rachman's analysis, as he seems to be aware, is his explanation of the initial occurrence of ruminative thoughts. It is easy enough to say that everyone has unpleasant thoughts, but that some find them exceptionally distressing on account of their prevailing mood or the way in which they were brought up. This may well be true, but does not really explain the high frequency of thoughts or the rather restricted range of themes which form the content of ruminations (Beech, 1977). Nor does it take into account the possiblity that the content of thoughts precipitating ruminations is atypical and is not experienced by other people. Rachman, himself, has suggested (1973) that ruminative thoughts may be quantitatively distinct from the morbid preoccupations which commonly occur in depression. Therefore it is surprising that he seems to be making the assumption that everyone's bad thoughts are very much the same. This part of his explanation of ruminations needs to be re-evaluated, preferably in the context of comparative investigation of the nature of their thoughts. Fortunately, the question of the genesis of the thoughts does not affect the remainder of his theoretical views.

As a direct deduction from his theoretical evaluations of ruminations, Rachman (1976) suggested that treatment may involve three components: medication to restore normal mood, followed by habituation (satiation) training to deal with continuing ruminations and response prevention if neutralizing rituals are in evidence. Satiation training was not described in detail although some procedural requirements were defined in a series of postulates (Rachman, 1971a) most of which seem to have been based on knowledge of habituation training with phobic patients (see, for example, Watts, 1971).

The most important of these hypotheses appear to be that habituation will be facilitated by a calm mood state; that if ruminations are highly distressing, long exposures will result in quicker habituation than short exposures, the reverse being true if the thoughts are mildly distressing; and finally, that there may be a temporary increase in the disturbance caused by the rumination during the early stages of training. When combined, these predictions result in the procedure outlined sketchily by Rachman and described above. The unfortunate omission of necessary detail has been pointed out already.

One indirect way to evaluate the adequacy of Rachman's theoretical account of satiation training would be to inspect the clinical outcome of using the technique. At least, if patients showed improvement in their ruminations there would be evidence that some component of the procedure was having an effect although it would not demonstrate that habituation was the effective process. To date, as has been seen, there is no viable clinical evidence to use in such an endeavour.

A more direct approach would be to observe individual patient's responses to the evocation of ruminative stimuli during sessions in order to determine whether they changed in a way which would be predicted by an habituation model. Rachman was not explicit about the changes which should take place. In 1971, he asserted that the effects of habituation training would be assessed in terms of the amount of psychophysiological disturbance produced by the occurrence of the ruminations, whereas in 1976, increases in latency and fading of thoughts were held to be associated with progress. These later indices seem to have little to do with habituation, appearing to be related more to the effects of conditioned inhibition described below.

On the other hand a reduction in subjective distress and psychophysiological response to ruminative stimuli appears to be a defining feature of habituation. Equivalent changes in response to phobic stimuli have been observed already (Watts, 1971). The idea of a decrement in response during training seems to be inherent in Rachman's (1976) description of the procedure as one of 'detoxification', by which the rumination loses its disturbing intensity. It seems that he may have had the habituation model in mind despite his reference to increased latency and fading.

Therefore it may be inferred from Rachman's account that subjective ratings of distress in response to a rumination should decrease over trials, except in the initial stages of treatment, when a temporary light increase in distress might occur. Parallel changes in psychophysiological responses would be predicted.

Recently, changes in subjective report during satiation training have been investigated in two patients with seven intrusive thoughts treated by the author (M.V.). For both, subjective distress following evocation of a thought was assessed in terms of a 0 to 100 scale with 0 being quite calm, and 100 the worst the patient had ever felt (the worst experience relating to the thoughts as described by the patient). In both cases it was possible to determine several variants of the rumination which elicited slightly differing amounts of distress. However the range of variation was small so that all thoughts were rated 85 to 100 at the outset. In view of this it was decided that there was little to be gained from starting with any other than the most distressing items. With the patient's help a tape-recorded description of the rumination was compiled to facilitate the repeated presentation.

(a) Case histories

The first patient was a 39-year-old mother of three, who was plagued by instrusive thoughts about death, especially her own, but had no neutralizing rituals. The thoughts were nearly always with her although she continued to work. On the Leyton Obsessional Inventory she obtained a symptom score of 31 and trait score of eight, both being consistent with those obtained by obsessional patients. During treatment she was taking Anafranil (25 mg at night) although she denied feeling depressed and was assessed by her psychiatrist as being only mildly so.

Initially, thought-stopping was attempted but was discontinued because no improvement was achieved. After this, it was decided to introduce satiation training with the patient's most distressing rumination as the target thought. This was determined to be imagining herself dead and lying in a coffin, waiting for cremation. The thought that she could almost feel, hear and see things around her although dead was most frightening. A tape was made of the therapist repeatedly describing this scene, as the patient found that this helped her to evoke the thoughts.

The patient was seated in a reclining chair and was asked to relax as much as possible. She was able to make herself comfortable and free from excessive tension without difficulty. She listened with her eyes closed to a 30 to 50-minute continuous presentation of the rumination tape, trying to conjure up each scene as it was depicted, as clearly as possible. She found that she experienced some difficulty in obtaining the image fully towards the end of each session but she reported that this never prevented her from obtaining an adequate representation.

During the first session she rated distress response after each presentation of the rumination. However, during subsequent sessions she rated only every

Table 3 Subjective distress ratings: first patient

Presentation	Session 1	Session 2	Session 3
1	50		
2	50	80	70
3	60		
4	50	85	70
5	45		
6	45	85	75
7	45		
8	45	85	75
9	80		
10	80		75
11	80		
12	80		75
13	70		

alternate one, as she had found that the procedure interfered with her concentration. Her ratings during the first three sessions are given in Table 3. The first eight presentations of session one were of a less upsetting thought (her own body being cremated), as initially the patient had been reluctant to evoke the most distressing rumination. Satiation training was discontinued after the third session because there was no real sign of reduction in ratings and the patient's detailed records of thought frequency at home indicated that there had been no improvement there either.

The second patient, a woman in her mid-30s, had an eight-year history of excessive worry that she might contract a variety of serious diseases, accompanied by mild touching and checking rituals which appeared to have a neutralizing function. In the past, her concern had been allayed temporarily by authoritative medical reassurance that she was not ill. On coming to treatment, she was preoccupied by the possibility that she might develop ulcerative colitis, despite the fact that full medical examinations in hospital had proved negative.

This concern led the patient to investigate her bowel movement minutely each day. If it appeared soft or there seemed to be the slightest suspicion of blood or mucus she would ruminate all day about the likelihood of developing ulcerative colitis and would imagine herself at different stages of the illness. She frequently asked for reassurance from her family and consulted medical texts or, when extremely upset, her GP and the local hospital which specialized in the treatment of cancer.

Thought-stopping was tried without effect. Satiation was, therefore, introduced, using thoughts of the patient in hospital during the early stages of the illness for one session, and ruminations about inspecting a soft motion for the remaining two.

The patient showed no signs of tension and quickly relaxed in a comfortable chair. She listened to the tape-recorded ruminations without a break for 30 to 50

Table 4 Subjective distress ratings: second patient

Presentation	Session 1	Session 2	Session 3
1	97	90	90
2	98	90	90
3	98	90	90
4	98	90	90
5	98	91	90
6	98	92	91
7	98	92	91
8	98	92	91
9	98	92	92
10	97	92	92
11	97	92	
12	96	92	
13	96	92	
14	96	92	
15	95	92	
16	95	92	
17		92	

minutes, concentrating on conjuring up the thoughts as clearly as possible. She reported some difficulty in doing this towards the end of each session but was never unable to evoke the thought. Her ratings are given in Table 4. The patient was not allowed to seek reassurance during sessions but response prevention at other times was not introduced at this stage. Shortly after the third session, the patient reported an improvement in her ruminations and asked that treatment should be suspended. She relapsed within three weeks with a marked exacerbation of her thoughts and neutralizing rituals.

The ratings in Tables 3 and 4 fail to show either any consistent reduction within sessions or the predicted increase in level at the beginning of treatment, which would have been predicted by Rachman (1971a). In addition, the first patient's ratings (Table 3) show no clear sign of improvement over sessions. (The second patient's ratings might not be expected to do this as response prevention was not employed with the neutralizing rituals.) Overall none of the predictions derived from the habituation model appear to have been upheld. It could be argued that the sessions were terminated too soon and that the ratings obtained reflect a plateau (rather than initial rise) in distress which would have dissipated had the rumination trials been continued. This could be the case, but if so it would place limitations on the use of procedure through practical considerations. The patient's sessions were terminated after an average of 40 minutes of uninterrupted rumination presentation, at the end of which they were finding it increasingly difficult to evoke vivid ruminations. Their reports indicated that it would have been hard for them to continue for very much longer. On the other hand their unchanging ratings demonstrated that a considerably longer session might be necessary for change to occur. It is felt that the requirements of the treatment procedure would go beyond the resources of the patients.

It is possible that satiation training would have been more profitable if less distressing ruminations had been employed. Certainly the use of a moderately upsetting thought initially with the first patient coincided with a slight decrease in the rating of distress during the session. However Rachman does not suggest that lesser ruminations should be treated first. Indeed, his 1976 statement that the 'most troublesome' obsessions are treated, seems to imply the opposite.

Taken together the failure with these two cases appears to indicate that satiation training, as Rachman described it, is not conducive to habituation. Of course this conclusion is based on fairly limited observations drawn from only two patients seen on a routine clinical basis without any of the frills usually attendant on research. There is far too little evidence here on which to discard Rachman's approach entirely. However, it is hoped that the role of habituation training will be given more formal attention, before any understanding of the theoretical bases of the treatment is assumed.

As a postscript which may add still further to all existing states of confusion, Rachman (1976) occasionally appears to feel that satiation training involved flooding rather than habituation as conventionally described. In particular he commented that the procedure is like a process of 'detoxification' and suggested that habituation could proceed when the rumination loses its disturbing intensity. This seems to be reminiscent of Rachman's (1969) account of flooding which he felt involved a period of intense responding to anxiety-evoking stimuli followed by a paradoxical quiescence during which habituation may take place. The probable bases of this method are discussed in Chapter 5. As Rachman did not mention flooding directly, this oblique reference may not have been intended as a suggestion that flooding and satiation training may be related.

2. Conditioned inhibition

An alternative possibility, suggested by Beech (unpublished report), is that satiation training could have its effect by promoting the development of conditioned inhibition in the manner which has been thought to account for the effects of an apparently similar treatment method, negative practice. As Broadhurst's (1976) application of the procedure demonstrates, negative practice too involves repeated evocation of the unwanted thought or act over a prolonged period of time. The rest periods as applied by Broadhurst are thought to be desirable but treatment may be given without them (Kendrick, 1960). When practice sessions are omitted, and the repeated evocations are made in one sustained series, the procedure seems to be indistinguishable from satiation training. It therefore seems likely that an account of one treatment's effectiveness would be applicable to that of the other.

Negative practice was developed by Dunlap (1932) and was applied, apparently successfully, to a number of minor problems including stuttering. Dunlap put forward three hypotheses to account for the effectiveness of repetition (see Lehner, 1960), but favoured one of them—the 'beta hypothesis'—as being the most likely explanation. This states that repetition does not affect the probable recurrence of the response except in as much as other factors operate through it. These other factors were thought to include motivation, ideational and affective influences. The theoretical inadequacy of this formulation is apparent and led to its rejection by Kendrick (1960), amongst others, in favour of a more convincing alternative, conditioned inhibition.

A full account of the theory of conditioned inhibition as an explanation of the effects of negative practice has been provided by Kendrick (1960). His model was based on the elaborate form of learning theory developed by Hull (1943), in which the performance ($_sE_r$) of a response is considered to be a function of drive (D), habit ($_sH_r$), negative drive (I_r) and negative habit ($_sI_r$). Jones (1958) modified Hull's original statement of the relationship between these variables to one which has been widely accepted:

$$_sE_r = (D - I_r) \times (_sH_r - _sI_r)$$

The negative drive, I_r is generated by performance of the response and only dissipates after it has ceased. Drive reduction reinforces to the negative habit of not emitting the target response, leading, after repeated trials, to a special form of extinction: conditioned inhibition. It follows from Jones's (1958) formula that when conditioned inhibition exceeds habit strength, the response in question will cease to occur.

Kendrick (1960) suggested that conditioned inhibition, occurring in this way, may be responsible for observed effects of negative practice. Eysenck (1956) has argued that when performance of a response is continuous I_r builds up to a critical level at which point an automatic resting response is produced, allowing I_r to dissipate and consequently $_sI_r$ to increase. Negative practice, in which the trials are close together, resembles continuous performance and may produce the same effect. Deliberate rest pauses, it is argued, may promote conditioned inhibition since they would facilitate I_r reduction and, therefore, the development of $_sI_r$. Kendrick tested several hypotheses derived from Hull's model (with Jones's (1958) modification) in experiments with rats. Despite one or two inconsistencies in his findings, his overall conclusion was that the development of a negative habit in the way described was the most viable explanation of the ultimate extinction of a habit repeated in the same stimulus situation.

The use of conditioned inhibition as an explanation of habit decrementation when the behaviour in question is an obsessive thought or rumination, encounters two main difficulties. The first lies in the doubtful status of such thoughts as reinforced responses, while the second is that these target events are very often associated with considerable anxiety and upset, a fact which sets them apart from many other responses investigated.

Rachman (1971a, 1976) described obsessive thoughts as stimuli, pointing out that they evoke a variety of responses when they arise, although he offered no account of their frequent and unwanted occurrence.

Whilst it is reasonable to assume that such thoughts do function as stimuli, it may be argued that they are primarily responses, evoked under definable circumstances. Some obsessive thoughts can very clearly be seen to be associated with environmental events, as when a patient sees a pushchair and subsequently wonders if she has harmed the child. The fact that such eliciting stimuli have not been identified in more cases probably reflects the lack of adequate investigation in this area. Comprehensive self-monitoring similar to that used by Slade (1972), with patients experiencing auditory hallucinations, could provide relevant information. The observed associations between obsessions and depression (Gittleson, 1966; Kendell and Discipio, 1970) indicates that stimuli arising from adverse mood as well as environmental cues may be influential in evoking obsessive thought responses. At best, morbid thoughts may be seen as stimuli only in relation to a very complex sequence of stimuli and responses.

In several ways, obsessive thoughts or ruminations seem to behave like emotional responses, particularly in respect of anxiety. Like anxiety, the occurrence of a thought of this nature is unpleasant, unwanted and beyond the control of the patient (although it is noteworthy that many patients seek out the situations which 'trigger' the ruminative response). This apparent similarity between the two forms of response seems to suggest that the occurrence of an unwanted thought may arise through classical conditioning rather than any form of instrumental learning. This cannot really be either verified or refuted until the cues associated with the response have been identified. However, the possibility that instrumental learning is involved seems to be reduced still further by the fact that many obsessive thoughts do not seem to be accompanied by any form of positive reinforcement. By no means all unwanted thoughts are associated with 'putting right' rituals which could serve a reinforcing anxiety-reducing function. Perhaps surprisingly, the lack of definitive status of obsessive thoughts and the apparent absence of reinforcement does not seem to preclude them from consideration in terms of conditioned inhibition. Gleitman, Nachmias, and Neisser (1954) state that Hull maintained that both negative drive (I_r) and negative habit $(_sI_r)$ are a necessary result of the evocation of the response, whether or not positive reinforcement is present. It is clear from this that there is no restriction on the manner in which the response is evoked, as long as it does occur, and that positive reinforcement is not essential.

The second difficulty in aligning the treatment of obsessive thoughts with conditioned inhibition is less easy to counter. By virtue of their content, these thoughts are accompanied by unpleasant emotional responses including anxiety, which may be of considerable intensity. No direct provision for concomitant responses such as these was made in Hull's (1943) model, nor in Jones's (1958) revision, and it is unclear how anxiety would affect the necessary development of both negative drive and negative habit. However, there is some indirect evidence which indicates that the eventual cessation of the target response may be delayed in the presence of anxiety.

Kendrick (1960) reported the results of an experiment in which he had manipulated the thirst level of rats and had given them repeated trials in a runway, reinforcing them with small quantities of water. All the rats eventually stopped running although they were still water-deprived. The animals who had been most deprived (high drive) continued to run for more trials than those tested at a lower drive level. It was considered unlikely that this occurred merely because the more deprived animals sought more reinforcement as, in another experiment, animals receiving partial reinforcement stopped running sooner than others at the same drive level which received water on every trial.

This latter, paradoxical, result confirmed Kendrick's view that the extinction observed was not ordinary experimental extinction (Gleitman, Nachmias, and Neisser, 1954) but rather was a function of drive level and massing of trials which controlled the tolerance threshold of inhibition. High drive tends to increase the tolerance threshold so that a greater build-up of inhibition is required before any response decrement is observed. Thus, subjects with high drive levels will take longer to achieve this form of extinction, regardless of the presence or absence of positive reinforcement.

It is possible that the anxiety which accompanies obsessive thoughts may function as a generalized drive so that patients may be considered to be at high drive levels during treatment. They might, therefore, be expected to require many more trials in order to achieve a cessation of their target thoughts than subjects working on neutral responses. This hypothesis is eminently testable even with a single patient, as obsessive thoughts evoking measurable anxiety should prove to be more refractory than those concerned with pleasant themes.

If anxiety and distress may be counted as drives, their probable effect in increasing the number of trials before response cessation takes place, may help to account for the extremely protracted treatment required by Broadhurst's (1976) patient in order to achieve only modest gains. This seems to indicate that negative practice may be of limited effectiveness unless care is taken to ensure that drive levels, including thought-induced anxiety, are low. One means of achieving this would be to sedate the patient mildly during treatment sessions. Alternatively, an attempt could be made to flood the patient to his thoughts until they ceased to evoke an emotional response, and then to embark upon negative practice. Both these suggestions are made on the assumption that the presence of anxiety will act as a drive and impede progress. This assumption requires experimental confirmation before the procedure can became part of a treatment approach. However some indirect evidence in support of this idea comes from observations made during the treatment of a 30-year-old woman with persistent thoughts that something that she did would harm her young daughter. The phrase used for negative practice was 'something that I have done will cause harm to my daughter'. For the first 15 to 20 minutes of repetition she showed spontaneous and extreme emotional reactions to the thought, sobbing loudly, but this subsided so that by the end of 40 minutes (800 trials) she was repeating the phrase mechanically and only with great effort. At this stage she could entertain the thought without worry. The emotional outburst at the beginning was highly reminiscent of responses encountered during flooding.

CONCLUSION

Satiation training has neither a substantial theoretical basis nor the empirical confirmation of case reports which usually follow the publication of a new technique. Indeed, as Rachman (1971a, 1976) described it, the procedure has relatively little to commend it to the therapist.

Broadhurst (1976) has recognized the greater potential of utilizing the similar procedure of negative practice in the treatment of obsessive thoughts. Negative practice is, as yet, untested, but at least has a more viable theoretical basis in Hullian theory.

The theory itself, and some corroborative experimental evidence, appears to indicate that excessive drives, perhaps including thought-induced anxiety, may impede progress during treatment. Thus, the basic negative practice procedure described clearly by Broadhurst (1976) and Jones (1960) may have to be modified to include some means of anxiety control. Appropriate experimental adaptation of the procedure might possibly contribute towards an effective treatment for obsessive thoughts.

7

Thought-Stopping

Thought-stopping, as its name indicates, is a procedure which is specifically designed to eliminate unwanted distressing and repetitive thoughts. The technique was first brought to the attention of behaviour therapists by Wolpe (1958) although he attributed its development to Bain (1928) and Tayler (1950). He outlined the procedure as being one in which the patient is asked to shut his eyes and to utter a typical unadaptive thought sequence upon which the therapist shouts 'stop' and the patient's attention is drawn to the fact that the thought actually has stopped. Control of the 'stop' command is gradually transferred to the patient until he merely utters stop subvocally.

Wolpe also described a modified procedure in which the patient is told to try to keep his mind on pleasant things and to press a key, activating a buzzer, every time an unwanted thought occurs. On hearing the buzzer, the therapist shouts 'stop' and the sequence is repeated. This modified procedure merely affects the way in which the target thoughts arise. In the original method they are evoked on command whereas Wolpe's variation deals only with spontaneous thought occurrences.

In 1973 Wolpe reported a further procedural innovation which may be implemented. He suggested that electric shock may be used to accompany the stop signal, but did not offer any explanation why he felt this should be of aid.

Several other clinicians (see below) have introduced relaxation training and deliberate relaxation before and after each thought-stopping attempt, but again no real explanation has been offered for this modification. This may reflect the fact that the thought-stopping procedure has been developed in the absence of any preconceived theoretical rationale, a point which will be discussed in detail after published reports have been described.

PUBLISHED REPORTS

Wolpe (1958, 1973) considered that thought-stopping was particularly effective in treating episodic brooding, but on the whole did not alleviate chronic obsessional ideas. Perhaps this is why reports on the use of thought-stopping with adult obsessionals are relatively scarce, there being only a handful of single case studies, one larger series and two attempts at controlled trials.

The earliest properly documented account of thought-stopping seems to be by Stern (1970). His patient, aged 27 years, had an eight to ten-year history of obsessional preoccupations and fears. He worried about every action he carried out and afterwards would ruminate about whether he had performed it correctly. He was treated in fifteen sessions each of 45 minutes. An hierarchy of his obsessional fears was constructed, treatment commencing with the lowest item. The first half of each session was taken up with achieving a state of relaxation with muscle relaxation training, backed up for the first nine sessions only with intravenous Brietal. When the patient was relaxed, he had to imagine performing one of the acts which worried him—for example, turning off taps—to 'worry' as he usually would for five to fifteen seconds and then to indicate that he had done so by raising his hand. At this signal the therapist banged on the desk and the patient should 'stop'. The procedure was repeated with the other hierachy items until eventually it was only necessary for the patient to say 'stop' subvocally for the thought to cease.

Practice was also carried out *in vivo* with the patient performing feared acts and using thought-stopping until he was able to put the method into action on his own at home. He also had to practise relaxation at home. No quantitative evidence of reduced thought-frequency was given. It was merely stated that the patient became competent at thought-stopping, using it effectively to control his symptoms and that he could cope with his accountancy work better than before.

Kumar and Wilkinson (1971) also used relaxation training in their thought-stopping programme with four patients. The patients were treated individually and were given muscle relaxation training once a week for three to four weeks during which time they were taken off drugs and kept a weekly frequency count of thoughts. Five sessions of thought-stopping were given following a standard procedure. The patient had to think about pleasure-evoking thoughts whilst listening to tape-recorded birdsong and waterfall sounds. Following this the patient was asked to verbalize an unwanted thought, upon which the therapist shouted 'stop' on the first trial, pointing out that the thoughts had ceased, and thereafter restarting the tape of pleasant sounds. He was told to practise by himself by saying 'stop' subvocally and switching his mind to pleasant thoughts. In addition, he had to keep a record of the frequency of unwanted thoughts. It is unclear what role relaxation training played in this package; it can only be assumed that it was to be implemented in conjunction with the pleasant scenes and sounds, and possibly also between sessions, as a means of reducing general tension.

No quantitative results were reported, it merely being stated that the frequency of thoughts was reduced considerably during the four-week treatment period. Thoughts still occurred occasionally at the end of treatment, but they were divested of their intensity and pathological quality (undefined).

In addition to this unsatisfactory report of outcome, it is difficult to determine the relevance of the study to work with true obsessive–compulsive patients as the subjects did not appear to have this primary diagnosis. One, a male aged 44 years, was also treated for agoraphobia and presented with thoughts concerning heart attacks and public places. Two 25-year-old women had fears of cancer and other diseases, and a third, aged 22 years, suffered from a fear of death. Without further information, it is not possible to tell whether these thoughts and fears possessed the ruminative quality characteristic of obsessive preoccupation (see Chapter 6). It seems very likely that the fears of illness and death did so, but in the absence of real verification, slight doubt must remain.

The evaluation of Stern's (1970) and Kumar and Wilkinson's (1971) studies is complicated by the inclusion of relaxation techniques. In Stern's case, the use of relaxation and an hierarchical presentation of items could have amounted to systematic desensitization, with the thought-stopping procedure adding nothing to that effect. The potential contribution of relaxation training to Kumar and Wilkinson's procedure is less obvious as its use during thought-stopping was not stated. However, even if the patients did not use progressive muscle relaxation exercises during their sessions, the taped sounds and pleasant imagined scenes seem to have been designed to have a calming and relaxing effect. Therefore these patients too seemed to be evoking their unpleasant thoughts whilst in a relaxed state. Despite the absence of an hierarchy, some of the anxiety elicited by the unwanted thoughts could have been attenuated by the patients' quiescent stage. It is by no means certain that the thought-stopping sequence was responsible for the reduction in thought-frequency which was observed. In view of this neither Stern's case nor those of Kumar and Wilkinson can be taken as unequivocal evidence that thought-stopping has any effect.

The remaining reports to be reviewed can be taken as more certain evidence concerning the efficacy of thought-stopping, since no extra trimmings such as relaxation training have been added to the basic procedure.

Two reports of treatment of unwanted thoughts with religious connotations may be despatched easily. Lambley (1974) tried thought-stopping briefly with a religious 20-year-old student who was constantly repeating lines of prayer to herself. The patient found the procedure irrelevant and externalized and requested that it should stop. This is hardly a fair trial of thought-stopping nor is it likely that the girl was psychiatrically ill. She was seen two days after her first attempt at sexual intercourse with her boyfriend and recovered rapidly a day later after some instruction in covert reinforcement.

Gullick and Blanchard's (1973) intelligent male patient experienced the recurrent and distressing thought that he was blaspheming after he had been baptized into the Pentecostal Church without experiencing the expected feelings of being saved. After a three-day baseline recording period he was given once-daily sessions of psychotherapy for nine days, thought-stopping for five days, return to baseline for three days, three more days of psychotherapy, four days without therapy and attribution treatment for eleven days. The unwanted thoughts showed a consistent reduction, apart from on no-therapy days, being eliminated near the beginning of the attribution phase. There was no indication that the treatments were having different effects. At the very most it might be said that thought-stopping was doing as well as psychotherapy, but really this seemed to be far from clear.

Yamagami (1971) restricted himself to thought-stopping when treating an obsessional colour-namer, but systematically varied details of the procedure. He gave twenty trials in each of four conditions. Initially he shouted 'stop' one to three minutes after the patient evoked an unwanted thought then the patient was relaxed after the stop signal had been given. Thirdly, shock was given instead of a shout of 'stop', and finally both 'stop' and shock occurred and the patients had to shout 'stop' immediately after the shock. After seventeen sessions, thought-frequency had decreased by 95 per cent and later disappeared and the thoughts were still absent seven months later. Anthony and Edelstein (1975) also only employed thought-stopping in treating a rather atypical patient who experienced unwanted thoughts related to a fear of having seizures. The 24-year-old girl had suffered from several seizures a few years previously, but these were well controlled by drugs. However, she had begun to ruminate over seizures and these thoughts made her panic; in turn this panic had tended to precipitate seizures, so that she was having them several times a week at the time of coming to treatment.

After two weeks of baseline recording, she was asked to ruminate about seizures overtly and the therapist interrupted her thoughts. Gradually the patient's thoughts were made covert and she took over control of the stop signal. She was asked to practise at home at least twice a day. She was symptom-free by the end of the week and experienced no more seizure-related panic attacks during the six-month follow-up period.

Despite the encouraging outcomes, very little may be said about the efficacy of thought-stopping from the case reports, as no attempt was made to include any control or placebo stages in the treatments used. Only three larger controlled trials have been conducted, in each of which thought-stopping was compared with an alternative condition. The earliest of the three by Stern, Lipsedge, and Marks (1973) involved a placebo treatment control, whereas Hackmann and McLean (1975) compared thought-stopping with flooding and Emmelkamp and Kwee (1977) used exposure in imagination.

Stern, Lipsedge, and Marks (1973) treated eleven patients who had obsessive ruminations as a major problem although six of them also had compulsive rituals. The time for which they had suffered from their ruminations ranged from four to 35 years (mean twelve years). The treatment instructions were tape recorded. For the thought-stopping procedure, relaxation instructions were given for four minutes, the patient was told to think an obsessive thought for 25 to 45 seconds, a loud metallic noise sounded (stop signal) and after a 45-second rest interval thought-evocation and stop signal were repeated for a total of twelve trials. The control tape was the same except that the patient was instructed to think of a blank television screen instead of obsessive thoughts. A cross-over design was used in which each patient alternated between the two conditions receiving two sessions of each. The patient took the cassette home to listen to once a day between sessions.

Psychophysiological recordings were made during sessions, and interviews were conducted each week. Daily ratings of thought-frequency, evaluation (three evaluative semantic differential scales) and 'danger' (three danger semantic differential scales) were made for one month before and during the trial. A fourth scale was rated at the same time; this was called 'distress', but was labelled 'troublesome', 'disgusting', or 'disturbing' for patients who found these names more appropriate. The group means on these scales, therefore, represented an averaging of slightly heterogeneous material. This would not necessarily affect an examination of change over time but would make an interpretation in terms of absolute magnitude difficult.

It was found that four of the eleven patients showed marked improvement at the end of treatment, but results for the rest of the group were described as disappointing. This outcome resulted in overall non-significant changes. There was a tendency for the patients to improve more during the thought-stopping phases than during the control phases, but this was not statistically significant either.

These disappointing results do not necessarily indicate that thought-stopping is ineffective. It is extremely unlikely that only two sessions of genuine treatment at the clinic, separated by two weeks would be sufficient to produce much change in symptoms of the severity that the ones treated appear to have been. Although the patients were instructed to listen to the treatment tape at home once a day, the authors gave no indication as to whether this was done. To comply with these instructions the patients would have to sit down and deliberately evoke the thoughts which they were wishing to eliminate. This action would guarantee immediate discomfort with only the delayed rewards of improvement. It is now clear from work with smokers and overeaters, that often people do not inflict discomfort on themselves for the sake of future reward (see Chapter 8). Therefore it cannot be assumed that the patients did what they were told. Even if a patient was conscientious, he would only have had a total of fourteen sessions with the tape and this still seems to be remarkably few.

In addition, it is difficult to assess the effects of using tape-recorded sessions. As some of the patients are reported to have had difficulty even in filling in the rating scales, it seems possible that they did not find it easy to follow the taped instructions. It is not stated whether there was a therapist present during the session at the clinic, but it would have been helpful if one was there.

Finally, the study may have militated against revealing any improvement, as not all the rating scales used to evaluate outcome appear to be entirely relevant. The frequency rating was of obvious importance and the rather heterogeneous rating, labelled 'distress', can be seen as being concerned with frequency as well as severity of thoughts. The use of the 'danger' and evaluative semantic differential scales is more puzzling as they seem to tap only qualitative aspects of unwanted thoughts and not the frequency with which they occur. It is difficult to see how these scales would reflect changes brought about by thought-stopping. The techniques are intended to reduce the frequency of unwanted thoughts. There is little to indicate that the quality of the thoughts would change as a result of someone shouting 'stop' or making a noise, unless a classical conditioning paradigm is involved, in which case the thoughts should become even more upsetting. In any event, there seems to be no good reason to suppose that the semantic differential scales would represent a direct means of assessing therapeutic change. Taking all these points into account, it is clear that the failure of this study cannot be taken as a firm indication of the weakness of the technique. However, the methodological deficiencies do not seem to be sufficient to mask a convincing treatment effect. Had thought-stopping exerted a powerful influence on thought-frequency, it is probable that it would have become apparent if only in attenuated form, despite the inadequacies of the design. The fact that no clear change was evident, does not augur well for the future of thought-stopping.

Hackmann and McLean (1975) compared thought-stopping with flooding rather than with a placebo control. Once more a cross-over design was implemented with ten patients (length of illness three to seven years), with half of them receiving four sessions of thought-stopping followed by four of flooding, and the remaining patients having the treatment in the reverse order. The flooding procedure was similar to the flooding, plus modelling treatment, described by Rachman, Hodgson, and Marks (1971) (see Chapter 5). Thought-stopping was conducted without relaxation. The patient was asked to signal when he had evoked an obsessive thought. The therapist then hit the desk with a ruler and shouted 'stop' after which the patient had to keep his mind blank for 30 seconds before the next trial was commenced. If thoughts intruded in the 30-seconds period, 'stop' was repeated. Gradually, over trials the therapist's 'stop' and noise were faded out and were replaced by the patient's verbalization of 'stop' uttered at first overtly and then subvocally. The outcome measures were Leyton Obsessional Inventory and Eysenck Personality Inventory scores, self and independent raters' assessments on seven point scales for obsessional anxiety, avoidance, time consumed by rituals and preoccupation with obsession, a similar global rating of severity of illness made by the assessor, and diaries kept by the patient.

At the end of treatment there were no significant differences between flooding and thought-stopping on any of these scales. In describing their sample, the authors identified three patients for whom thought-stopping was the more helpful treatment, and one for whom both helped; the remaining patients were either aided most by flooding or neither treatment had much effect. The effect of each treatment was evaluated on its own. The patients, who received thought stopping first, improved significantly ($p < 0.05$) as a result of this treatment on Leyton Obsessional Inventory symptom scores and diary recording of frequency of rituals (but not on a corresponding one of thoughts). Those who had thought-stopping second showed improvement over and above the effects of their preceding flooding on Leyton Interference and Resistance scores and global severity ratings made by the independent assessor. Taken together, the treatments yielded a degree of improvement which Hackmann and McLean felt to be comparable to that achieved in other studies using a variety of treatments, including Hodgson, Rachman, and Marks (1972) with modelling, flooding and response prevention and Rack (1973) with clomipramine.

As the study was designed to compare thought-stopping with flooding plus response prevention, the number of sessions which were devoted to each was fewer than would be required to evaluate the effectiveness of either treatment on its own. Therefore the rather meagre results arising from thought-stopping must be considered to be comparable to those which would be obtained at most half way through an ordinary treatment programme. As several other scales indicated improvement, significant at the ten per cent level after thought-stopping, it is possible that improvement would have been evident on a wider range of measures if the treatment had been doubled in length. This, of course, assumes that change would not have reached a plateau by half way through the course.

In addition, Hackmann and McLean may have reduced the chances of establishing a clear-cut effect of thought-stopping or flooding by using a heterogeneous group of patients. Stern, Lipsedge, and Marks (1973) and the case report authors cited selected patients in whom intrusive and unwanted thoughts were prominent for their investigations. Conversely, Rachman, Hodgson, and Marks (1971) used only patients with compulsive rituals when working on flooding and modelling. Hackmann and McLean did not select in either of these ways, but instead used a group which it seems from their case descriptions included both patients with elaborate rituals and those whose main difficulties were related to thoughts. It appears from the report that of the five patients who improved with thought-stopping, three suffered primarily from unwanted thoughts and two from thoughts and checking rituals. In contrast, four of the five who did not respond well to thought-stopping had fears of contamination with associated avoidance and washing rituals; the fifth suffered from images of relatives burning in hell and did not respond to flooding either.

Although no firm conclusion may be drawn on the basis of the results obtained from only ten patients, it does seem that thought-stopping may be of little value in the treatment of patients with fears of contamination and compulsive rituals, but that it may have more effect when intrusive thoughts predominate. There seems therefore to be a slight indication that thought-stopping may have some beneficial effect.

Hackmann and McLean's procedure was modified slightly by Emmelkamp and Kwee (1977). They used the sound of a loud hooter as the 'stop' signal and instructed the patients to think of neutral or pleasant thoughts when the ruminative thoughts stopped. As described in the previous chapter, their presentation and analyses of results do not allow any conclusion to be drawn about the efficacy of the treatments used. It appears that three of the five patients did show some reduction in thought-frequency following five one-hour sessions of thought-stopping. However, as two of these were also the only ones who improved following the alternative treatment, exposure in imagination, any specific effects of thought-stopping may be questioned.

DISCUSSION

Taken together, all the studies cited represent the treatment of only 35 patients by thought-stopping. This is scant enough evidence on which to evaluate the effectiveness of the technique. But, in addition, the number of cases has to be reduced still further by the exclusion of Stern's (1970) patient, and the four treated by Kumar and Wilkinson (1971) on the grounds that the use of relaxation would have had an unknown, but probably beneficial effect, and also of Lambley's (1974) student who appeared to have been acutely distressed, but not disordered. As no conclusions could be drawn from Emmelkamp and Kwee's (1977) results, their patients cannot be included. Without these, 24 patients remain.

Exactly half appear to have benefited from thought-stopping, the rest either remaining unchanged, or in the case of some of Hackmann and McLean's patients, doing rather better with another treatment. At face value, this success rate is hardly one which inspires great confidence in thought-stopping as a therapeutic tool. However, it may be that this judgment is a little hard as Stern, Lipsedge, and Marks's (1973) patients who received too few sessions and Hackmann and McLean's (1975) four patients who suffered from washing rituals, more than thoughts, formed the bulk of the failure groups. Thus it is possible that under more favourable conditions thought-stopping could have been shown to have a higher rate of success.

Taking this into account, there seems to be just about sufficient positive evidence to continue the enquiry into the effect of thought-stopping, but rather than ploughing blindly on with applied research, it would be as well to consider the rationale on which the procedure is based as this aspect of the package has been ignored up till now.

THEORETICAL BASES OF THOUGHT-STOPPING

Very little seems to have been recorded about the development of the thought-stopping procedure. From Wolpe's (1958) account it seems that it may have been devised on the basis of face validity, in that it seems sensible to attempt to stop unwanted thoughts, backed up by some evidence that it could be effective. The procedural variations, added later, also bear little more than the hallmark of common sense. Therefore any search for a learning-based explanation of why the modest successes achieved by thought-stopping should have occurred, is confronted with a puzzle in which operative learning processes have to be inferred from an aggregation of treatment procedures. In an attempt to unravel this problem, only the basic thought-stopping procedure will be considered, the effects of procedural variations will be discussed where it is felt that they may be influential.

The basic thought-stopping procedure is one in which the patient is seated, but not deliberately relaxed, and is asked to evoke his usual unwanted thought-sequence. At a variable interval after he has signalled the initiation of the thought, the therapist shouts 'stop', and draws the patient's attention to the cessation of the thought. After a short pause the procedure is repeated and over successive trials the patient gradually takes over control of the stop signal, eventually uttering it subvocally. There appear to be five component parts in this procedure which potentially could contribute to a beneficial therapeutic outcome. These are, controlled exposure to the unwanted thought, positive reinforcement, punishment, the use of distraction or incompatible responses, and interruption of the behavioural chain. The possible contribution of each of these will be discussed in turn.

1. Controlled exposure to the unwanted thought

During the course of a session, the patient is exposed to repeated short presentations of his thoughts, whilst he is seated comfortably in the presence of a therapist, whom it is assumed, he trusts. It is likely that this procedure would be conducive to habituation to the thought stimuli or to reciprocal inhibition of anxiety elicited by them. Both occurrences would be expected to be facilitated by the introduction of deep relaxation both whilst experiencing the thought and afterwards as for example in the studies by Stern (1970) and Kumar and Wilkinson (1971).

However, the exposure would be only to the initial stages of a prolonged rumination as there is no indication that the starting point in thought-evocation is varied. This means that many parts of the thought-sequence would never be presented. Some stimulus generalization might be expected to occur so that some of the thoughts in the sequence, similar in content to those dealt with in sessions might lose their anxiety-evoking potential. Nevertheless, it seems unlikely that the anxiety associated with all unwanted thoughts would be eliminated so that it may be necessary to search for additional effective components of thought-stopping in order to account for patients who become symptom-free after treatment.

2. Positive reinforcement

In 1958, Wolpe offered no explanation of the effectiveness of thought-stopping, but in 1973 he discussed it under the heading of 'Positive Reinforcement'. He considered that the habit of thought inhibition is reinforced by the anxiety reduction following each successful attempt to stop the thought. This analysis rests on the assumption that termination of the unwanted thought will result in anxiety reduction. Although this may be so in many cases, it has been argued in the previous chapter that stopping some ruminations, at least, at an early stage could result in distress. This would be the case if the patient usually followed the unwanted thought with ones aimed at putting it right (Rachman, 1976) or if the thought was the first part of a prolonged rumination embarked on in an attempt to reduce discomfort occasioned by the initial thought. For cases such as these, it may be necessary to modify the procedure in order to ensure that the consequences of thought cessation do not appear aversive.

In this context it may be questioned whether a sudden shout of 'stop' sometimes accompanied by a loud noise (Hackmann and McLean, 1975; Stern, Lipsedge, and Marks, 1973) or an electric shock (Wolpe, 1958, 1973) should be employed. At the very least such stimuli would be likely to evoke a marked startle response in the patient, as has been demonstrated in changes in psychophysiological responses recorded by Stern *et al.* (1973). As the stop signal provides the stimulus for both startle response and thought cessation, the latter two would tend to occur together. Thus the termination of the thought could easily become associated with an immediate increase in autonomic response rather than a diminution of the same. It would follow that rather than giving a dramatic stop signal, any startling effect should be minimized so that the patient experiences as little adverse change as possible in his state.

This would not solve the problem of continuing anxiety resulting from thought cessation. The immediate introduction of progressive relaxation exercises, soothing music, or perhaps appropriate medication after the stop signal, might enable sufficient anxiety reduction to occur for the procedure to have a positively reinforcing effect. In addition, the knowledge that the thought has indeed stopped may be reinforcing for patients who had felt previously that their thoughts were beyond control. The impact of this information seems to be maximized in the routine thought-stopping procedure by the therapist pointing out to the patient that his thought is no longer present.

3. Punishment

In several respects thought-stopping resembles the sort of procedure which is used in aversion therapy (McGuire and Vallance, 1964) or covert sensitization (Cautela, 1967). The patient is seated comfortably and imagines a prohibited response, in this case a thought, whereupon a sudden noxious stimulus is administered. Termination of the noxious stimulus is associated with inhibition of the unwanted response. It may be argued that thought-stopping using the procedure described by Wolpe (1958, 1973) falls short of the aversion paradigm, as a mere shout of 'stop' cannot be said to be in any way comparable to, say, an electric shock. This objection is quite reasonable, but cannot be applied as readily to the procedure used in the two controlled treatment trials in which the shout of 'stop' was supplemented with a bang on the table (Hackmann and McLean, 1975) and a loud metallic sound (Stern, Lipsedge, and Marks, 1973) or to Wolpe's (1958, 1973) suggestion of using electric shock. Stern *et al.*'s psychophysiological recordings indicated that their stop signal had a considerable impact on the patients. They reported that all patients showed a marked startle response, as evidenced in tachycardia and deflection of skin conductance at the onset of the noise.

In view of this, it seems quite probable that the patients found the noise decidedly unpleasant, so that potentially it could serve as punishment. In operant terms, this would mean that it would serve to decrease the occurrence probability of the unwanted thoughts.

If it is assumed that some variations of stop signal do provide required aversive consequences, the adequacy of thought-stopping as a punishment paradigm may be examined. Ideally the aim of thought-stopping is to inhibit totally and permanently the unwanted thoughts so that they never occur at all in any situation in which the patient finds himself. In order to meet this aim the procedure must achieve complete suppression of thoughts and extensive generalization of that effect outside the clinic.

The thought-stopping procedure does not seem to be designed to engender total thought-inhibition. Usually the patient is allowed to elaborate the unwanted thought for intervals varying from a few seconds up to two to three minutes before the stop signal is introduced. Thus punishment follows a period of thinking rather than thought initiation.

The classic work of Solomon, Turner, and Lessec (1968) with beagle pups indicates that punishment initiated when a prohibited act is well under way is unlikely to suppress the behaviour entirely. Hungry puppies who were slapped on the nose with rolled-up newspaper 30 seconds after they had started feeding, continued to approach the food dish and to feed, although they showed signs of anxiety whilst doing so. From this it seems possible that patients who receive a shock signal whilst already experiencing their unwanted thoughts would continue to think about them but, if anything, with increased anxiety.

In contrast, some of Solomon *et al.*'s puppies were hit on the nose just as they were about to touch the food and these refused to approach the bowl at all. It would follow that it might be more beneficial to 'stop' the patient just as the thought is about to emerge, so that eventually it may be inhibited permanently. In practice, of course, this will not be possible as neither patient not therapist will be able to detect the thought until the initial stages of it have occurred. However the patient can be asked to signal as soon as a thought starts so that he may be stopped as near to the beginning as possible. Only Hackmann and McLean (1975) seem to have asked their patients to signal immediately a thought occurred.

The problem of generalization is not so easily resolved. Clearly the patient will be able to discriminate between the consulting room, where the therapist exudes stop signals, and the rest of the world, where there is nobody to make a noise every time he has a prohibited thought. In order to anticipate that thought-stopping will generalize, either some form of learning beyond the control of discriminative stimuli has to be postulated, or some means of applying the procedure at any time, in all situations, has to be contrived. Those who have published reports of the use of thought-stopping seem to have paid little attention to the first possibility, as on the whole the number of sessions with the therapist have been too few to expect much learning beyond conscious control to become established (see, for example, Kumar and Wilkinson, 1971; Stern, Lipsedge, and Marks, 1973; and Hackmann and McLean, 1975).

Rather, most workers have seemed to emphasize the transfer of control of the stop signal to the patient at an early stage of treatment, and home practice of the entire procedure, in addition to use of the stop signal, should an unwanted thought arise. The main advantages of having the patient as therapist like this is that he is always present when a problem thought occurs and by responding subvocally, should never be prevented from uttering a contingent 'stop'. But by making 'stop' subvocal and by abandoning all accompanying loud noises, its function as a punishing stimulus may be lost so that a punishment paradigm may no longer apply. Even disregarding this possibility and assuming that the subvocal 'stop' could function as punishment, there is considerable reason to doubt whether it would be effective.

The theoretical and practical problems associated with self-punishment, that is with applying an aversive stimulus contingently to oneself, are discussed at length in Chapter 8. In the present context, suffice it to say that not only has Skinner (1953) suggested that self-punishment is unlikely to have an effect comparable to punishment administered by others, but that it is now apparent that people are often reluctant to apply aversive stimuli to themselves (see Whitman 1972). Overall the use of self-punishment is not likely to be viable.

Having discarded the possibility of the patient treating himself, the only hope for generalization lies in the establishment of an automatic autonomic response to thought onset. The development of such a response has been one of the main aims of aversion therapy for other problem behaviours and so the probability of achieving this with thought-stopping may be estimated from the degree of success in these related areas. The record of aversion therapy has not been impressive even though more powerful aversive stimuli have been used than thought-stopping workers have employed (Eysenck and Beech, 1971). There seems to be no reason to expect that thought-stopping would do any better. Therefore it may be concluded that although the thought-stopping procedure could be modified to make it consonant with a traditional punishment paradigm, the results which are likely to accrue from doing so would be unlikely to be worth the effort involved. It would be preferable not to cast the stop signal as punishment, but rather to investigate alternative roles which it might play.

4. The use of distraction or incompatible responses

One possible reason for the therapist to shout 'stop' loudly would be in order to distract the patient and thereby interrupt his ongoing train of thought. When transferred to the patient's control, the stop signal would retain its distracting properties but would also serve as a response which would be incompatible with continuing to think the unwanted thought.

In using a loud 'stop' as a distracting stimulus, it seems to be assumed that the same stimulus spoken in a softer voice would fail to have the desired effect. There seems to be very little evidence on which to base this view and indeed there are some observations which seem to contradict it. Patients who are receiving desensitization or any of Cautela's covert procedures (1970) experience no difficulty in terminating unpleasant scenes or thoughts in response to a quietly spoken request and there seems to be no good reason why people with obsessive thoughts should differ from them.

It could be argued that the compelling nature of obsessive thoughts are likely to make them particularly difficult to stop and thereby set them apart from other intrusive internal stimuli. But it has yet to be demonstrated that the thoughts of obsessional patients are unique in that respect, as phobic patients also experience repeated and unwanted thoughts about their fears. Until proven otherwise, it seems conservative to assume that an obsessional's ability to control his thoughts in response to instruction will be the same as that of other neurotic patients. Thus the apparent belief that the command to stop must be loud if it is to be effective may be unfounded. This point is not merely one of detail as it has been suggested earlier that the shout of 'stop' may produce an autonomic response which is incompatible with anxiety reduction following thought-cessation. If there are reasonable grounds for believing that the shout is dispensable, then a quieter alternative is certainly to be preferred.

The usual thought-stopping procedure also places great emphasis on transferring the stop signal from the therapist to the patient so that eventually the latter supplies his own stop command. In fact, it is difficult to see why the therapist has to say 'stop' in the first place, as it is the patient who gives the cue for the procedure to take place. In raising his finger to indicate that a thought has occurred, the patient is giving a signal for the stop command to be made. This seems to be an unnecessary complication of a simple chain of events. Instead of raising his finger, the patient could say stop, either out loud or subvocally without involving the therapist at all. Generally this is what occurs at an advanced stage of thought-stopping, but there seems to be no reason why it should not happen from the start.

It seems to be immaterial whether the patient says 'stop' aloud or to himself at first except that an audible response in the initial stages of treatment would help the therapist to monitor his attempts. Although not actively involved in the procedure, the therapist may by his presence ensure that the patient practises dutifully and can also answer queries which arise. Practice with the therapist is therefore thought not to be dispensable.

Once issued by the patient, the stop signal may take on a slightly different function. It is difficult to look upon it merely as a distraction as it is now uttered by the patient, and thereby as a concomitant response must come into conflict with the ongoing train of thought. Apart from the fact that attention to saying 'stop' is likely to detract from concern with the unwanted thought, the imperative connotations of the word may arrest other ongoing activity, at least temporarily. For these reasons the patient's response of 'stop' may prove to be incompatible with the continuation of unwanted thoughts, causing them to cease.

It is not clear why it should be expected that the thoughts would continue to be suppressed for any length of time after the signal had finished. It would seem to be much more likely that, left to their own devices, the thoughts will reoccur spontaneously as soon as there is nothing of importance occupying the patient's mind. In order to ensure that the thoughts do not re-emerge, it may be necessary to institute a continuing incompatible response following the patient's 'stop' command. Wolpe (1969) suggested that such a procedure should be adopted. Kumar and Wilkinson's (1971) use of imagined beautiful scenery would seem to be suitable as it involves thoughts which are likely to be incompatible with those which are unwanted, by virtue both of their differing content and of their anxiety-reducing (rather than anxiety-arousing) quality.

5. Interruption of the habitual behaviour chain

Before the patient starts treatment, the occurrence of an unwanted thought is likely to lead to complex and prolonged rumination. It has been suggested that at least some ruminations serve to reduce anxiety temporarily in so far as they are terminated when the patient feels that he had reached a solution or compromise. The fact that satisfaction with the solution is only transient does not detract from the short-term relief which is experienced. The postulated anxiety reduction on termination of the ritual would reinforce the execution of the rumination and probably make its performance more compelling.

The use of a stop signal by therapist or patient serves to interrupt the reinforced sequence of thought so that the habitual chain of events between thought initiation and eventual reinforcement is disrupted. From a strictly Skinnerian viewpoint this might be considered to be sufficient to prevent the rest of the rumination from occurring. In his terms the first ruminative thoughts must surely provide the discriminative stimuli for the occurrence of those which follow. Therefore the introduction of an interrupting stimulus would alter the stimulus situation so that the ruminative thoughts would no longer necessarily be the most likely to be evoked.

This must assume that the interrupting 'stop' signal has one or more prepotent response already associated with it; if it has not, then there seems to be no reason why the ruminative thoughts should not continue to occur. Although by its meaning 'stop', said subvocally or otherwise, may tend to halt ongoing behaviour, it does not seem to evoke any active alternative response. Therefore there seems to be no reason why the progression of the rumination should be suspended indefinitely. Again there seems to be a strong case for believing that saying 'stop' would be most effective if followed immediately with a response incompatible with distressing thinking.

An operant analysis of the thought sequence provides one further piece of information. In his discussions of chaining Skinner (1953) indicated that the elements in the behavioural chain which are closest in time and often in space to the eventual reinforcement are the most powerfully reinforced. The behaviours which initiated the chain are less strongly reinforced. It follows, then, that it should be easier to disrupt the chain of behaviour in its early stages than towards the end when maximal reinforcement has nearly been achieved. Bergin (1969) has made use of this observation successfully in treating unwanted appetitive responses, for example, homosexual approach behaviour. He has advised patients to analyse the behaviour chain which leads up to the prohibited response and then to introduce incompatible adaptive behaviour as early in the chain as is possible. It seems likely that a similar procedure could facilitate thought-stopping. Instead of waiting for seconds or minutes after thought initiation before saying 'stop', the patient could be encouraged to stop himself as soon as the first inkling of a thought arises. By doing this he would break the chain at its weakest point and maximize his chances of being able to substitute an alternative response.

DISCUSSION

Consideration of the possible factors operative in thought-stopping has led to the conclusion that three components of the procedure may be responsible for most of the improvement following treatment which has been observed: (a) the interruption of the chain of thought upon initiation, (b) the institution of an incompatible response, (c) and positive reinforcement in the form of anxiety reduction are all thought to be operative. It is felt that the thought-stopping procedure in its usual form fails to maximize the effectiveness of these components and that this may in part account for the very limited success with thought-stopping which has been achieved.

The factors thought to be effective during thought-stopping suggested that a modified procedure might prove beneficial. The patient, when seated comfortably, should be asked to evoke a distressing thought. As soon as the thought arises, he should say 'stop' in a voice just loud enough to interfere with his thoughts and should switch to an incompatible response, preferably one which is conducive to anxiety reduction. Relaxation training may be necessary to provide him with such a response and the therapist's presence during the early stages of treatment is probably essential to ensure that the procedure is carried out correctly. The patient's attention should be drawn to his success in terminating his thoughts. Further he should be asked to concentrate on the cues associated with the onset of the thoughts so that he may become skilled in detecting the first signs of their occurrence.

Rachman (1976) has pointed out that ruminations are often accompanied by overt rituals and that these should be treated in addition to the unwanted thoughts. Response prevention instructions should be given following thought-stopping sessions. Failure to do this could have been responsible in part for the limited success of thought-stopping reported in the published accounts. Although both controlled treatment trials included some patients with overt rituals as well as thoughts, neither involved the control of rituals in the context of thought-stopping (Stern, Lipsedge, and Marks, 1973, Hackmann and McLean, 1975).

So far this modified thought-stopping procedure has not been evaluated empirically, so no statement about its effectiveness can be made.

CONCLUSION

The outcome of the published work on thought-stopping is not promising, but several of the studies contain serious deficiencies which could have limited the efficacy of the procedures used. It is possible that appropriately designed studies would yield more favourable results.

However, it is felt that even these would fail to provide entirely satisfactory outcomes because of deficiencies inherent in the thought-stopping procedure itself. An alternative procedure, emphasizing positive reinforcement, interruption of the thought chains, and incompatible responses has been suggested, but as yet is untried.

The fact that this chapter ends with the discussion of a totally unvalidated procedure reflects the sadly limited range of behavioural techniques which may be applied to intrusive thoughts. Neither thought-stopping, nor satiation training (see Chapter 6) seems to have much potential as treatment techniques. Although the alternative procedure, proposed above, may prove to be a little more effective, it is very unlikely to become a panacea for obsessive thoughts. A completely new approach to obsessive thoughts and their modification is required urgently. It is to be hoped that this will be given some priority in behavioural research.

8

Self-Regulation, Self-Control, and Self-Reinforcement Procedures

This chapter will be concerned primarily with the way in which the patient directs his own behaviour when no-one is present to supervise or observe him, particularly when his control involves temporary discomfort. Both during and after behavioural treatment the patient is given instructions which are to be carried out unsupervised. For example, the patient may be asked to record his rituals, to refrain from washing and to watch television as a distraction from unwanted thoughts.

It is usually assumed that the patient will carry out the instructions and experience no real difficulty in doing so. In fact this is not always the case, so that the progress of treatment may be impeded. Any aid which the patient could be given to enhance his chances of following the instructions would have a beneficial effect on his programme.

In most cases, self-supervised procedures have been used merely to supplement sessions with the therapist or to facilitate transfer from hospital to home. However, in a few instances the entire treatment has been carried out by the patient, contact with the therapist being confined to discussing progress and planning the next stage of the programme. In these cases, the patient's ability to carry out the treatment instructions is of paramount importance. The case studies in which the patient has treated himself are discussed below.

The attempts which a patient makes to change his behaviour, either by carrying out instructions or on his own initiative, may be classified into three broad groups. He may have to refrain from doing something which he wishes to do, like seeking reassurance, washing his hands, or checking. In doing so he will have to forego the temporary reduction in discomfort following performance of the ritualistic act in order to avoid the punishment of lasting handicap from his symptoms. Conversely, the patient may have to perform some acts which he would rather avoid like contaminating himself and his possessions prior to

117

response prevention. Here he will have to tolerate a short-term discomfort for the sake of future reward in terms of symptom reduction. Finally, the patient may have to perform treatment exercises, which whilst not unpleasant may be inconvenient or time consuming, for example, record keeping and relaxation practice. Here again, the patient would have to put up with the mild punishment of inconvenience in order to secure the longer-term benefits of improvement.

It is clear that to a greater or lesser extent all three groups of self-initiated behaviours are subject to conflicting reinforcement. In each, immediate punishment (discomfort) is followed, later, by reward. It is under this special reinforcement condition that Kanfer (1971) maintains that a person may exhibit self-control by performing the response that will avoid future punishment at the expense of present reward thereby refraining from the tempting response which would bring immediate gratification. Kanfer took over this view of self-control from Skinner (1953) adding only the requirement of temporal delay between outcomes to Skinner's conflicting reinforcement paradigm.

Skinner had stipulated that in self-control situations, the individual could either refrain from the tempting response by doing nothing or by executing an alternative response which would decrease the probability that the prohibited response would be performed. The way in which such a controlling response was to achieve this end is to be described below. Kanfer agreed with Skinner's analysis and carried it further by describing how the individual might come to interrupt his habitual chain of behaviour by performing a controlling response rather than his preferred indulgent act. Some understanding of the circumstances under which an individual is likely to execute a controlling response may provide an indication of when a patient will be able to carry out his distressing treatment procedures on his own.

Kanfer's discussion of self-control followed directly from that of self-regulation of the means by which the individual maintains his habitual behaviour patterns. Therefore self-regulation must be described so that the factors associated with the exercise of self-control may be understood fully. The following description is based on Kanfer (1971), Kanfer and Karoly (1972a and b). No attempt will be made to assess the theoretical adequacy of Kanfer's model as to do so would necessitate a lengthy discussion of the general cybernetic approach to behaviour, which would be far beyond the scope of this book. However, criticism of elements of the model which have been adopted by clinicians in their self-control work with obsessional patients will be made in the context of discussion of the clinical work.

Kanfer and Karoly postulated that the sequence of self-regulation starts with input, in the form of environmental and internal cues, following the execution of a response. If the response just performed is part of a well-practised, smooth-running pattern of behaviour, then the next response in the chain is performed without conscious evaluation by the subject. If, however, some judgment about the adequacy of the last response is required (as, for example, in the acquisition of new chains), deliberate self-regulation is brought into play. The cues resulting from execution of the response are observed deliberately by the subject (self-monitoring) and are compared with internalized performance standards based on past experience and instruction. Kanfer called this comparison 'self-evaluation'. The outcome of self-evaluation is the subject's judgment that his performance exceeds, equals or falls below the comparison criteria. This judgment serves as a discriminative stimulus for positive self-reinforcement or self-punishment, the determination of which will be influenced by the motivation of subject and the characteristics of the task. The consequence of self-reinforcement will either be the repetition of the same response until it is improved to meet criterion or the immediate introduction of the next response to be performed.

The three stages of self-monitoring, self-evaluation and self-reinforcement are considered to be the main components of self-regulation and all have been used as the bases of treatment techniques in their own right. These will be discussed below.

Self-control was conceptualized as a special instance of self-regulation in that the individual changes his pattern of behaviour rather than maintaining it. Kanfer and Karoly (1972a) considered that an individual's sudden behaviour change results from the introduction of a new standard for self-evaluation (a performance promise) to replace the one which had previously condoned the new prohibited response. Thus, a patient who is resolved to control his excessive washing would replace his old standard of 'hands contaminated, wash five times', with one decreeing 'no washing in response to dirty hands'. The performance promise may be developed by the subject on his own, but is more likely to be implemented if public commitment to the new behaviour is given. The introduction of this new standard for self-evaluation, leads to self-reinforcement of a different set of behaviours and hence to the introduction of new responses. The response which is initiated following self-reinforcement in a self-control situation may be either one of doing nothing or something else incompatible with the prohibited response (knitting instead of washing, for example), or may be a response designed to reduce the probability that the unwanted response will occur. Kanfer and Karoly considered that these latter, controlling responses correspond to those described by Skinner (1953).

Skinner maintained that the controlling responses serve to modify the variables which govern the occurrence of the response to be controlled. He did not state clearly the nature of these variables, but Vaughan (1975) reviewing his discussion, concluded that the most important are:

(1) the motivational state of the organism;
(2) the presence of appropriate discriminative stimuli;
(3) the positive reinforcement and punishment contingent upon performance of the response to be controlled.

Several different forms of controlling response are associated with each of these three sets of variables and most have some potential use in the self-control of obsessive–compulsive behaviour. They will be described in the context of the practical application of self-control techniques.

The clinical evidence for the effects of self-monitoring, performance standards, self-evaluation, self-reinforcement and controlling responses will be reviewed separately. Very little work has been done in any of these areas with obsessive–compulsive patients, so that the scant information arising from them has been supplemented with some of the more numerous observations from research into the control of smoking behaviour. Although the situations in which obsessional patients have to exhibit self-control have just been shown to be equivalent to those in which self-control over other forms of behaviour is exerted, the grossly pathological nature of the patient's condition may sometimes make generalization from people controlling smoking and eating misleading. Therefore the inclusion of results from non-obsessional groups is intended to provide a note of caution when initiating work with patients, rather than to specify precisely what is likely to be achieved.

SELF-REGULATION

1. Self-monitoring

During the course of any behavioural treatment, patients may be asked to record the frequency and duration of their unwanted thoughts and acts as a means of detecting changes in their behaviour. Such self-monitoring is usually undertaken by the patient with the understanding that it will provide relevant information for the therapist rather than in the belief that it constitutes a form of treatment on its own. However, there is some indication from work on smoking reduction that self-monitoring may be reactive, producing a reduction in the frequency of the unwanted response which is being recorded. McFall and Hammen (1971) noted that in smoking control studies there tended to be a dramatic drop in smoking frequency near the beginning of treatment which stabilized at about 30 to 40 per cent of baseline until the programme ended, regardless of what method of treatment was used. They suggested that this characteristic smoking reduction curve could be a function of three components which are common to all smoking studies: (a) the subjects are motivated volunteers; (b) they are instructed that they will stop smoking by the end of treatment, and (c) the subjects self-monitor their smoking behaviour and periodically report their progress to the therapist. (All these points would apply to obsessional patients monitoring their ritualistic behaviour.) McFall and Hammen (1971) carried out an investigation of several different forms of self-monitoring and demonstrated that the familiar pattern of smoking reduction could be achieved with the three non-specific factors alone. Kanfer's (1970) review also reaches the conclusion that self-monitoring may be reactive.

Reports of the reactive properties of self-monitoring have led to a few attempts to use it as the only active treatment in the control of obsessive–compulsive behaviour and thoughts.

Frederiksen (1975) treated ruminations in an intelligent 25-year-old woman with self-monitoring only. For six years the patient had suffered from thoughts of breast and stomach cancer, occurring in episodes of about fifteen minutes' duration. She was asked to graph the frequency of episodes, and on doing so showed a decline from thirteen to two bouts a day over the first week. Two more weeks of monitoring produced no further change. During the succeeding weeks the patient was asked to perform intensive monitoring, recording frequency, date, time, overt activity, antecedent stimuli, content, consequences and ratings of severity. Social reinforcement was given for following the instructions. She reported only five episodes in 25 days of recording, showing further decline over the first two months of follow-up and no ruminations at all for four months thereafter.

Bass (1973) also observed a reduction in obsessive thoughts during treatment mainly involving self-monitoring. The patient was a 43-year-old man who experienced violent thoughts, including one concerning strangling his wife. This thought had first arisen when one of his children, who was ill, had died because of his wife's negligence. Although subsequently divorced, the thought had persisted preventing him from achieving a satisfactory adjustment with another partner. He had been taking chlorpromazine for fifteen years and had been hospitalized for a long time. A single session of electrical aversion failed to have any positive effect and may even have made him worse. The patient was then given an elastic band to put on his wrist and was told to twang it each time he had a strangling thought. In addition, he had to self-monitor the thoughts. His strangling thought frequency dropped from 30 to fewer than five thoughts a day in the first week. The frequency fluctuated somewhat over the succeeding weeks, but by week 33 the thoughts of strangling had disappeared completely. He was free from this thought at a thirteen month follow-up but other, untreated, violent thoughts remained. As traditional aversion therapy had had no beneficial effect and the elastic band can have provided at the most a mildly aversive stimulus, it seems to be extremely unlikely that the improvement could have been due entirely to the self-punishment. The introduction of self-monitoring must have contributed to the observed treatment effects.

In contrast to these two accounts of successful thought-reduction, Le Boeuf (1974) found that self-monitoring on its own had no effect. The patient was a 45-year-old man with a 25-year history of hand-washing, who was considered to be well motivated. His washing did not show any reduction during a baseline phase of self-monitoring, although it was subsequently eliminated with an elaborate aversion procedure.

Three case reports of which one indicated failure, are far too few on which to base any evaluation of the effectiveness of self-monitoring. Our clinical impression is that it has little impact on patients with overt rituals, but occasionally patients with intrusive thoughts indicate that self-monitoring procedures may alter the quality of their ruminations. For example, one 39-year-old woman, suffering from anorexia nervosa and a mild obsessive–compulsive disorder said that having to record and describe her intrusive thoughts of carbohydrate orgies, altered them so that they became automatic, evoking no feeling. She felt that this had occurred because she had been made to scrutinize and analyse her thoughts. This sort of observation indicates that self-monitoring may have an effect in some cases, but it remains to be seen how great it may be and how commonly encountered. Even if it is proven, eventually, that self-monitoring modifies that target behaviour, there seems to be no theoretical or empirical grounds on which to predict that the effects which are demonstrated will prove to be large. It seems more likely that, if present, the effect of self-monitoring will act as a hindrance in establishing baseline information rather than as an effective treatment on its own.

2. Performance standards

The term 'performance standard' refers to an individual's internalized criterion of behaviour by which he judges the adequacy of his present performance. In the case of habitually performed behaviour, this standard will have been built up with past experience of success and practice. An experienced cook will continue to knead dough until it feels right, in accord with the knowledge of correct texture, and appearance arising from past cooking.

In contrast, Kanfer and Karoly (1972a and b) maintained that when behaviour is changed a new standard (not based on previous experience) is introduced and responses are modified to correspond to its requirements. (The cook may decide to make a different form of bread and modify her kneading to suit her new requirements, for instance.) Similarly, a treated obsessional patient, discharged home, may modify his habitual avoidance of contamination by instituting a standard of approach to dirty objects and acting accordingly.

Although experimental evidence is lacking, there seems to be some face validity in Kanfer and Karoly's assertion that the introduction of a new standard of performance is necessary precursor of behaviour change. It is difficult to imagine how self-controlled behaviour change could proceed without some awareness of the criterion performance which is to be attained. A patient controlling his behaviour or carrying out treatment exercises on his own will require some standard of performance if he is to succeed. This being so, the source of the performance standard and the conditions under which it will be reinstated become of central relevance.

Kanfer and Karoly felt that in self-control the standard is provided by a kind of 'performance promise' or contract made by the individual, either with himself, or in interaction with another person (often a therapist). The performance promise involves a resolution to change the probability of the response to be controlled; for example, to practise relaxation or not to wash. In order to be effective, the promise must include not only the intention to change, but the means of succeeding. There will be little to be gained from the patient saying that he will not wash, if he has no way of resisting temptation when it occurs. He must be able to specify controlling responses that are within his capabilities to use when necessary. Thus the performance promise may be looked upon as a plan of campaign which must be formulated before temptation strikes. The more explicitly the plan is stated, the more successful will be the outcome.

Although the exact nature of the performance promise and the role it plays in self-control have yet to be established empirically, Kanfer and Karoly's description clearly spells out the need for the subject both to be aware of the goals of his behaviour change and to know the means by which he may attain them. It follows that in clinical practice care should be taken that the patient has all the relevant information at his or her disposal. It may be insufficient to instruct the patient to clean the house without excessive repetition, as she may not possess an appropriate new standard of normal behaviour. To her, normal cleaning may involve an unknown number of repetitions with the vacuum cleaner so that she would be uncertain when her behaviour matched her new, but ill-defined criterion.

It may be necessary to inform the patient precisely of the range of numbers of repetitions accepted as being within normal limits so that she can match her behaviour exactly with her performance standard. Although patients may gain a great deal of information about appropriate performance standards from discussion and modelling by the therapist, there has been no attempt to assess the effects of precise and deliberate definition of standards. It would seem to be a fairly straightforward matter to compare the effects providing patients with clearly defined criteria for their target behaviours with leaving them to draw their own conclusions from their ordinary therapeutic interactions. It could be predicted that the former provision would result in greater desired behaviour change. However, modification would be expected only if the patients had available responses which would engineer the change.

Again, Kanfer and Karoly's discussion suggests that progress will be facilitated if the patient is made aware of the exact responses which will be required rather than leaving them to his imagination. These responses will include not only the new target set of behaviours, but also responses which will enable him to control the behaviours which he wishes to eliminate. Probably instruction and practice in both groups of responses will prove more effective than discussion or listing of them alone. New target behaviours may be practised and discussed after demonstration by the therapist. This occurs spontaneously during the course of many behavioural programmes, but its deliberate use in treatment has not been assessed. The provision of controlling responses and their subsequent use have been investigated more formally in single case investigations. These are described below under the heading 'Controlling Responses'.

The emphasis on practice as well as prescription of clearly defined performance standards makes clear that their provision on its own is thought to be unlikely to engender change. However, when accompanied by appropriate behaviour rehearsal, a comprehensive performance standard may constitute an aid to treatment, the usefulness of which has not been explored in detail.

3. Self-evaluation and self-reinforcement

Kanfer and Karoly's (1972a and b) model requires that self-evaluation will always be followed by positive self-reinforcement or self-punishment, depending both on the outcome of self-evaluation and the individual's idiosyncratic standards for self-reinforcement. Further, it is asserted that it is self-reinforcement and not the judgmental outcome of self-evaluation which 'motivates' the individual. The subject is inspired to further action by the praise and/or material reward he gives himself and not by the mere knowledge that he is doing better than past experience had led him to expect.

This analysis appears to be at odds with everyday experience. For example, a mathematician may work his way through page after page of addition sums without once praising himself for his accurate performance. However, he may check that each addition is correct before progressing to the next. His behaviour seems to be maintained successfully by knowledge of results, not self-reinforcement. Occasions on which behaviour may be self-evaluated, but not self-reinforced have also been noted by Bandura (1971b). At this level, it appears that Kanfer (1971) may be incorrect in assuming that self-reinforcement is responsible for continued endeavour in the absence of external consequences. Subjective evaluation of performance may be sufficient to maintain behaviour. It has yet to be determined whether self-reinforcement, when it occurs, adds anything to this effect.

There appear to have been no studies with obsessive–compulsive patients concerning the behaviour-maintaining properties of self-evaluation. It seems probable that the clarity with which the performance standard is defined would be of importance, but so also would be the absolute level of perfection which it depicted. One of our obsessional patients adopted excessively high standards for housework, based on what she believed (erroneously) would be her husband's level of achievement. Consequently she would not attempt many of her duties as she considered, correctly, that she would not be able to attain her self-imposed goals. Had she either adopted more realistic standards or accepted greater deviations from her existing ones, she would have been able to perform her housework quite adequately. It is possible that this inhibiting combination of unrealistic self-determined standards and a reluctance to fall short of them may complicate self-modification in other patients who tend to be perfectionists.

The maintaining or motivating role now denied of self-reinforcement and attributed to self-evaluation is quite distinct from the function more usually associated with reinforcement. If considered as a special case of reinforcement administered by others in an operant context, positive self-reinforcement following a response would be expected to increase the probability of that response occurring on the next occasion, and similarly self-punishment should bring about a diminution in response probability. If self-reinforcement were to be proved comparable to that administered by others in these respects it could be powerful means by which the patient could control his own behaviour himself.

Unfortunately, even Skinner had grave doubts about the efficacy of self-administered reward and punishment. He discussed both in some detail in a chapter on self-control (Skinner, 1953). He pointed out that (positive) self-reinforcement of a response presupposes that the individual is able to obtain reinforcement, but does not do so until that response has been performed, giving the example of a man who denies himself all social contacts until he has finished a particular job. Whilst acknowledging that this sort of behaviour does occur, Skinner questioned whether it is really operant reinforcement. He felt that it differed from reinforcement administered by others in that the man was free to stop work and to reinforce himself at any time, yet did not do so, probably because of the guilt that would be engendered by non-contingent indulgence. Under these conditions, Skinner considered it to be unlikely that the consequences (social contact) would have any strengthening effect on the behaviours which preceded it. He was no more confident about the effects of self-punishment and appeared to indicate that neither that nor self-reward deserved much place in the consideration of self-control.

It might well be imagined Skinner's (1953) lukewarm enthusiasm to have had a restraining effect on investigations of self-reward and punishment. This does not seem to have been the case, as a number of laboratory experiments with college students and clinical studies have been published, in most if not all of which Skinner's reservations appear to have been ignored.

Vaughan (1975) reviewed the published laboratory experiments and found that only a small proportion (six studies) of the total were related to the problem of the effects of self-reward or punishment on response probability. Only one of the six, a study by Marston and Cohen (1966), provided any evidence that subsequent responding was affected by self-administered consequences in college students. *Post hoc* analyses did indicate that self-punishment (a self-operated flashing red light) did reduce the likelihood of the response being repeated in a nonsense-syllable learning task. However, insufficient data was given to allow any assessment of the magnitude of the effect. The other five studies failed to yield any positive results.

Overall there was too little evidence to accept the proposition that self-administered reward and punishment affects the probability of response occurrence on subsequent occasions. Similarly, the results of the few studies in the more clinical areas of smoking, studying and overeating were found to be disappointing (Vaughan, 1975).

The work on self-reinforcement in obsessive–compulsive patients has been restricted exclusively to self-punishment. No attempt appears to have been made to ask patients to reward themselves after non-compulsive behaviour or successful contamination during a self-treatment exercise. Instead, the emphasis has been on the punishment of ritualistic behaviour and thoughts.

Mahoney (1971) used a curious form of self-punishment in the treatment of a young man with ruminations about brain damage and worthlessness, after counting backwards—intended to disrupt the rumination—had instead produced an initial increase in the number of thoughts per week. The patient was asked to wear an elastic band on his wrist and to snap it hard on his skin every time a thought occurred. He remained well at four-months follow-up. Bass (1973) obtained success with one patient using the same procedure, combined with self-monitoring.

Rubin, Merbaum, and Fried (1971) described a procedure which they called self-punishment and which they used in the treatment of a female patient who experienced 'dirty' thoughts which precipitated hand-washing. As systematic desensitization had failed to have any effect, the patient was given a portable shock box and was told to shock her hand after a 'dirty' thought in order to 'buy a ticket' to carry out her hand-washing ritual. Her frequency of hand-washing was reduced from 100 to ten times a day in less than a week. A second patient, treated in the same way involved the shock box in her rituals by washing it. Supervision at home was necessary to ensure that she carried out the required programme, but she moved house before the end of her treatment.

The model on which this procedure was based is not at all clear. Rubin, Merbaum, and Fried (1971) seemed to explain the procedure to their patients in terms of using shock as a direct means of controlling the overt rituals (i.e. buying a ticket) as if the main interaction would be between these two elements of the situation. As the shock preceded the hand-washing and was in no way contingent upon its occurrence, there seems to be no justification in calling the procedure self-punishment. This label would be appropriate only if the shock was intended to punish the thought which was considered to precipitate washing. Certainly shock was made contingent upon the experience of a thought, so perhaps this is what Rubin et al. had in mind in naming the procedure.

Apart from these two accounts, the use of self-reinforcement with obsessional patients seems to have received little attention. At a stretch, some parts of the thought-stopping procedure could be classed as self-punishment, as the patient is asked to say 'stop' to himself in the absence of the therapist when an unwanted thought arises. Such a classification is based on the assumption that the treatment effect (if any) is brought about by the mildly aversive nature of the command 'stop'. However, the effects of thought-stopping are open to alternative interpretation (see Chapter 7). Further, the usual thought-stopping procedure based on Wolpe (1958) involves considerable training and practice with a therapist before the patient utilizes the procedure on his own. The published accounts (for example, Stern, 1970) do not disentangle the effects of self-controlled implementation from practice with the therapist, so that the utility of thought-stopping as a self-reinforcement procedure cannot be evaluated.

Similarly, Cautela (1970) described home practice and the self-controlled use of reinforcing imagined scenes in the context of target behaviour in his discussions of his various covert reinforcement procedures. Again, the effects of self-controlled aspects of these treatments have not been separated out from those of sessions with the therapist, so that, for instance, in Wisocki's (1970) account of a patient who was compelled to fold clothes over and over again, any effect of self-reinforcement cannot be singled out.

It is clear that there is no convincing empirical evidence on which to base any conclusion about the probable usefulness of self-reinforcement as a treatment technique. Skinner's (1953) misgivings indicate that caution should be exercised in its use. To this may be added another warning, in that there is some evidence that subjects do not always use the self-reinforcement procedures they have been asked to employ. For example, in smoking control studies. Powell and Azrin

(1968) found that subjects would not wear their portable shock boxes when the shock was intense and Whitman (1972) found that his clients only used an aversive tasting pill on three per cent of smoking occasions, although they were supposed to take one with *each* cigarette.

This reluctance to self-reinforce appropriately does not seem to be restricted to self-punishment, as McReynolds and Church (1973) discovered that 40 per cent of self-contracts made by their students in an attempt to increase study behaviour were broken. Each student was supposed to set a study time goal and to self-reward fulfilment of it with small privileges. The contracts were broken by the students either taking reinforcement when not warranted, or withholding rewards which had been earned.

None of the subjects in these studies could be said to have been suffering from any disorder approaching the severity of obsessive–compulsive neurosis, so that it is possible that they were less motivated to tolerate the demand imposed by their treatments than an incapacitated obsessional would be. However, in the absence of any evidence from relevant patient groups, it would seem prudent to exercise the greatest care in the design and conduct of self-reinforcement programmes. Indeed, in the light of Skinner's remarks it seems questionable whether the outcome of even an optimally conducted study is likely to be substantial enough to justify all the time and effort involved in execution.

4. Self-control

Skinner (1953) gave the name 'self-control' to the subject's performance of a response other than the one which habitually gained substantial immediate reward and delayed punishment. The response executed served to modify the parameters of which the reinforced act was a function, so that the unwanted behaviour would be less likely to be performed. Skinner called such acts of restraint 'controlling responses'.

In his account he failed to acknowledge the possible distinction between the use of a controlling response and its efficacy. He seemed to assume that as long as the response was performed, its effectiveness was guaranteed. In clinical practice, it may be necessary to distinguish between the two components. Even though an individual uses a controlling response, his efforts may not be sufficient to prevent him from executing a particularly compelling act. In fact if the urge to perform is too strong, he may fail to attempt control in any form.

In any consideration of self-control, the probability of occurrence of the response used for control and its effect, once executed, must be evaluated separately. The latter may depend upon the nature of the response which is employed, but the former will almost certainly be related to the individual's motivation to change. In the discussion which follows, the efficacy of various forms of controlling response will be reviewed on the (unlikely) assumption that a means of control, once provided, will be used. After that, the circumstances under which a response is likely to be adopted will be appraised.

CONTROLLING RESPONSES

Skinner (1953) used the classes of responses utilized by an individual in the control of other people as a basis for determining the types of self-controlling responses which, potentially, will be available to the subject. He identified nine possible categories of self-controlling responses, illustrating each with anecdotal examples drawn from everyday experience.

In his theoretical discussion, Skinner stipulated that the controlling responses serve to modify the variables which govern the occurrence of the response to be controlled. He did not provide any explicit list of these variables, but it may be inferred from his discussion that the most important are (see also page 119):

(1) the motivational state of the organism;
(2) the presence of appropriate discriminative stimuli;
(3) the reward and punishment contingent upon performance of the response to be controlled.

Most of Skinner's categories of controlling response can be classified as affecting at least one of these three variables. The only exceptions are the categories of 'Physical Restraint and Physical Aid' and 'Doing Something Else' (see Skinner, 1953). The first may be dismissed rapidly as responses in this class seem to have no place in clinical work. Skinner gives as an example of physical restraint the response of placing one's hand across one's mouth to restrain laughter. This form of response seems to have little application with obsessional patients. Doing something else, and the other seven types of controlling responses, grouped in their three classes, will be discussed more fully.

(a) Doing something else

If an obsessional patient refrains from his rituals or deliberately contaminates himself as a treatment exercise, he is quite likely to experience discomfort and distress which will continue to tempt him to perform his rituals for some time (Rachman, De Silva, and Röper, 1976). A response of doing something other than the ritual behaviour is most likely to be successful, if in addition to replacing the prohibited response it reduced the resulting discomfort in some way. Either the patient should become engaged in any activity which is sufficiently absorbing to distract him from his state, or he should make some attempt to relieve his unpleasant feelings directly.

The influence of distracting occupation has not been evaluated in its own right, although such activities may be used during the response-prevention stage of treatment. Patients may be encouraged to attend occupational therapy, talk to the nursing staff (on non-symptom topics) or read a favourite book after a treatment session. These strategies seem to be adopted partly on the commonsense grounds that distraction will alleviate a worry, and partly because patients sometimes comment that involving themselves in interesting activities is helpful. The assumed efficacy of distraction needs to be verified formally. There has been very little more in the way of thorough investigation of the use of responses which will serve to reduce the discomfort being experienced. Relaxation exercises have obvious potential as reducers of discomfort, but it is unclear to what extent they would be appropriate. Although the patient may experience anxiety and tension when refraining from his rituals, this may occur concomitantly with feelings of hostility and depression and indeed, may not be predominant (Walker and Beech, 1969).

In cases where tension or anxiety is the main feeling experienced, the use of relaxation exercises could have some effect. Alban and Nay (1976) treated a young male shop assistant who checked all his activities. After a week of complicated baseline recording and relaxation training, the patient was told to impose a delay between the urge to check whenever it occurred and checking, during which he was to relax himself. The length of delay was increased over successive weeks. In the twelfth week he checked only three times and was symptom-free at follow-up in week forty. It is not possible to disentangle the effects of relaxation from the other components of treatment in this case so that much more, unequivocal, evidence is needed before its efficacy can be confirmed. Rather than asking the patient to institute an alternative behaviour straight away, several workers have attempted to achieve a change in response pattern by modifying the chain of behaviour associated with the response. Alban and Nay's (1976) treatment, in fact, could be taken as an example of this, as at first the patient was asked only to delay his checking, rather than to replace it with relaxation.

Instead of interrupting the behaviour chain directly, Worsley (1970, Case 4) attempted to weaken it by varying the order in which the component parts were performed. The patient, a student with rigid and prolonged ritualistic behaviour patterns associated with many aspects of life, particularly using the lavatory, had to practise varying the order in which the acts in each rigid chain were performed. Any increase in flexibility which· the patient found difficult to institute was rehearsed in imagination first. The patient was still symptom free at six to seven months' follow-up. In varying the chain, the patient was doing something else, other than the response which occurred habitually. The only anomaly was that the replacement act was another part of the ritualistic sequence and not a response which would detract from or be incompatible with the behaviour to be controlled.

1. Controlling responses which alter the discriminative stimuli for the response to be controlled

(a) Changing the stimulus

This category includes any responses which create or eliminate the occasion for a response. To achieve this, the subject must manipulate either an eliciting or a discriminative stimulus. For example, a slimmer may put a box of chocolates out of sight in order to avoid eating, or an absentminded person may ensure attendance at a forthcoming meeting by writing the date in his dairy.

There seem to be very limited possibilities for an obsessional patient to reduce the likelihood of his unwanted behaviour occurring by removing or avoiding the eliciting stimuli. In theory, he could stay out of the kitchen in order to keep away from the taps which he checks, but in practice it seems to be extremely difficult for an obsessional patient to avoid most, if not all, the stimuli which are associated with his rituals (Meyer, 1966).

The patient may have more success in instituting control by introducing stimuli which evoke responses incompatible with unwanted thoughts or rituals. Playing a favourite record or watching television may prohibit ruminative thinking and many 'doing something else' activities may serve a similar function. Perhaps more important, the patient could introduce another person to oversee his behaviour in ritual-evoking situations. Some patients seem to be able to suppress much of their undesired behaviour in the presence of others, so that this tactic may have some effect. However, other people are not always available so that the scope of this procedure is likely to be restricted. Overall it seems that attempts at control by changing the stimulus have very little to offer the obsessive–compulsive patient.

(b) Using aversive stimulation

Skinner (1953) maintained that aversive stimulation may be used to promote the occurrence of desired behaviour (and therefore the non-occurrence of the obverse, undesired behaviour). Setting an alarm clock may be given as an example. The unwelcome bell will prompt rising, if only to switch it off, rather than lying in. The closest parallel in clinical work with obsessionals seems to come in Rubin, Merbaum and Fried's (1971) use of self-imposed shock to 'buy a ticket' to perform the ritual. This procedure has been described under 'Self-Reinforcement' (page 125). In essence, the patient has to tolerate shock if she wishes to indulge in ritualistic behaviour, but may avoid it if she pursues some alternative course of action. There is too little evidence available to assess this form of use of aversive stimulation.

2. Controlling responses which modify the 'drive state' with respect to the response to be controlled

Patients who are confronted with stimuli and events which evoke compulsive behaviour are likely to experience unpleasant feelings and emotions before and during their rituals. Such feelings are commonly of anxiety, tension, depression or hostility (Walker and Beech, 1969). In addition some may suffer from more persistent anxiety or depression affecting them over weeks or months. The presence of either temporary or longer-term distressing states may have an adverse effect on the patient's unwanted thoughts and rituals (Walker and Beech, 1969). This being so, controlling responses which reduce these adverse states may reduce the probability of the ritual acts occurring, or at least increase the ease with which they are controlled by other means.

(a) Depriving and satiating

Skinner (1953) maintained that an individual may manipulate his drive level so that he may regulate the occurrence of the response to be controlled. For example, an impecunious person may skip lunch so that he will eat a great deal at a free supper. On the other hand, if he does not wish his host to know of his poverty, he may eat as much as he can before arriving so that he will not appear to be ravenous. Skinner also considered that a person may satiate one form of behaviour by indulging energetically in another related one.

Both direct and indirect satiation or drive reduction seem to be of much relevance to obsessive–compulsive patients. Beech (1977) has postulated that there may be a general 'pool' of drive which can be channelled in various ways and which in obsessional patients probably contributes to the level of pathological behaviour exhibited. Paralleling Skinner, it was also suggested that two strategies could be adopted to restore stable behaviour.

The first would be to reduce the drive level and the other would be to redirect the drive into constructive and healthy action and thought. The reduction of drive level can be achieved by attempting to ensure that two seemingly different drive states are brought under control. The first may be thought of as specific appetitive drives (sex, hunger, thirst, and so on) while the second may be seen in terms of general push or energy level. The idea is to keep these drives at a low level by obvious means in the first case, but by using alternatives to pathological behaviour and thought in the other. The second requires some clarification. There seems to be some 'build up' in the tendency to engage in pathological behaviour which the patient can come to recognize. Having done so he can learn to direct his energy into more normal activities which are energy consuming. Prompted by drive signals, he can switch to alternatives such as crossward-puzzle solving, gardening, painting or any other activity of an absorbing kind. In effect, he can 'do something else' *specifically* of a drive-reducing nature. The emphasis is upon the demanding nature of the alternative task, since it must allow no scope for pathological thought or behaviour to be engaged in simultaneously.

The notion of a general 'pool' of drive of the sort being described, and the means by which it may be rechannelled and reduced are recent developments in the understanding and care of obsessional patients. Therefore they have not been evaluated formally so far.

(b) Manipulating emotional conditions

Skinner suggested that people may induce emotional conditions in themselves for the purpose of control by presenting and removing stimuli. The angry man who walks away may be reducing his rage in order to control the response of hitting his antagonist. Conversely, if wishing to become angry, he may reread an offending letter before he sees its author. In this case he is presenting himself with stimuli which evoke the desired state.

This may be one way in which to describe the utterance of relaxation instructions by a patient to himself. His relaxing phrases act as cues for the physical responses which have been learnt with the therapist and may be used to reduce persistent tension or anxiety in ritual-evoking situations. Although patients are often told to practice relaxation exercises at home, and more important to perform them when feeling tense, no investigation of their self-instructed use and utility in anxiety-evoking situations has been made.

A little relevant evidence may be drawn from Alban and Nay's report of a relaxation delay technique described previously. The patient's checking was eliminated by asking him to relax deliberately (presumably to reduce discomfort) during increasing delays before allowing himself to check. In this case, the effects of relaxation cannot be separated from those of delay. Similarly, relaxation effects are confounded this time with those of social reinforcement, in the successful treatment of another patient with checking rituals, reported by Melamed and Siegel (1975) and described under 'Operant Conditioning' (section 3 (a) below). Clearly the use of relaxation exercises as controlling responses still needs to be established. However, they seem to be amongst the most promising of the responses which would be available to the patient, as their use, if effective, should bring about a direct reduction of discomfort, thereby giving them inherent reinforcing properties.

Apparently related to relaxation instructions are the self-statements of the kind described by Meichenbaum, Gilmore, and Fedoravicius (1971), which are designed to be incompatible with fearful or depressive statements. Again evidence for or against their effectiveness with obsessive–compulsive patients is lacking, but by their nature they would seem to have considerably less potential than relaxation instructions. In the latter case the patient has learnt both to give himself instructions and to perform an appropriate and probably effective response. It is the relaxation response following instruction which would be expected to produce the beneficial effect and not the self-statement on its own.

In contrast, no deliberate response follows incompatible self-statements. Presumably it is assumed that the exclamation of statements of fearlessness or good spirits will both render the whispering of incompatible fearful self-statements very difficult and evoke emotional responses which are sufficiently strong as to override existing anxiety. It seems very likely that the second of these assumptions, in particular, will not prove to be the case. Even if the anxiety-reducing properties of the word were to be enhanced by aversion-relief techniques (Wolpe, 1958, Solyom et al., 1971), it seems doubtful whether their utterance, alone, would be sufficient to combat the severe aberrations of mood which are experienced by obsessive–compulsive patients. Indeed it is possible that their unsuccessful use could make the patient worse. Statements such as 'I am calm' or 'I can cope', which are not followed by an appropriate change in emotional state, may make the patient more aware of his lack of control and hence increase his panic and distress.

Rather than utter incompatible self-statements, it may be better for the patient to make use of music, poetry or any other preferred form of art in order to induce a more relaxed or cheerful state. Although many patients report that this is effective, the strategy has the limitation that the necessary apparatus may not be available just when relief is needed.

(c) Drugs

Skinner contended that drugs may be used to simulate the effects of other self-control responses. For example, tranquillizers may be taken to decrease anxiety and thereby avoidance. Antidepressants, also, may be taken over a longer term, to alleviate adverse moods. As it is rare for the patient to be supervised when taking his drugs, their administration is entirely under his own control.

3. Controlling responses which alter the reinforcing consequences of the response to be controlled

(a) Operant conditioning

Under this heading, Skinner discussed the potential of positive self-reinforcement. His strong reservation about it and the pertinent studies with obsessive–compulsive patients have been described under 'Self-reinforcement' (page 124). That account involved only studies in which the patient administers reward to himself in the absence of anybody else. However, there may also be situations in which the patient programmes social reinforcement to occur contingently when he controls an undesired response and executes an appropriate alternative.

Melamed and Siegel (1975) provided an example of this in which a 63-year-old man involved his wife in the self-determinated reinforcement for not checking. The patient performed up to three hours of checking rituals prior to going to bed and had several other incapacitating problems. He was instructed to leave out one room at a time from his rituals, and at the same time to reduce gradually the time spent checking the remaining rooms. Specific goals were set for each night's performance and if these were attained his wife gave him a hug and a kiss, he took time to do the crossword, practised relaxation for fifteen minutes, and in some instances a dollar was dropped from the therapist's bill. He responded well and apart from one very minor relapse was symptom-free at eight-months follow-up.

It is impossible to sort out the effects of the wife's attention from the other reinforcers, particularly the reduction in the bill. Assuming that the couple enjoyed a good relationship, the wife's affection may have been powerfully rewarding, although it seems possible that the mutual knowledge that the hug and kiss were planned in advance could have detracted from their effectiveness. In addition, the involvement of the wife in treatment probably instigated much interest in the programme and discussion of it by the couple. The wife would have known precisely what goal her husband was to achieve, possibly increasing his feelings of obligation to achieve it. Interactions such as these between the patient and another person during treatment seem to be important determinants of the motivation to succeed which is discussed below.

The logical extension of involving another person in reinforcement programmes is to have the reinforcement determined entirely by the other person,
usually a therapist. Of course, this goes beyond the realms of self-control to
operant conditioning and possibly token economies.

Perhaps not surprisingly the only reports of such programmes with
obsessive–compulsive patients have involved very young patients. For example,
Hallam (1974) used withdrawal of attention (ignoring and physical isolation) to
eliminate repetitive questioning in a teenage girl. More appropriate social
responses were taught and rewarded. It seems doubtful whether operant
programmes would be as viable with adults, as extreme environmental manipulation would probably be more difficult.

(b) Punishment

Skinner's doubts about self-punishment have been described already. One
additional problem seems the reluctance of the patient to administer to himself
anything which is inherently unpleasant.

One alternative to self-administration would be to arrange for someone else to
carry out the punishment. Melamed and Siegel's (1975) patient's wife could have
refused to kiss him and torn up the crossword-puzzle if her husband had failed in
his task. Once more the wife's involvement in treatment and the contrived nature
of punishment might prove influential. In the absence of a second person,
punishment may be dispensed automatically.

Le Boeuf (1974) gave a male patient with hand-washing rituals an automatic
shocking device. In the first treatment the patient was given a pocket timer with
an alarm, set for twenty-minute intervals. He was not to wash his hands during
that interval, but could do afterwards if he wished. His behaviour did not change
and so a shock box was added to the device. He wore electrodes on his fingers and
shock was administered automatically if he washed whilst the timer was in
action. The timed interval was increased gradually up to two hours. At this stage
the shock box was removed without any deterioration in his condition. At
follow-up after a year abnormal hand-washing was still absent.

One major problem with this kind of approach is that some people will not
exercize the controlling response of wearing the shocking device, particularly
when the shock is too strong (Powell and Azrin, 1968).

CONCLUSION

There is insufficient evidence about the controlling responses reviewed to
conclude that any of them work. That is, it is far from certain that if used they will
serve to prevent the occurrence of the response to be controlled. Throughout it
was assumed that if available a controlling response would always be used in
tempting situations. However, there is some strong evidence which indicates that
this may not always be the case (Whitman, 1972, McReynolds and Church,
1973). This could mean that patients sometimes failed to use their controlling

responses in the case studies which have been described, in which case the evidence for or against the efficacy of self-control procedures becomes even more tenuous. At the very least therapists should attempt to check if the responses prescribed are being put into use.

FACTORS ASSOCIATED WITH THE USE OF A CONTROLLING RESPONSE

It has been recognized already that patients may not utilize their controlling responses on all occasions. As a controlling response cannot be effective if it is not used, the factors which affect its implementation are of some importance. The account which follows seems to apply to the control of most forms of obsessive–compulsive behaviour except obsessive thoughts of an unpleasant nature and some ruminations. As indicated in Chapter 6, these may present theoretical problems of their own.

Perhaps the simplest example of the need for a self-control response may be when a successfully treated patient comes in contact with contamination at home and is tempted to wash. Whilst in hospital he was told to refrain from washing for several hours. Therefore he is faced with the choice of refraining from washing and enduring the distress which this causes, but also moving nearer his goal of cure, or obtaining immediate relief (or at least lessening the distress) by washing, but thereby jeopardizing his progress. First the case in which the patient has no controlling response will be considered: that is when not washing means doing precisely that, with no means of making the restraint easier. The following analysis of the factors affecting the patient's response was influenced by the work of Skinner (1953) and also by Mausner and Platt's (1971) precise delineation of influential variables in smoking cessation research.

The following factors appear to be important in determining whether the discomfort will be tolerated on any one tempting occasion.

1. Discomfort

(a) Intensity

If abstaining from washing is likely to prove extremely unpleasant, the patient may wash, regardless of the ultimate consequences.

2. Reward (remission of symptoms and its associated assets)

(a) Length of delay

If recovery is likely to occur only in months' or years' time, it may seem too remote to be related to present behaviour.

(b) Value

That is how much the patient wishes to be rid of his symptoms and wants the social and occupational rewards or removal of punishment which will result. If the patient is not entirely averse to all his rituals or has no powerful rewards to be gained on their remission, their removal may not be worth the distress involved.

(c) Overall expectancy

This is the patient's subjective probability of attaining symptom remission and the other rewards. If the patient believes that there is no hope of recovery, he may not even try.

(d) Subjective probability of attaining the reward if the patient fails *in this particular control attempt*

This means the chances of eventually losing symptoms if he allows himself to wash on this occasion. If the patient believes that lapses in control can be made up by additional effort subsequently, so that long term outcome is not affected, he may not refrain from washing on all occasions.

(e) Subjective probability of attaining the reward if the patient succeeds *in this particular control attempt*

It, for example, the patient believes that early success when he returns home will be essential to complete recovery he may struggle hard for success in the first few days.

2. Conclusions

Of these factors, the discomfort and subjective probability beliefs are likely to have been influenced by experienced of response prevention exercises during treatment and discussions about treatment effectiveness and prognosis with the therapist. The patient is likely to have evaluated information of this sort in terms of his appraisal of his own abilities. Within the limits of truthfulness, a therapist may maximize his estimates of the patient's chances of success and of the necessity of practising control on all occasions, in an effort to instil similar estimates of subjective probability in the patient. Beyond that, there seems to be very little that can be done to modify those particular variables. Reward value is more amenable to manipulation in that the therapist may be able to ensure that important goals can be realized when symptoms have been eliminated. The realistic possibility of a job may be helpful in this context. The rewards for control may be boosted further by continued, fairly frequent, contact with the therapist or by involvement of a valued friend or relative to praise successful attempts and to disapprove of failures. This will also reduce the delay between control and reward as the patient will be praised for his efforts long before the ultimate goal is reached.

In instructing the patient in the use of a controlling response, the intention is usually to make self-control easier for him to accomplish. It has been recognized for a long time in other areas (such as smoking control), that some people, after deciding to change, are able to control their undesired behaviour without seeming to utilize any of the listed controlling responses and certainly without requiring any specialist aid. To some extent, similar people are to be found in clinical groups.

Several attempts have been made to define and explain the peculiarly strong motivation which is characteristic of such people, but none have been entirely successful (see, for example, Premack, 1970, Logan, 1973). Therefore, in the absence of any further information, the occasional occurrence of such pheno-menal individuals is merely to be acknowledged before attention is returned to the majority who will have heeded their instruction in the use of a controlling response.

Excluding controlling responses which change the stimulus situation, which are considered not to be relevant in work with obsessionals, the remaining controlling responses seem either to alter the amount of reward or punishment which the patient receives or to reduce the discomfort which he experiences in controlling himself. (Doing something else may be included in the latter category, as most alternative acts involve at least distraction.) If used effectively, any controlling response from these groups will enable him to put up with more distress than he would tolerate otherwise, either by giving the promise of increased reward or by directly reducing his discomfort.

Successful practice with controlling responses prior to discharge may produce an upwards re-evaluation of subjective probability of success, whereas discovery that the responses are only partially effective would probably result in a down-ward evaluation of expectancies. Apart from such changes, the introduction of a controlling response would not alter the number of factors which determine the occurrence or non-occurrence of control.

Just like merely refraining from responding, a controlling response will not be used thus allowing the prohibited behaviour to occur if:

(1) the distress resulting from restraint is too great for the response to combat, or the response produces unpleasant consequences;
(2) the reward is insufficient or too delayed;
(3) the overall subjective probability of success and/or those following success or failure on this occasion are low.

Although stated simply here, the relationships between these factors in determining control is likely to be complex. For example, if a highly valued reward is going to be attainable after only a short delay, the patient may persist despite his own misgivings about his chances of success.

Like the effectiveness of the controlling responses, none of the hypotheses which may arise from this outline have been investigated in any systematic way. The model is presented merely as a reminder that even when a controlling response has been shown to be effective (and to date no relevant demonstrations have been made), there are many complicated factors to be considered in the seemingly simple task of instructing a patient how to control his own behaviour when alone.

9

Adjuncts to Treatment

A number of behavioural treatments have been described in Chapters 1 to 8. Throughout, most attention has been given to the formal behavioural components of the procedures, but, it is hoped, without any suggestion that these are the only aspects of treatment which may contribute to the therapeutic change. There are a number of ways in which the therapist may augment the effects of behavioural intervention, and these are discussed in this chapter.

Change in obsessive–compulsive behaviour during treatment may be facilitated by the provision of adequate instructions and information and by tuition in self-control techniques for patients as well as training relatives as therapists. Adverse mood states and anxiety may require treatment by appropriate physical methods. In addition, it may be necessary to deal with problems of work, marital and sexual adjustment before an acceptable level of social adaptation can be said to have been attained. Here psychotherapy may have some part to play. In the discussion which follows, additions to the treatment of the obsessive–compulsive symptoms will be dealt with before the management of other problems is described.

ADJUNCTS TO BEHAVIOURAL TREATMENTS

Additions to the main behavioural package fall into two categories, those involving procedural variations and shifts of emphasis within the original model, and those constituting the introduction of a second distinct form of therapy (psychotherapy or drugs). The first group may involve both patient and relative, the second nearly always encompasses the patient alone.

1. Procedural additions

Many of the ideas outlined in this section crystallized in a series of discussions which one of the authors (M. Vaughan) had with G. Röper concerning a paper presented by the latter in 1976 (Röper, 1977). Most are based on clinical experiences and await empirical investigation. They are best viewed as hypotheses founded on, at the least, some common sense rather than as anything resembling established facts.

As there are some essential differences between the instructions and training given to patients and those given to relatives the two will be described separately. However, it should be remembered that the two tend to be strongly related so that in many cases, the implementation of one automatically involves the other.

(a) Aids for patient

As the patient is always actively involved in the treatment, he may find it helpful to be given a clear outline of the rationale on which the treatment is based. This is especially likely to be the case if he finds that he is to be asked to engage in activities which he dislikes and avoids, as in flooding. The provision of a rationale for treatment may give some reason for an otherwise seemingly senseless and very upsetting pursuit. In addition, the treatment description provides a framework on which the patient may begin to construct his own treatment schedule, as described below.

The level at which the explanation of treatment is pitched, will depend upon the ability of the patient to deal with the ideas to be presented. At least it should include some account of all the major components of the treatment which is to be used. Hand-outs do not seem to have been used in this context, but could serve as useful references, especially for patients who are likely to take over control of their own treatment.

It seems to be important to explain the role of seeking reassurance in the context of discussing the rationale for treatment. Many patients frequently ask for reassurance concerning their fears and behaviour from relatives, therapists and friends. The repeated requests are irritating and upsetting to those who receive them and seem to bring no enduring relief to the patient. They may be characterized as rituals in their own right in so far as they temporarily serve to reduce or avoid the anxiety evoked by the thought or act with which they are concerned. Conceptualized in this manner requests for reassurance may be treated in the same way as other avoidance behaviour. Response prevention may be attempted by requesting and reminding the patient not to ask for reassurance. Should this fail and reassurance be sought, reinforcement in the form of temporary reduction in discomfort may be withheld by a polite refusal to respond to the patient's request (a view shared by Rachman and his collaborators, see Rachman, Hodgson, and Marks, 1971). An explanation of this sort enables the patient to understand refusals to reassure rather than perceiving them as unexpected and somewhat perverse rebuffs. A mutual agreement not to seek or to give reassurance based on understanding of the effects of each, may help the patient and his relatives to enter into less pathological interactions.

It has been suggested already that one of the incidental effects of modelling, flooding, and response-prevention procedures may be to provide the patient with appropriate standards of behaviour. It may be that the introduction of clearly defined standard setting into any form of behavioural programme would be of benefit to patients with excessive repetitive rituals of several years' standing. It is not uncommon to find that patients are no longer aware of how other people act in situations where their own rituals are excessive. Although it is quite likely that relatives and friends have frequently told them that, say, their washing or cleaning is inordinate, it is quite possible that nobody has defined clearly how much of each activity would ordinarily be considered to be sufficient. Unfortunately, most of the behaviours which obsessive–compulsive patients indulge in to excess cannot be eliminated entirely if acceptable levels of hygiene and orderliness in daily living are to be maintained. It is considered desirable to wash one's hands briefly after using the lavatory, to keep carving knives away from small children and to be fairly careful that the gas has been turned off. Any behavioural programme which is designed without due recognition of such limits runs the risk of engendering behaviours which lie outside the confines of prevailing social norms. This being the case, it seems to be preferable to make a deliberate statement of standards as necessity arises during sessions, rather than relying on the patient's ability to take advantage of chance comments and of modelling arising as treatment progresses.

The form in which the standards are given may vary depending on the nature of the behaviour to be retained. In some instances a precise verbal definition may be sufficient. One patient of the second author's (M. Vaughan) had difficulty in modifying her excessive use of toilet paper. Once the number of sheets normally used was specified, she was able to reduce her consumption immediately.

On the other hand, Rachman (1974) found that straight verbal instructions produced only a little improvement in a patient who cleaned his teeth in small groups, taking about 45 minutes to complete the task. Once appropriate brushing had been demonstrated by the therapist, rapid improvement was observed. This was supplemented by a number of practice trials in which the patient aimed to meet agreed time goals.

The differing effectiveness of verbal instruction in the two cases may have been a function of the ease with which the standard performance could be described. Whilst the instruction 'only four sheets' clearly defined the criterion of performance for the first patient, it would be more difficult to give a detailed description of how to brush one's teeth. In the second case, a demonstration preceded by instructions informing the patient the salient points to be observed might be expected to be a more effective procedure.

The exact contributions of instruction and demonstration (modelling) have not been determined. Although it is felt from clinical experience that clear setting of standards may be an influential aspect of treatment, it has only been mentioned directly in accounts of two cases. Rachman (1974) mentioned the treatment of two patients in his discussion of 'primary obsessional slowness'. The fact that the second of these is also described by Hodgson and Rachman (1976) and is cited by Marks, Hodgson, and Rachman (1975) suggests that his response to treatment may have been exemplary rather than typical, thus placing some restraint on the generalization which may be made from the results. Both patients spent excessive amounts of time in washing, dressing and showering and so on. The prolonged tooth-brushing of the first patient has been described already. Both patients were slow because of their extreme meticulousness and repetition. (It is questionable whether this behaviour should really be described as slowness.)

The provision of standards, both in terms of times to be taken and of activities to be performed, served to reduce their care and number of repetitions made and therefore the time taken over the tasks. However, it was found that the initial instruction had to be backed up with considerable practice before full therapeutic gains were achieved. These observations underline the view that explicit standard setting represents an adjunct to treatment rather than a therapeutic intervention on its own.

The provision of appropriate standards would be expected to influence not only treatment changes, but also the maintenance of improvement after discharge. It would be hoped that the patient would incorporate the new standards into his existing set of attitudes and would use them as criteria against which to regulate his own behaviour.

Kanfer (1971) has suggested that in undertaking any form of behaviour which is not entirely habitual, but which requires some concentration or thought, the individual will compare his actions with some pre-existing (internalized) standard or criterion of performance. This self-evaluation will inform the subject whether or not he has acheived his goal. Kanfer stipulated that this self-evaluation leads automatically to self-reinforcement, which in turn provides discriminative stimuli for the next act in the sequence. The subject continues with what he was doing or changes his behaviour depending on the self-reinforcement received. In fact the function of self-reinforcement may be disputed (see Chapter 8) and its exclusion does not seem to detract significantly from Kanfer's model. The knowledge of results ensuing from the comparison of performance with the standard (self-evaluation) may provide sufficient discriminative stimuli for the next act to take place.

Although Kanfer's approach to self-regulation may not be accepted universally, it seems clear enough that individuals tend to use some standard of performance to guide their behaviour and that such standards may on occasions be adopted from information provided by highly valued and respected therapists or friends. The reduction of rituals using many behavioural treatments involves some degree of self-control on the patient's behalf, both in tolerating the discomfort aroused by non-performance of the ritual as in, say, response prevention, and in resisting the compulsion to carry out the ritual. A similar need for self-control is likely to be experienced after treatment each time the patient encounters an unforeseen contaminating situation or experiences a mild relapse. The difficulties in introducing formal self-control procedures have been discussed in Chapter 8. These should not necessarily deter the therapist from attempting to give the patient some self-control techniques, but should provide warning that such methods should not be considered to be treatments on their own. The most natural time to give instruction is when problems of self-control arise as treatment progresses. This tends to occur spontaneously even during treatments in which formal tuition has not been planned.

A more systematic approach would be to give the patient one or two treatment sessions, following the chosen behavioural programme, and then to observe and question him carefully about problems experienced in carrying out the instructions either during sessions or at home. A careful behavioural analysis of the patient's difficulties should indicate which form of self-control procedure would be likely to have the most effect. The optimal procedures could then be taught to the patient by verbal instruction, modelling and guided practice. Subsequent treatment sessions could include some time set aside for discussion of the patient's use of the self-control techniques.

In this way, by the time the patient was left to fend for himself at home, he would not only know that he possessed a repertoire of responses to use in difficult situations, but also that he was already proficient in their use. On several occasions it has been found that the mere knowledge that he possesses a potential means of coping will give a patient sufficient confidence to enter a situation which he fears. In addition, successful practice during treatment will tend to boost the patient's expectations of success and hence to increase the chances that he will implement the response if a taxing situation is encountered again. On occasions, the patient's own attempts at self-control may prove to be insufficient. If this occurs during treatment, additional guidance and surveillance from the nursing staff may provide the required external control, as appears to have been the case in the supervised response prevention used by Meyer (1966) and Meyer, Levy, and Schnurer (1974). Once at home, extra supervision may be difficult to arrange, so that an alternative form of externalized control will be required.

The possibility of using tokens or points as reinforcers administered by relatives or through the post by the therapist does not seem to have been explored. It is questionable whether the tokens would need to be backed up by material reinforcers. More likely, they would become reinforcing in themselves as symbols of success evoking anticipation of praise from therapist or friends. When used as an adjunct to other behavioural treatments a point or token system could be directed at any aspect of the patient's behaviour with which he was having particular difficulty.

The introduction of this form of sub-programme into treatment would serve to increase the patient's attention to the designated aspect of his problem, and probably to increase his motivation to deal with it. The extent to which such general factors rather than the use of tokens effected any change observed would need to be unravelled.

Even after successful treatment, the majority of patients, if not all, will remain vulnerable to at least temporary phases of relapse. The patient may be able to deal with minor recurrences of symptoms by himself if he has gained some understanding of the therapeutic procedures during his initial treatment. This is where a clear explanation of the rationale for treatment may play an important role.

Once the more able patient has helped the therapist to plan programmes for several major symptoms, he might be encouraged to formulate the procedures for additional symptoms on his own, referring back to the therapist for approval of his plans and for aid when difficulties were encountered. In this way, the patient could be taught to detect and record his pathological behaviour and to identify both the stimuli which evoked it and the reinforcement by which it is maintained. Having thus described his behaviour, he should be able to apply the therapeutic procedures previously controlled by the therapist.

Many patients may find it hard to achieve this level of sophistication in the time that is available during treatment, and further, some may find it difficult to implement any form of procedure without external encouragement and aid. In these cases it may be possible to train a relative, rather than the patient, as therapist, as described below. Otherwise, a great deal of reliance will have to be placed on the maintenance of very close contact between the patient and his therapist.

Some patients seem to find it helpful to have the possibility of mild relapse explained, as they are then less upset by what, otherwise, may seem like failure when symptoms re-emerge. In addition, they will probably find it less difficult to contact the therapist again if they are aware that he is expecting to see them again from time to time as difficulties arise. Full discussion of 'emergency procedures' to be used in time of relapse may help to obviate the need for the patient to waste time in trying to decide whether his symptoms are or are not severe enough for him to contact the therapist.

(b) Preparation of relatives

Nearly all the family members living in close contact with obsessive–compulsive patients have been suffering for several years, at least, from a severe and incapacitating disorder—not their own, of course, but that of the patient. Some have had to tolerate for as long as twenty years the rules and restrictions imposed by the fears and rituals of the afflicted person. Very often they will have been forced into colluding with the patient, performing endless, pointless checking and cleaning rituals in an attempt to keep him relatively calm. Physical contact between spouses is likely to have been severely limited and sexual intercourse may be prohibited.

Once treatment has reduced or substantially eliminated the patient's major symptoms, the family is faced with the task of altering their daily life to suit the new requirements of their now ritual-free member. This readjustment appears to affect two main areas of relatives' functioning: their attitudes and feelings towards the patient, and the organization of their leisure life.

After years of restricted living, it is not surprising that some close relatives develop feelings of resentment and hostility towards the patient. More remarkable is the fact that many relatives do not express any negative views. At least in some cases this seems to arise because the relative considers the patient to be ill and in need of special care and protection. Therefore his infuriating eccentricities are perceived as being part of his illness for which he cannot be blamed and must not be rebuked.

Having stoically born the burden of what was thought of as a chronic illness for years, sometimes despite repeated treatment attempts, caring relatives may be amazed to see the patient abandon most of his more spectacular rituals within the space of three short weeks. In the face of an amazing 'cure', the onlooker has either to give thanks to the deity, or to doubt the authenticity of the symptoms which have been lost. At least some relatives seem to opt for the latter course. They appear to argue that if rituals can disappear that quickly then they cannot have been as severe as had previously been supposed. It may be thought likely that the patient could have recovered at some earlier date, had he tried harder at that time. Thoughts of the time and effort spent in co-operating with rituals which the patient could have abandoned may lead to resentment and anger.

This line of reasoning was particularly clear in the husband of the patient previously described who achieved a rapid remission in her toilet rituals and subsequently in others associated with cleaning the house. Having expressed a view similar to that outlined above to the therapist, he told his wife repeatedly that she could get over her remaining residual rituals if she tried. Further, after years of over-solicitous care, he seems to have lost all belief that she is in any way handicapped and gives her no support or encouragement in any form during her bouts of mild depression with their concomitant temporary re-emergence of some rituals.

Cases such as this make it apparent that some attempt should be made to help close relatives to realign their attitudes and feelings towards the successfully treated patient. No satisfactory method of doing this has been developed. It is possible that informing the relative before the beginning of treatment that a fairly rapid reduction in symptoms could occur may make him more prepared for the event. If the relative is given a reasonable explanation of rapid improvement before it takes place, he may be more able to accept it than if one is provided afterwards when it may appear to be a *post hoc* rationalization. Certainly, discussion after treatment did very little to help the husband just described. A considerable amount of time was spent in explaining the nature of treatment including the possible reasons for rapid improvement as well as in reassuring him of the severity of his wife's initial complaints. This did not seem to influence his new belief that she was just like everybody else.

On the other hand the same husband did appear to derive some short-term benefit from his sessions in that he was able to discuss some aspects of his hostility towards his wife which he would not have felt able to mention to his friends or family. Possibly this enabled him to restrain his anger at home to a greater extent than would otherwise have been the case. For this sort of reason it may be necessary to give close relatives a great deal of support towards the end of formal treatment, just before and after the patient is discharged home.

Once the patient has returned home and has taken over at least some appropriate household duties, the closest members of the family will probably find that they have more free time at their disposal. For the first time in a long while they will have time to pursue their own leisure interests rather than spending hours involved with the patient's rituals and in doing the chores which the patient has been unable to perform.

Some relatives already possess lively interests and hobbies and welcome the opportunity to engage in them to a greater extent, but this is not always the case. Many spouses have had to devote the greater part of their married life to the care of their partner and have either lost, or never developed, interests of their own. In such cases the removal of the patient's rituals may come as a relief, but may also leave a void which the spouse finds difficult to fill.

If the relative and probably also the patient have too much unfilled time, they may become over-aware of the difficulties which each is experiencing in adjusting to their new life together, and this in turn may lead to increased tension between them. It may prove to be important to discuss the probable change in life-style with the relative before treatment commences. If the anticipated amount of new free time is estimated, with the patient's approval, the relative could be given the task of preparing himself for his altered routine, whilst the in-patient phase of treatment is taking place. With the patient in hospital, the relative would be free to make the necessary trips to the library, to join clubs, to negotiate for allotments or to do whatever else was necessary to initiate his new pursuits.

Quite apart from supporting the relative and preparing him for the patient's improvement and return home, it may be necessary to stop him from involving himself in the patient's rituals, wittingly or otherwise. Perhaps the commonest form of involvement in the patient's complaint is the relative's earnest attempts to provide reassurance in response to the patient's repeated anxious questions about contamination, the adequacy of checking, chances of possible harm and so on. The relative is unlikely to see his collusion as in any way detrimental, as his reassurance is invariably based on a genuine desire to calm the patient (and probably also to gain a little peace himself). However, it is probable that he will agree that his reassuring utterances bring no more than momentary relief, and that the patient soon resumes his questioning with as much fervour as before. In fact, some patients seem to become increasingly agitated the longer requests for reassurance are allowed to continue and none are reassured by the answers which they receive. Moreover, withholding reassurance and thereby stopping their requests seem to have a beneficial effect. After an initial increase in distress or not being reassured, patients tend to calm down rapidly, so that they achieve a less distressed state than had reassurance been allowed to continue. For this reason, it may be explained to the relative that reassurance, although well intentioned, usually does not help the patient and indeed can become very upsetting for everybody. Because of this, the relative should be encouraged to stop responding to the patient's demands.

No attempt made by the relative, alone, is likely to be successful as any sudden withdrawal of reassurance by a usually responsive source is likely to mystify and distress the patient and thereby to play an additional strain on relationships with the family. It is essential that the reasons for withdrawing reassurance are explained to both parties. In addition, an agreement should be made that whilst the patient will endeavour to refrain from asking for reassurance, the relatives will ensure that none is given.

This new mode of interaction may prove to be difficult to achieve at first. Marks, Hodgson, and Rachman (1975) have found that role-playing practice may be helpful in a discussion group for patients and relatives. Patients with fears of contamination were asked to request reassurance from their spouses in front of the other group members. The spouse was taught to reply, 'hospital instructions are that I don't answer you'. The question and answer were rehearsed several times. The use of role-playing has not been evaluated formally, but some intervention of that nature may well be necessary in order to engineer a radical change in an habitual ritualized interaction.

A few relatives, particularly spouses, are more directly involved in the patient's rituals. They are ordered or coerced into taking over some of the excessive cleaning and checking or to help whilst the patient performs her rituals, by for example overseeing the patient's bath-time activities. This form of involvement is more likely to be recognized by the relative as being undesirable than is giving reassurance, hence he may be more able to see the need to change his behaviour. However, it will still be necessary for the changes to be made to be agreed upon by both partners as the patient may otherwise resent her spouse's sudden refusal to co-operate.

It may still need some supervised practice for the relative to become accustomed to refusing to participate. In isolated cases, the spouse may oppose the suggestion that he should refrain from either helping in the rituals or supporting the patient in performing them. This seems to arise when the relative himself possesses many obsessional traits, if not florid symptoms. For example, Catts and McConaghy (1975) described one patient who cleaned excessively, but whose husband admired the cleaning and engaged in spring cleaning several times a week whilst the patient was in hospital. The therapists commented that the husband had to be retrained in order for the patient to be treated successfully. In extreme cases, retraining the spouse could involve a substantial behavioural programme in itself.

As the relative learns to disengage himself from rituals and from requests for reassurance, he begins to take an active part in the patient's management. In theory, there seems to be no reason why he should not be taught to extend his intervention by taking on the role of therapist for at least part of treatment. The use of a spouse or close relative as therapist has obvious advantages during home treatment sessions, as treatment could be conducted during all waking hours, and in particular whenever an unexpected crisis arose. By involving the relative as well as the patient in discussions of treatment rationale and in training in the development of intervention programmes, the two could work as a team in planning and executing further treatment.

The extent of co-operation achieved between relative and patient, particularly if the former is to take a directive therapist role, will depend upon the nature of the existing relationship between the two. If the patient's behaviour has reduced the spouse to a state of hostility and antagonism, as was the case in the couple previously described, it is extremely unlikely that an attempt by the spouse to act as therapist would meet with any success. Besides being firm, the therapist must be able to understand and sympathize with the patient's distress. Many relatives have been tormented by the patient's rituals for so long that they may well be unable to show the necessary appreciation and concern during treatment. Those relatives who are able to recognize the discomforts which the patient experiences during treatment, may achieve some success as therapists. They might benefit from observing the therapist at work with and then taking over from him for several sessions and being given feedback on performance.

As the role of relatives as therapists is of practical importance, their training should be given priority. Some energy should be directed towards controlled investigation, not only of the efficacy of relative therapists, but of their selection and the way in which they are trained.

2. Additional disorders

An obsessive–compulsive patient's fears and rituals are only part of the problem with which she or he may require assistance. Broadly speaking the areas of abnormalities of mood and/or anxiety levels and of difficulties in everyday living (marital and social relationships, etc.) may need attention. These two groups of disorders require very different forms of treatment. In some cases abnormalities of mood and anxiety may be best helped by physical methods, probably drugs. On the other hand, problems in daily life might be tackled with specially constructed behavioural programmes and the possibility that psychotherapy might prove beneficial should not be ignored. Because of their differing treatment requirements, the two groups of disorders will be considered separately and appropriate treatment evidence reviewed.

(a) Disturbances of mood and/or anxiety

Gittleson's (1966) study indicated that obsessions occur relatively frequently in the context of depression (present in about 31 per cent of depressed patients). This is consistent with Beech and Perigault's (1974) view that adverse fluctuations in mood state are a primary influence in the genesis and maintenance of obsessive–compulsive disorders. They postulated that obsessive–compulsive patients possess a pathological state of arousal and provided initial psychophysiological data that indicated this is likely to be the case. It is possible that this heightened state of arousal tends to manifest itself, in terms of psychiatric symptomatology, as a fairly distinctive form of depression.

Vaughan (1976) attempted to define the characteristic features of depression associated with obsessional symptoms. Patients with obsessions occurring during depression were compared with those with depression alone with respect to eight qualitative aspects of depression. Patients with obsessions were more likely to experience rapid mood changes, anxiety and agitation and less likely to exhibit retardation than patients with depression only. The groups showed some differences in agitation, but the numbers with this symptom were small for both groups. In fact anxiety was not distributed uniformly across the patients with obsessions in depression. Paradoxically, patients with previous obsessional personalities were no more likely to show anxiety if they had obsessions in depression than if they did not. In contrast, patients without premorbid obsessional personalities were highly likely to experience anxiety associated with obsessions in depression. This study may be criticized on several grounds, two of which are of particular relevance here. First, the patients with obsessions who were studied were not necessarily primarily obsessive–compulsive neurotics, but were selected for inclusion because of the presence of obsessions during depression. In fact just over half the patients (about 54 per cent) with obsessions in depression did have obsessions prior to their depressive illness. Therefore the group was heterogeneous comprising both obsessive–compulsive patients and those without obsessions prior to their depression. Because of this, it cannot be said with certainty that the pattern of depressive symptoms that emerged defined the form of depressions experienced by obsessionals with complete accuracy. However, as a good 50 per cent of the sample were obsessive–compulsive patients, the observed pattern of symptoms is highly likely to bear a close resemblance to their typical state of depression.

The second objection is that the data studied was taken from the coded entries on Institute of Psychiatry (London) item sheets completed by many different registrars. The reliability of these observations is unknown, although Kendell (1968) has defended the use of such material by pointing out that unreliability of data will decrease the probability of obtaining significant results from statistical analyses and thus will lead to conservative hypothesis testing. It was felt that the results obtained in this study could be accepted on these grounds. Overall it was considered that the presence of obsessions in depression was associated with an identifiable form of depression, namely one in which agitation, rapid mood changes and in many cases, anxiety, were present and in which retardation was rare. Not all obsessional patients seem to suffer from depressive episodes, but even amongst those who do not feelings of anxiety and tension are extremely common, causing great distress.

The occurrence of depression in the context of obsessive–compulsive disorders is sufficiently frequent to merit the careful monitoring of mood state in all obsessional patients, particularly as mood may fluctuate so that depression may not be prominent at the time of initial assessment. Any distressing deterioration of mood which occurs is likely to precipitate the need for some appropriate form of physical treatment. Alternatively, or occasionally in addition, feelings of anxiety and tension will require attention.

Sternberg's (1974) review of the literature revealed remarkably few clues as to optimal physical treatments for either of these two problems. A search through the remaining literature up to mid-1977 similarly failed to be helpful. One of the most conspicuous features of the studies in Sternberg's review was that a simple physical method tends to have been used to treat the entire complex of symptoms which constitute obsessive–compulsive disorder. In most cases no attempt has been made to differentiate between depression or anxiety on the one hand and rituals and obsessive fears on the other, as targets of treatment. Similarly, no distinction seems to have been made between these aspects of the disorder in many of the reports of treatment outcome. More discouraging still is the fact that there has been a dearth of reports of controlled trials combining the use of physical treatments for depression and anxiety with behaviour therapy for compulsive behaviours and fears. In this deplorable situation only tentative suggestions about care can be made in most instances.

Symptoms of anxiety and tension may occur in depressed states, such as described by Vaughan (1976) or on their own. In the former case, treatment may be directed at depression as a whole with no independent consideration of the component symptoms. However, in the absence of depression, anxiety and tension may require attention in their own right. The physical treatment of anxiety/tension and depression will be considered separately.

(i) Anxiety and tension. Some patients may experience anxiety and tension specifically associated with their rituals and fears. This may be reduced substantially without specific treatment after successful behaviour therapy when most of the distressing thoughts and compulsive behaviours have been eliminated. However, as excessive anxiety during treatment may make it more difficult for the patient to co-operate, some direct reduction of anxiety may facilitate the smooth running of treatment, at least in the early stages.

Although Jacobsonian-style relaxation training seems an obvious approach to anxiety reduction in a behaviourally orientated treatment programme, its efficacy with obsessive–compulsive patients has not been documented fully. The most comprehensive account of its use comes from Rachman, Hodgson, and Marks (1971) and Hodgson, Rachman, and Marks (1972) who gave their patients fifteen sessions of relaxation training spread over three weeks as a control condition prior to modelling, flooding, and response prevention treatments. They failed to find any change in assessor and self-ratings of anxiety associated with rituals. It is difficult to assess the relevance of these findings as the ratings were made before and after relaxation training and not whilst the patient was relaxing deliberately. This is not a criticism of Rachman *et al.*'s work as the design was appropriate for their purpose. Nevertheless, in the present context it means that the lack of change cannot be interpreted as indicating that anxiety levels were not reduced whilst the patient was relaxing. It can merely be said that relaxation training showed no effect in a situation where the patient was making no deliberate attempt to relax. Had the patient been instructed to try to relax himself, and then to rate her anxiety, the results might have been different. It has been suggested already that the patients may have derived some benefit from their relaxation training and that this might be evidenced in the differences in outcome for the patients given modelling, flooding and response prevention with and without prior relaxation training (Rachman, Marks, and Hodgson, 1973).

In addition, Rachman and his colleagues used tape-recorded relaxation instructions to which the patients listened in the absence of a therapist. Although tape-recorded instructions have been shown to be moderately effective (Mathews and Gelder, 1969), it is doubtful whether they could be applied as easily with obsessive–compulsive patients. In our experience and in that of colleagues, it is not uncommon for obsessional patients to show one or other of two extreme responses during relaxation training.

Some patients follow the instructions so exactly that they tense all muscles with extreme vigour and do not 'let go' until puce in the face and gasping for breath, and then unbend slowly, eventually arranging themselves carefully in a 'correct' relaxed position, whilst remaining exceedingly tense. In contrast, other patients fail to start training at all, as each attempt at instruction is interrupted by many queries and questions and requests for confirmation that the patient has carried out the instruction properly. In many cases it is possible for the therapist to overcome both problems, but it seems extremely unlikely that training would proceed smoothly if the patient was just given the tape recorder and left to her own devices. For this reason, it is felt that the use of tape-recorded instructions by Rachman *et al.* may have reduced the efficacy of relaxation training quite substantially.

This objection seems to be countered by Röper *et al.*'s (1975) finding that there was no change in rated anxiety after training in which a therapist was not only present, but also actively demonstrated relaxation exercises, obeying tape-recorded instruction. The patient imitated the therapist's actions and then discussed her performance. Again change was assessed after treatment without a deliberate attempt to relax, so the non-significant results may not be surprising. Further, the inclusion of all the therapist's gymnastics must have left very little time in each session for the patient to have a go as well, so that supervised practice time may have been limited.

Overall the effectiveness of Jacobsonian-style relaxation training with obsessional patients seems to be unknown. There is still ample room for investigation of therapist-conducted instruction, and the use of biofeedback training (EMG, heart-rate, for example) has not been studied at all. Without contrary evidence, some form of relaxation training, with emphasis on self-controlled use in anxiety-evoking situations, could be attempted with patients suffering from anxiety specifically associated with their obsessional fears and rituals.

As an alternative to relaxation training, one of the minor tranquillizers could be prescribed as a 'cover' during behavioural treatment sessions. Obviously, this would be more expedient in terms of time and effort, and would probably do all that was necessary unless a longer-term reduction in anxiety and tension was required.

Many obsessive compulsive patients seem to experience high levels of anxiety and tension, which although they may be exacerbated by fears and rituals, are not eliminated by the removal of the abnormal behaviour. These patients may require attention for their anxiety over a long period of time. Although relaxation training with instruction in self-administration may help them to sustain some anxiety reduction, it is extremely likely that this will not be sufficient in the majority of cases.

Despite the evident need for tranquillizers in many obsessive–compulsive patients, there are depressingly few reports of research in this area. Sternberg's (1974) review lists nine tranquillizers, citing fourteen references in total (less than two per drug), very few of which reported the comparison of one active drug with another. The differing designs and measures adopted made comparison across studies impossible. In this state of knowledge it appears that the choice of tranquillizers will have to be made almost entirely on the basis of the informed personal preference of the prescribing agent.

The only viable alternative to tranquillizers appears to be a leucotomy of some sort. Sternberg (1974) has reviewed the main methods of surgery and their associated advantages and risks. He concluded that there is an appreciable possibility of serious consequences of leucotomy including epileptic fits and wound complications. Nevertheless about half the obsessive–compulsive patients who have some form of leucotomy seem to benefit greatly from it. The improvement seems to come from adjusting the patient to the disorder rather than from ameliorating the disorder itself.

It seems to be abundantly clear that leucotomy can only be considered as a last resort. Then if it is successful the patient's tension and anxiety may be reduced substantially but his obsessive–compulsive symptoms will remain. At this stage, behavioural intervention may be beneficial even if it failed before the leucotomy was performed. There are several reports of patients who responded to behavioural treatments after a leucotomy, but not before it. Conversely, it has been recorded that some patients do not improve (see, for example, Walton and Mather, 1967). The actual success rate of behaviour therapy after leucotomy in obsessive–compulsive patients has not been determined, nor has the optimal temporal relationship between the two treatments been established.

The probable efficacy of behavioural intervention after leucotomy must be an important consideration in making the decision whether or not a leucotomy should be performed. As even a successful leucotomy does not eliminate compulsive behaviour, the patient is not symptom-free after surgery. Although his rituals may be performed with less anxiety and more mechanistically than before, he may still be handicapped considerably by them. Unless the rituals can be reduced satisfactorily behavioural techniques, the advantages gained from a hazardous leucotomy may be very limited indeed.

(ii) Depression. Although not all obsessional patients suffer from persistent severe depression, most experience adverse mood states which require attention at one time or another. Untreated, depressed mood may impede the progress of behaviour therapy (Teasdale in Rachman, 1976) or precipitate a re-emergence of symptoms after therapy. As with depression without obsessive–compulsive disorder, the main choice of treatment lies between electroconvulsive therapy (ECT) and antidepressant drugs. ECT has been found to alleviate depression in patients with obsessional disorder (Slater and Roth, 1969) and in some cases a reduction in rituals has followed the improvement in mood. However, it has been suggested that ECT should not be used with obsessional patients who are not

depressed as lasting memory impairment, depersonalization or anxiety may occur (Sargent and Slater, 1950).

Unlike ECT, the anti-depressant drugs have not been studied as treatments for depression occurring in obsessional patients, but rather as remedies for the compulsive disorders themselves. There appears to be no evidence concerning the efficacy of either tricyclic antidepressants or monoamine oxidase inhibitors in treating the depression experienced by obsessional patients *per se*. Again the therapist must draw on his knowledge of the effects of the drugs in other clinical groups when selecting the medication most likely to be of use with the patients exhibiting depressive symptoms.

Interestingly, some positive findings have emerged from studies of the effects of tricyclic anti-depressants on obsessional thoughts and rituals. These have come from studies involving clomipramine (Anafranil) in which a considerable reduction, and even a cessation in some patients, of compulsive behaviour has been observed (Sternberg, 1974). The studies are few in number involving small samples in uncontrolled trials so the results may not be taken as being conclusive. However, favourable results have been obtained by Capstick (1971), Marshall and Micev (1975), and Waxman (1975) amongst others. In these studies, clomipramine was administered intravenously. This procedure often appears to be surrounded by considerable ceremony and medical attention, with in some instances supportive group contacts with others receiving the same treatment. In view of this, it is clear that appropriately controlled trials are particularly necessary.

Capstick (1975) observed that clomipramine may precipitate moderately severe depressive episodes, secondary to side-effects of tensions and agitation in some patients. Although Capstick asserted that this effect may be alleviated quite readily, it seems likely that it could jeopardize the patient's co-operation with treatment.

Finally, an initial attempt to evaluate the relative effects of clomipramine and behavioural techniques on patients with rituals has been described by Marks (1977). The analyses of results had not been completed at the time of writing so that no definite statement of outcome could be made (Marks, personal communication).

3. Conclusions

'The literature' provides very little in the way of guidelines for the treatment of depression, anxiety and tension occurring in the context of obsessive–compulsive states. Now that the full importance of mood and arousal level in the genesis and maintenance of obsessive–compulsive behaviour is beginning to be realized (Beech and Perigault, 1974), the need for a comprehensive investigation of physical methods becomes imperative. In particular, the combined use of drugs and behaviour therapy warrant close attention, as it seems likely that eventually it may be demonstrated that neither treatment is entirely effective on its own.

PROBLEMS OF ADJUSTMENT IN EVERYDAY LIVING

Besides their fears and rituals, nearly all obsessive–compulsive patients experience difficulties in adjustment in most areas of life, and these are manifested in their behaviour and emotional responses. It is conceivable, but far from proven, that 'intrapsychic disorder' (Cawley, 1974) may underlie not only these associated problems, but the obsessive–compulsive symptoms as well. To the extent that any or all these difficulties are causing distress, the patient will require additional aid with them, after or during treatment for his obsessive–compulsive symptoms.

The treatment of 'intrapsychic disorder' may be distinguished from that of the other problems, as by their nature such problems, if indeed they exist, may only be accessible to 'formal psychotherapy' (Cawley, 1974). Any investigation of intrapsychic disorder is bedevilled by the intrinsic impossibility of testing all hypotheses based on psychodynamic theorizing, so the relationship of any such disturbances to obsessive–compulsive disorders has not been established. There is not even the indirect confirmation of their influence which would arise through the demonstration that psychoanalytically based formal psychotherapy is an effective treatment technique. Cawley (1974) concluded that the required research in this area has not yet been done.

It is of interest that dynamically oriented psychotherapists have begun to recognize the usefulness of behavioural techniques. Meyer, Levy, and Schnurer (1974) have dealt with several patients referred to them by psychotherapists; in this case the main reason for referral was to rid the patients of their disabling rituals which prevented them from attending their psychotherapy sessions.

More recently, Murray (1976) has suggested that obsessional and other patients should be treated with behaviour therapy or psychotherapy (psychoanalytically based) or a combination of the two, depending on the degree to which their disorders were controlled environmentally or were a function of intrapsychic disorder. He offered no case studies to support this suggestion, but Lipper and Feigenbaum (1976) writing in the same journal reported a case in which the aim had been to provide both forms of treatment in the case of a nineteen-year-old girl with compulsive washing rituals associated with thoughts of being dirty and related to two previous abortions. Her hand-washing was reduced to normal frequency and duration after three weeks of modelling, flooding and response prevention (after Rachman, Hodgson, and Marks, 1971). At this stage supportive psychotherapy was introduced to help her build up her ego defences of intellectualization and isolation of affect, which it was felt had been broken down by her second abortion. (A full dynamic interpretation of the development of the disorder was given at the end of the report.) The patient broke off treatment after only four sessions of psychotherapy, but despite this was found to have maintained her symptomatic improvement and to have achieved a level of satisfactory adjustment in the main areas of her life. It is exceedingly tempting to agree with this patient that dynamically orientated psychotherapy is not worth pursuing, at least until such a time as its advocates have proven their case.

Setting aside the almost mystical intrapsychic disorders, there are many observable difficulties in adjustment which may beset obsessional patients. Work, leisure and sexual activities, and social, marital and other family relationships may be affected, although not all may be impaired in any one individual. Each area of difficulty will be described in detail below, but first some common factors operative in all will be mentioned.

Cawley (1974) considered that people with either of two groups of maladaptive personality traits will encounter pervasive difficulties in everyday living. One cluster of traits includes obstinacy, rigidity, moroseness and irritability, the other comprises uncertainty, indecisiveness and over-submissiveness.

The first group of traits may overlap to some extent with those possessed by the patients whom Beech (1977) has called 'oppositional' in character and who both appear to find it difficult to accept interference from an authority figure and who seem to be disposed to adopt a contrary viewpoint. Beech felt that patients like these may have a poorer prognosis in treatment, and it seems quite likely that their ability to function well in other areas of life will also be reduced.

A second major influence on the patient's adjustment, at least after treatment, will be the substantial change in life-style arising from the reduction or elimination of unwanted thoughts and rituals. Perhaps for the first time in years the patient will have time for work, leisure and social activities and will be able to contemplate closer sexual contact with his spouse. Unless well prepared for this change, the patient is likely to find it difficult to adapt. Now that it may be expected that at least some symptom reduction may occur with behavioural interaction, posttreatment readjustment becomes more important than previously. In some cases, patients may experience problems in everyday living which are not readily attributable to personality, rituals or sudden change in life-style occurring after treatment. Marital disharmony, in which the spouse plays an active and antagonizing role, and dominating or maladjusted parents, may also make it difficult for the patient to respond adaptively to his environment.

To varying degrees, problems in everyday living involving any of these three factors should respond to intervention either through the use of behavioural techniques or through some form of psychotherapy. In this context, the approaches labelled 'informal psychotherapy' by Cawley (1974) would seem to be most appropriate. This classification covers directive, non-directive, client-centred counselling, and supportive and distributive forms of psychotherapy. Once again, there is little conclusive evidence concerning the general efficacy of these forms of psychotherapy.

Appraisals of outcome range in their opinion from, at one extreme, fervent enthusiasm of the practitioner, convinced of the veracity of his tool, as evidenced in the proliferation of psychotherapy journals, to cynical dismissal by a member of the other camp (Rachman, 1971b). Until informal psychotherapy has been shown unequivocally to be effective in dealing with life problems in obsessive–compulsive states, it seems to have no intrinsic appeal which would make it preferable to the alternative, behavioural approach.

No systematic evaluation has been made of the great majority of behavioural interventions which have been, or could be, introduced in an attempt to ameliorate the patient's everyday adjustments. Unless otherwise stated, it may be assumed that the procedures described are untested, and therefore should constitute the material for further research and not the basis of routine clinical practice.

Although the pervasive and often adverse effects of the patient's personality on his everyday adjustment may be observed without difficulty in those with obsessional or oppositional traits, no formal attempt has been made to modify traits by behavioural means. It is possible that some of the behavioural programmes aimed at symptom reduction may affect associated personality traits; for example, extensive flooding for excessive tidyness and cleaning could leave the patient less concerned about all aspects of neatness and cleanliness than before. However, there seems to be little indication that this is the case as Leyton Obsessional Inventory trait scores do not appear to change after successful treatment (Rachman, Hodgson, and Marks, 1971).

Instead of attacking personality traits indirectly in this way it might be possible to design a treatment programme which was aimed specifically at their modification (given of course that the patient expressed the wish to change). The oppositional patients, described by Beech (1977), seemed to be characterized by a marked tendency to find counter arguments to any suggestion and 'good reasons' why any instruction should not be carried out. Not only may this make treatment difficult, it is also likely to interfere with social and work relationships. It is not clear to what extent these patients realize that they are presenting this obstructive approach, or the effect that it is having on others. It is possible that feedback, in the form of tape-recorded examples of the patients' behaviour, backed up by comments from the therapist, would make them a little more aware of the problem. Whether it would change their ensuing behaviour is another question. Probably extensive practice with modelling and feedback would be required before any discernible improvement was achieved.

Every maladaptive trait possessed by the patient would have to be handled separately, as each would require a different approach. For example, a particularly rigid individual might be taught to vary his routine deliberately, in the manner which Worsley (1970) and Mills et al. (1973) have adopted in the treatment of some of their patients' symptomatic behaviour. As many patients possess more than one undesired trait, so that virtually all aspects of behaviour are affected, the chances of achieving any sustained improvement seem remote.

Although worth considering for patients in whom only one trait is conspicuously maladaptive, behavioural intervention is probably as limited a tool when many grossly aberrant traits are involved, as any other form of treatment. The therapist working with the patient on his problems of everyday living may be best advised to tailor the treatments to accommodate the maladaptive traits, rather than to attempt to tackle the traits themselves. He will still have problems to choose from as the patient may experience difficulty with any or all of the following aspects of his life.

1. Work

Many obsessive–compulsive patients will have had to give up formal employ-ment and/or cease doing routine household chores at some time prior to treatment, because of their handicapping disorder. Some may have been unable to work for many years. If treatment is even moderately successful, they should be free sufficiently from their rituals to contemplate resuming employment or normal domestic duties.

The institution of some form of work is important in at least three respects. First it may reinstate the patient in his or her old role as breadwinner or housewife, helping to establish an ordinary family structure again. Second, going out to work may bring an isolated patient into contact with other people, and third, the occupation will help to distract him from his obsessional concerns. The third is probably the most important function of formal employment, considered in terms of the patient's needs (setting aside provision of finances).

The authors have often observed that patients who are moderately in-capacitated at home, especially those with obsessive thoughts, may derive enjoyment and a respite from their thoughts at work. A married woman seen frequently, was plagued with thoughts about death whilst at home, but was able to keep these thoughts out of her mind and to maintain an active interest whilst at work. As this example indicates, housework may not distract the patient effectively, and the main function of its reinstitution in this case, would be to create an appropriate family structure.

The practical problem of finding employment for someone who has been out of work for a considerable time is not one which is amenable to behavioural intervention. However, the process may be facilitated slightly, at least for those of clerical grade upwards, by ensuring that the patient will perform adequately when interviewed. In particular, it will help if he has a ready prepared explanation for his absence from employment (this problem is not nearly as acute for married women as most will be expected to have had time off to raise children). If preliminary enquiry indicated that the patient has inadequate interviewing skills, some role-playing sessions may provide the required experience, or at least give the patient sufficient confidence to attend the interview.

Having obtained employment, with or without interview, the patient must be sufficiently skilled at the job to keep up with his fellow employees. A 'refresher' course in requisite skills may be required prior to employment for patients who have been unemployed for a long time or who have never worked. In addition to learning to do the job, the patient may have to be reminded of work 'rituals' such as tea-breaks and clocking-on so that he will know how to behave in order to be like his fellow workers. Most patients are aware of the need to disguise or postpone any residual rituals which they possess. Involving the patient in ordinary domestic chores may present slightly different problems. A housewife on her own or with only a young child for the greater part of every day is removed from any public observation and distraction which might help her to restrain her remaining compulsive acts and thoughts. In many cases, rehabilitation is made more difficult by the fact that the patient's obsessive–compulsive complaints had originally been centred upon the very cleaning, tidying and cooking to which she has had to return. (Although patients' rituals may be related directly to their formal employment, for example, a clerk checking files, this appears to occur most frequently with housework, probably because of the boring nature of the work.) Both these factors militate against the development of a satisfactory routine.

In some cases it may be preferable for the patient to take a part-time job, and resume only some household duties. This would mean that her husband would have to continue performing a number of mutually agreed-upon chores. Often the resulting improvement in the patient's health and the additional income arising from her job make this an acceptable compromise for her husband. Whether the patient resumes all her duties or only some, she may need some help in establishing appropriate domestic skills. Modelling, practice with explicit feedback, and realistic standard setting may facilitate her progress.

2. Leisure

Nearly all patients who have achieved some improvement will find that they have more time on their hands for leisure pursuits. A few will have hobbies and interests which were merely suspended while they were totally handicapped by their rituals and thoughts.

The introduction of new leisure activities seems to proceed in two stages. First the patient has to be interested in a hobby and then he must be persuaded to convert his interest into action. The first stage may require a great deal of salesmanship from the therapist, and any available family or friend. Although not yet attempted, the generation of leisure pursuits and interests could be introduced as a formal component of in-patient treatment care. Full use could be made of occupational therapy facilities, not so much merely to occupy the patient, as to allow him to sample as widely as possible from all the pursuits which he would be able to continue when at home. He could be dispatched to the local library to gain additional information both about hobbies and about societies to join. As an additional effect, these preparatory activities could contribute to his progress as they would provide discharge-orientated occupation between sessions and during periods of response prevention. A programme like this would probably equip some, but not all, patients with an interest to take home with them.

The second stage of hobby development would be to try to ensure that the patient actually pursued some interest when he returns home. For these patients who had developed an interest, self-control could be supplemented by a verbal or written commitment given to the therapist (Kanfer, 1971). A series of hobby-related exercises could be specified before discharge and an agreement made for the patient to carry out each in turn over the follow-up period. This arrangement should be represented as an important continuation of treatment and progress should be monitored at regular follow-up interviews where the therapist's praise or disappointment would probably act as reinforcers. All aspects of this procedure should help the patient to fulfil his commitment to change.

Patients who had no stated interests could be treated in the same way, if their commitment entailed sampling a number of hobbies (those to which they had least objections) and then definitely deciding on one to pursue. Patients starting in this way would probably find it more difficult to live up to their commitments, as initially the task would have little intrinsic appeal. However, it is possible that in some cases at least the hobby would be found to be more enjoyable than imagined and that this would enhance the patient's motivation to continue. Unfortunately, even the most skilled promotion campaign is unlikely to succeed with some of the more 'oppositional' patients who seem to possess an ability approaching genius in always being able to think of a reason why they could not possibly undertake to do whatever had been suggested.

3. Social activities

Many patients, especially those who are single, are found to be extremely socially isolated, so that one of the main tasks of post-treatment adjustment is to establish them in some form of social group. For some, the reduction of symptoms may be all that is needed to allow them to find their own friends competently. Unfortunately, very few seem able to act with this degree of independence, many more seeming to possess a retiring or unsociable personality which militates against deliberate social action. These patients frequently exhibit either anxiety or lack of skill in social situations or more probably both. Several attempts have been made to tackle both social anxiety and deficient skills, using systematic desensitization with the former and social skills training for the latter.

Social skills training typically involves role-playing common social situations with discussion of performance and sometimes video-feedback of selected parts of the interaction. Marzillier, Lambert, and Kellett (1976) and Hall and Goldberg (1977) have compared the effects of systematic desensitization and skills training in psychiatric patients whose main problem was one of inadequate social skills. Taken together, their results seem to indicate that patients receiving either treatment tend to improve. However, only Marzillier, Lambert, and Kellett's study had a control group of any sort and their treatment groups improved more than this waiting list controls on only two of a number of measures. Nevertheless, both studies indicate that systematic desensitization tended to increase frequency of social contacts or participation. Marzillier, Lambert, and Kellett's study showed a similar effect for skills training, but Hall and Goldberg indicated that this may also improve social strategies and decrease 'problem behaviour'. Despite this, Hall and Goldberg's patients failed to improve to the level of normal controls and at three-months follow-up only the systematic desensitization group showed any sign of having generalized their social participations.

These results are not very encouraging for people working with even moderately ill patients. Even allowing for the fact that research in this area is in its infancy and that the studies mentioned ran into many teething troubles as a consequence, there is little reason to belief that 'socialization' is likely to be anything other than an uphill struggle with, at least, only moderate chances of success.

4. Family interactions

The incapacitating rituals of the patient are likely to have had some adverse effect on the way in which the rest of the family behave at home. A reduction in the patient's symptoms will give the family the opportunity to readjust their own lives. In some cases the adoption of a freer life-style may come automatically, but in others the transition may not be attained spontaneously. It seems possible that difficulties will be particularly likely to occur with adults, when the patient's illness has persisted for years, creating a rigid routine which has become habitual and with children who, having been involved with a parent's ritual, continue to act in accord with her old demands. The need to help adult relatives to readjust their lives has been mentioned already, and so the present discussion will be concerned solely with the children. Several undesirable consequences may accrue from a mother involving her child in her rituals over a prolonged period. First, the mother may forget or fail to learn appropriate ways of dealing with her child so that she will reveal a lack of basic skills when her symptoms are alleviated. In addition, either the child may have imitated or have been taught some of her mother's pathological behaviours and beliefs, or may have adopted an unduly restricted pattern of life to fit in with her requirements.

In dealing with the first sort of difficulty, Marks, Connolly, and Hallam (1973) have suggested that appropriate maternal behaviour may be acquired through observing a skilled model. They cite the case of a 27-year-old woman who compulsively picked scabs off her eighteen month-old son's face and body and who was observed to show no maternal behaviour towards the boy. Maternal behaviour was modelled by a female therapist with the mother being encouraged to participate, and being praised liberally for her efforts. The mother gradually took over care of the child under supervision. Both maternal behaviour and scab-picking showed sustained improvement. The full extent to which modelling of this nature may be beneficial has not been investigated.

The possibility that the children may need assistance to overcome habits acquired as a result of their mother's behaviour appears to have been neglected. Sometimes the treatment of the mother may also fortuitously help the child. For example, Marks, Connolly, and Hallam's patient had restricted her boy's freedom, not allowing him to climb, run on gravel paths, or engage in other dangerous pursuits. Part of the patient's maternal training was to allow the child to do these things. This may have acted as *in vivo* desensitization of any anxiety which had been engendered in the child by repeated prohibition. Older children who have adopted a parent's irrational beliefs may be able to modify their attitudes and behaviour without help when the patient's conduct changes. Nevertheless some attention should be paid to the welfare of such children, particularly those whose parents have been handicapped for a long period. For, in theory, they would seem to be vulnerable to developing a similar complaint. In fact, surprisingly little interest has been shown in establishing empirical links between an obsessional parent and the behaviour of the child, so that the incidence of even transient disorder in the children of obsessive–compulsive patients in unknown.

5. Marital problems

Not only may the patient's symptoms provoke conflict with her spouse, but they may also serve to mask discord unrelated to them. It is not uncommon for matrimonial unhappiness to become more evident as the patient's rituals are reduced, not necessarily because it is worsening, but rather because previously both partners were more absorbed by the patient's compulsive symptoms. The possibility that the compulsive symptoms are fulfilling some protective function in such cases should not be ignored, but appropriate consideration of this idea is beyond the scope of this book. Setting this aside, the observation remains that a fair number of patients experience considerable marital difficulties after their compulsive behaviour has been eliminated. In so far as any situation which evokes tension or distress is likely to increase the chances of relapse, the possibility of some form of treatment for the marital problem would be considered.

Some evidence for the possible effectiveness of marital therapies comes from Gurman (1973). He noted at that time that empirical investigation in this field was in its infancy and perhaps for the reason he found it necessary, in his evaluative report, to reject quite a few. Using stringent criteria for selection on methodological grounds he appraised the outcome of fifteen studies. All involved patients were attending university clinics and family counselling and guidance centres which seems to indicate that probably none of the patients or marriages were severely disordered. The therapies in the fifteen studies fell into four groups: behavioural, client centred, communication training, and dynamically orientated.

Gurman concluded that overall about 66 per cent of patients could be considered to be 'very much improved', 'a good deal improved' and 'somewhat improved' at the end of treatment. Moreover, there seemed to be some indication that behavioural treatments tended to be better than the others, although Gurman pointed out that this observation was based on a very small number of cases.

These findings appear encouraging but it should be remembered that no control groups were cited and the spontaneous remission rate for marital problems is not really known. Therefore, there was no way of knowing how the couples would have fared without treatment. Further, no follow-ups were undertaken so that there was no indication whether improvement was maintained. Perhaps more important in this context is the fact that it was unlikely that any of the patients were severely disordered. With couples including an obsessional patient, this can hardly be said to be the case. The obsessional spouse's condition is likely to introduce complication into husband–wife relationships of a kind not usually encountered in marital therapy. Because of this and of shortcomings of the studies reviewed by Gurman, it seems probable that marital therapy involving an obsessional patient is likely to yield rather more modest gains than the 66 per cent improvement rate suggested.

Stern, and Marks (1973) are the only therapists to report on behavioural treatment of marital problems with an obsessional patient. The patient and her husband were given contract marital therapy for a total of ten sessions. Each partner listed positive behaviours which were desired from the other mutually agreed upon contracts were arranged requiring the listed behaviours to be performed. The marital relationship was considered to have improved steadily, and in addition the patient's checking rituals which had previously been resistant to behavioural treatment virtually disappeared. A year after discharge the patient's husband left her, so that the treatment attempt cannot be considered to have been a long-term success. Nevertheless the improvement observed during treatment may be sufficient to allow others to give behavioural marital therapy another try.

6. Sexual dysfunction

Although some patients report a satisfying sexual life despite debilitating thoughts and rituals, many others report that intercourse has not been successful or even attempted for a long time. It cannot be assumed that normal sexual functioning will be resumed automatically when the patient's compulsive symptoms have been eliminated. Besides the possibility that sexual problems may have been present in addition to the obsessive–compulsive disorder from the start, a history of abortive attempts and rebuffs may lead to revulsion, avoidance or specific sexual dysfunction (of the sort listed by Bancroft, 1972) in either of the partners. In such cases, it may be necessary to provide some sort of formal treatment.

The sensate focus approach of Masters and Johnson (1970) is still very much in vogue and has been extended and made more flexible by several other sets of workers (Bancroft, 1975, for example). The success rates claimed have been impressive and although some of the necessary controlled trials have yet to be carried out, the general approach appears to contain some potential. However, it is unclear what rate of success should be expected when at least one partner is a psychiatric patient. The patients in the main outcome studies have not suffered from psychiatric illness. Bancroft (1975) obtained his clients from general practitioners, gynaecologists and Family Planning Association doctors, so it is unlikely that they included many (if any at all) with disorders as severe as obsessive–compulsive states.

The introduction of an obsessional partner may complicate treatment in at least two ways. Firstly the patient's symptoms may interfere with progress as patients often possess fears and rituals centred around bodily secretions. If treated successfully by, say, flooding and response prevention, avoidance may be reduced to a level of reluctance which may be dealt with satisfactorily by a sensate focus approach. If, however, fear and avoidance remain stronger than this, it may be difficult to ensure co-operation from the patient. In addition, in patients prone to depression, specific sexual dysfunctions may be exacerbated or may re-emerge when an adverse mood state is present.

Secondly, the patient's obsessional disorder may be associated with marital conflict which is intertwined with the sexual problems. Bancroft (1975) has suggested that the presence of interpersonal problems may complicate treatment, resulting in an increase in the number of sessions required. In view of these points, there is no clear indication of the degree of success which should be expected from the use of a sensate focus approach to the treatment of sexual dysfunctions in partnerships which include an obsessional patient. Despite this, the reports of patients and spouses indicate that there are occasions on which some form of treatment ought to be applied.

CONCLUSIONS

If read rapidly, this chapter could easily be interpreted as being a list of difficulties arising during treatment and the antidotes to apply, as if every patient will need all the 'cures'. It is certainly not intended that this should be the case; again it is emphasized that the care of any one patient would not be expected to involve all, or even a majority of, the strategies described. It would have been far clearer to have indicated the incidence of each ancillary problems and the probable success rate of the associated intervention. Unfortunately no information of this nature is available currently, so that all that can be stated is that an unknown number of patients will require additional treatment of uncertain validity in conjunction with their main behavioural programme. Apart from generating ideas, one main function of the chapter may be to point out that, contrary to the impression created by some published work, behavioural intervention and treatment in general does not begin and end with the application of desensitization or flooding, modelling, and response prevention techniques.

10

Conclusion

Obsessionals are only a small fraction of the total patient population, yet they are among the least amenable to treatment, and the distress which they suffer can be very considerable. It is usual, too, that the families of those afflicted are often subjected to very great hardship which, because of the typical secretiveness of the obsessional, comes to light only in extreme circumstances. Not infrequently the life-style adopted in the home of these unfortunate individuals is so grossly abnormal that, setting aside any genetic influence which there might be, it must contribute to the future adjustment (or maladjustment) of their children.

We have recently been involved in the treatment of a severely handicapped obsessional woman, abandoned by her husband several years earlier, who had raised her children in conditions of enormous deprivation. No food was cooked, and that eaten was of a limited kind; no heating was allowed, even in the coldest of weather; no comfort or affection could be shown since only the most perfunctory contact could be endured by the patient with her children.

In another typical family, while conditions were less harsh, the children were so restricted in play and social contacts that their lives could only be regarded as greatly impoverished.

It is important, we feel, that such consequences are identified since it is so often that the attention given by therapists is focused upon the patient alone, and the dire needs of the family are given little thought. Indeed, we have encountered cases where the families of patients have not only tolerated such conditions, but have made the most valiant and far-reaching sacrifices to accommodate the abnormalities of thought and behaviour which the patient displays. Little is known about these matters in any but an anecdotal and unsystematic way, but they are an important and sometimes horrifying measure of the severity of the problem. To us, it seems that the family of the obsessional is often neglected, their difficulties going unappreciated and, to add to their burden, when the investigator does approach their problem it is frequently without the genuine sympathy and understanding which is deserved. We have, for example, encountered patients whose families have been subjected to reproof and caustic comment for the part which they are alleged to have played in causing the obsessional's distress, whereas perhaps praise for effort made would have been more appropriate.

But while the family deserves help in coping with enormous difficulties, it is obvious that the obsessional patient and his therapy should be the focus of attention. Unfortunately, treatment has not proved to be particularly helpful, even when earnestly sought.

Cawley (1974), for example, has concluded that the problems of patients with obsessional disorders are in general unlikely to be helped on any large scale by formal psychotherapy. In Cawley's view, psychotherapy, along with all other treatment alternatives, might be considered for inclusion in a therapeutic programme, but each component would need to be adopted as a logical consequence of identified patient need, rather than of standard practice.

Similarly, Sternberg (1974), in his review of the physical treatments, concludes that these have not yet been properly evaluated with respect to obsessional states, and that we have only tentative evidence for the usefulness of such methods. Even that well-documented procedure, leucotomy, in its various forms, seems to offer little predictable value and considerable risk to the patient.

In disorders which are as crippling and tenacious as obsessions can be, it is hardly surprising that claims for an important advance in treatment should be welcomed. Indeed, where such treatment seems to be linked with an acceptable rationale and empirical evidence from therapeutic trials, the obvious appeal is immense. Behaviour modification certainly seems to offer the much-needed breakthrough and there is no doubt that the past few years have witnessed intensive investigatory activity in the area of obsessionality by psychologists. Both the mechanisms of the disorder and its treatment have received much attention. The published evidence, taken as a whole, has been encouraging and claims for the efficacy of behaviour modification procedures create a decidedly optimistic impression.

The problem to which we have addressed ourselves in this book is that of evaluating the work carried out in this area. In particular, we have made an attempt to assess the published evidence in terms of the ordinarily accepted criteria for experimental work, and to reach some tentative conclusions which will serve as a guide to clinical practice.

'SELF-CONTROL' TREATMENT

Taking first those procedures which can conveniently be grouped under the heading 'self-control', the conclusion which one must draw from published evidence is that such methods are adjunctive rather than main therapeutic techniques. In our opinion, however, there are two very important reservations which may be entertained in respect of 'self-control' methods in the context of obsessional states. First, for the most part they are relatively untried in any systematic and detailed way and hard evidence for their efficacy is lacking.

Second, in our view the theoretical bases of self-control methods, dependent upon Skinnerian formulations, are inadequate and have little to commend them. Furthermore, in terms of available evidence concerning the mechanisms of obsessional states one would have to conclude that these methods are unlikely to assume major importance in therapy.

Perhaps it is appropriate to say, however, that the particular value and place of these methods in the treatment of obsessionals is not known, rather than that they contribute little. Obviously more research is needed to clarify the issue and one would be reluctant to reject these methods prematurely since self-control has an important potential place in treatment. Most obviously they might be used as a means of bridging the gap between in-patient treatment and return to life in the community.

However, exclusive pursuit of isolated self-control approaches is unlikely to prove fruitful, as clinical experience indicates that dependence on one or two main techniques appears not to cater for the problems which affect the obsessional. It does not necessarily follow, of course, that the inclusion of a 'multi-modal' approach would confer any greater therapeutic benefit. Indeed it seems likely that to do so such an approach would have to encompass techniques beyond the range described here as it is apparent that these self-control methods are often inadequate even in combination.

SYSTEMATIC DESENSITIZATION

Indeed, in our view of the major techniques employed only systematic desensitization can be said to be underpinned by a well-developed theoretical basis, and even in this case there is considerable doubt that the rationale provided has stood up well to investigation.

In this sense perhaps systematic desensitization is at the kind of disadvantage to which a cogent theoretical model is exposed—it is reasonably clearly formulated and therefore amenable to test and disproof. Certainly, the same cannot be said for flooding, response prevention, and thought-stopping.

Perhaps more telling, however, is that there have been no controlled trials of systematic desensitization in obsessionals, so that any conclusions respecting efficacy depend upon case studies. While such conclusions must obviously be most tentative, these case reports suggest greater success if the mode of desensitization is *in vivo* and if the nature of the obsession is circumscribed.

MODELLING, FLOODING, AND RESPONSE PREVENTION TREATMENT

In spite of the inadequacies of theoretical basis, modelling, flooding, and response prevention have assumed great importance as the treatment strategies of choice for obsessional disorders. To some extent this prominence is explained by the fact that these techniques have generated the most systematic research into empirical treatment effects, but it is interesting to observe that this has tended to lead to the assumption that they have clearly established effectiveness. Such an assumption would be erroneous for a number of reasons.

In the first place it has not yet been established that modelling, flooding, and response prevention are responsible for changes observed since no adequate control data has been gathered. As we have pointed out in Chapter 5, for example, Rachman's use of a relaxation control, while useful, does not rule out the effects of other variables which could have affected the outcome. A further restriction on undue optimism about the value of results from the application of these techniques is that very few patients actually completely lose their symptoms, and improvement is largely limited to obsessive–compulsive rituals and the anxiety associated with them.

In general, improvements in mood state and in social adjustment are not well documented and, as we have argued elsewhere, the continuance of adverse mood allows the individual to remain vulnerable to further episodes of obsessional thought and behaviour. Indeed, 'booster' treatments have been frequently found to be required although the extent to which this is necessary is less well reported. Our own clinical experience indicates very clearly that patients who have responded favourably to behaviour modification continue to remain vulnerable and seldom appear to sustain improvements over lengthy periods of time. Naturally, we would not advance the argument that relapses of the kind observed should lead to the abandonment of treatment. Where behaviour modification techniques can be shown to provide even temporary relief from symptoms there is much to be said for their employment in an area where little else may be effective. Rather, our view is that it is appropriate to arrive at a balanced view of the contribution which such techniques afford, and the evidence suggests that such contribution, while valuable, is only partial and inclined to be temporary in nature.

SATIATION TRAINING

Satiation training is certainly of some interest but, so far as both theoretical basis or empirical evidence are concerned there is little to be said for the procedure. Indeed, the procedure itself is not particularly well-described as yet, but appears similar to the method which we have used and based upon early learning theory formulations respecting the development of conditioned inhibition. Briefly, the method has involved the selection of some central pathological idea which can be expressed in some relatively simple verbal format, or some behaviour which is both central and reproducible in continuous sequence.

The idea or behaviour is then rehearsed repeatedly, in a manner similar to that described by Yates (1958), taking the repetitions well beyond the point at which either emotional expression or simple capacity to reproduce in a mechanical way are found. In short, while negative emotion may be an early experience in the repetitious sequence, and while accurate reproduction is characteristic of the early stages of rehearsal, training (repetition) should continue to the point of patient exhaustion. Certainly, enforced (as opposed to elective) rest pauses should occur, as should errors in performance attributable to fatigue, and it should be abundantly clear that the patient has reached a stage in rehearsal which cannot be sustained, and a point at which he is compelled to rest. We have used this method on a number of occasions and over a lengthy period of years, but two cases may illustrate its application. In the first case we were asked to treat a patient whose abnormal behaviour stemmed primarily (and almost exclusively) from a fear that his work with animals may occasion him to become a carrier of a particular disease. This idea, which like many others had both meaning and emotional loading, was capable of being expressed in the space of a short sentence. The patient was instructed to repeat this sentence for some 35 minutes without rest pauses. He reported that the idea had, toward the end of the session, lost all significance for him and was merely a 'collection of words'; the emotional loading was apparently modest and was lost very early in the rehearsal.

In another case, that of a severe obsessional with fears of harm coming to members of her family through some action of hers, this control idea was rehearsed for 40 minutes before enforced rest pauses, blocks, and errors, became an important feature of her performance. In this case, too, the emotional impact of the exercise was noted to occur sporadically over the first half of the therapy session, and thus was more protracted as well as more intense than the case described above.

In yet a third case, that of a very severely disturbed obsessional boy of sixteen, the central idea was concerned with bowel functioning with an accompanying impulse to manually assist both forced and normal excretory functions. This has produced physical damage, and there was a real risk here of serious physical injury to add to a crippling psychological condition. The reaction to our conditioned inhibition training produced different results again from those just documented. The emotional reaction was almost immediate and very intense, so that the patient attempted to leave the room and screamed in an uncontrollable manner. Eventually he was able to continue with the repetition of the key phrase, but appeared to be very quickly prompted to engage in a 'parallel' ritual (rumination) which seemed to be carried out at the same time as rehearsal of the 'bowel functioning' thought. This, however, gave place to a quiescent phase which, in turn, gave place to a phase in which errors were repeatedly made, until he was asked to stop at the end of 40 minutes.

The important considerations, of course, are those of whether within-sessions and between-sessions progress is satisfactory and in accordance with the theoretical account offered; neither point has been confirmed in studies available to date. In addition, the contrast between the success of negative practice and the results presented in Table 3 (page 94) suggests that the mode of presentation of the thoughts should be investigated.

There is, however, a relevant clinical point which may be raised in connection with the conditioned inhibition therapy of obsessionals. It has become clear to us that the selection of the idea to be used in treatment must be given careful consideration. We have found that some verbal formulations, arrived at after discussion with patients, seem inadequate even though apparently encapsulating the elements of obsessional concern; some alternative which does not look essentially different from the 'unsuccessful' idea, however, may be entirely successful. It seems to us that the difference may lie in the degree to which the verbal formulation is a general one (as opposed to being tied to specific objects, situations, and the like). Some patients clearly are more 'at home' when the idea is more specific in its relation to recognizable situations and events although, for obvious reasons, one is tempted to make the idea sufficiently abstract to apply to many different specifics.

THOUGHT-STOPPING

Finally, where thought-stopping is concerned we must again conclude that the available evidence does not inspire confidence. Two of the three controlled trials available for this technique, for example, have been concerned with extremely brief treatment (Stern, Lipsedge, and Marks, 1973; Hackmann and McLean, 1975), and so do not provide much help.

CONCLUSIONS

Accordingly, in the light of our review of treatment evidence, we must reluctantly conclude that there is no conclusive evidence that behaviour modification offers a viable approach to the modification of abnormal thoughts in obsessionals. For the motor components of these conditions, however, the picture appears to be a little brighter—or at least to encourage a degree of cautious optimism. Here, flooding, modelling, and response prevention would seem to involve elements helpful to the patient, although it is important to say that these methods still require further careful, controlled experimental work. Nor of course, is there any convincing evidence about the mechanisms involved in these techniques and how they deal with the abnormalities of function to which they are directed.

Further there is no clear idea available as to which patients are likely to benefit from the strategies reviewed, although we may safely assume that it is the norm rather than the exception for obsessional patients to relapse following treatment, and to require 'booster' courses of therapy. In our view, too, the implication of adverse mood has been soundly documented in the context of obsessional disorder, as an important background variable as well as being involved in a causative role in relation to specific abnormal behaviours and relapses. Furthermore, it is our opinion that the scope of behaviour modification techniques has not been sufficiently great to encompass a number of abnormalities, including mood and social behaviours, which are characteristic of the obsessional patient.

Finally, we are in no doubt that much of the definitive work in this area remains to be done notably, we feel, in arriving at good answers to the question of the nature of obsessional mechanisms. In our view effective treatment must be related to real knowledge concerning dysfunction and, as yet, neither are available. We would not deny that behaviour modification has had considerable impact upon what had been a rather dismal treatment prospect, and our opinion would be that in certain particulars the benefit has been real as well as apparent. For example, in respect of reducing the habit component of the disorder, and in reducing anxiety, there are probably legitimate and important successes to count, but it is salutary to consider the aspects of malfunctioning which are not brought under control, the serious relapse rate, the dearth of evidence respecting the nature of the pathology, and numerous other matters. It seems to us of paramount importance that exaggerated claims for success in this area are avoided since, if they are not, a false impression of benefit conferred can only act as a brake upon much-needed research.

References

Agras, W. S., Leitenberg, H., Barlow, D. H., Curtis, N. A., Edwards, J., and Wright, 1971. Relaxation in systematic desensitization. *Arch. Gen. Psychiat.*, **25**, 511–514.

Alban, L. S., and Nay, R., 1976. Reduction of ritual re-checking by a relaxation delay technique. *J. Beh. Ther. and Exp. Psychiat.*, **7**, 115–155.

Allen, J. J., and Tune, G. S., 1975. The Lynfield obsessional/compulsive questionnaires. *Scott. Med. J.*, **20**, Supplement 1, 21–26.

Anthony, J., and Edelstein, B. A., 1975. Thought-stopping treatment of anxiety attacks due to seizure-related obsessive ruminations. *J. Beh. Ther. and Exp. Psychiat.*, **6**, 343–344.

Asso, D., and Beech, H. R., 1975. Susceptibility to the acquisition of a conditioned response in relation to the menstrual cycle. *J. Psychosom. Res.* **19**, 337–344.

Bain, J. A., 1928. *Thought Control in Everyday Life*. New York, Funk and Wagnalls.

Bancroft, J. H. J., 1972. Problems of sexual inadequacy in medical practice. In Mandelbrote, B. M., and Gelder, M. G. (Eds.) *Psychiatric Aspects of Medical Practice* (A collection of Oxford essays). London, Staples Press, pp. 243–259.

Bancroft, J. H. J., 1975. The treatment of marital sexual problems. Maudsley Bequest Lecture, Institute of Psychiatry, University of London, London.

Bandura, A., 1969. Principles of Behaviour Modification. London, Holt.

Bandura, A., 1971a. Psychotherapy based upon modeling principles. In Bergin, A. E., and Garfield, S. L. (Eds.) *Handbook of Psychotherapy and Behaviour Change: An Empirical Analysis*. New York, John Wiley, pp. 653–708.

Bandura, A. 1971b. Vicarious and self-reinforcement processes. In Glaser, R.(Ed.). *The Nature of Reinforcement*. New York, Academic Press, pp. 228–278.

Bandura, A. Blanchard, E. B. and Ritter, B. 1969. The relative efficacy of desensitization and modelling approaches for inducing behavioural, affective and attitudinal changes. *J. Pers. Soc. Psychol.*, **13**, 173–199.

Bass, B. A. 1973. An unusual behavioural technique for treating obsessional ruminations. *Psychotherapy Theory: Res. and Prac.*, **10**, 191–192.

Baum, M. 1970. Extinction of avoidance responding through response prevention (flooding). *Psychol. Bull.*, **74**, 276–78.

Beaumont, G. 1975. A new rating scale for obsessional and phobic states. *Scott. Med. J.*, **20**, Supplement 1, 27–34.

Beck, A. T., Ward, C. H., Mendelson, M., Mock, J. and Erbaugh, 1961. An inventory for measuring depression. *Arch. Gen. Psychiat.*, **4**, 561–571.

171

Beech, H. R. 1971. Ritualistic activity in obsessional patients. *J. Psychosom. Res.,* **15,** 417–422.

Beech, H. R. 1974. Approaches to understanding obsessional states. In Beech, H. R. (Ed.). *Obsessional States,* London, Methuen, pp. 3–18.

Beech, H. R. 1978. Advances in the treatment of obsessional neurosis. *Brit. J Hosp. Med.* **19,** 54–59.

Beech, H. R. and Liddell, A. 1974. Decision-making, mood states and ritualistic behaviour among obsessional patients. In Beech, H. R. (Ed.). *Obsessional States,* London, Methuen, pp. 143–160.

Beech, H. R. and Perigault, J., 1974. Toward a theory of obsessional disorder. In Beech, H. R. (Ed.). *Obsessional States,* London, Methuen, pp. 113–142.

Bergin, A. E., 1969. A self-regulation technique for impulse control disorders. *Psychotherapy; Theory Res. and Prac.,* **6,** 113–118.

Bevan, J. R., 1960. Learning theory applied to the treatment of a patient with obsessional ruminations. In Eysenck, H. J. *Behaviour Therapy and the Neuroses.* Oxford, Pergamon Press, 165–169.

Black, A., 1974. The natural history of obsessional neurosis. In Beech, H. R. (Eds.). *Obsessional States,* London, Methuen, pp. 19–54.

Boersma, K., Den Hengst, S., Dekker, J. and Emmelkamp, P. M. G., 1976. Exposure and response prevention in the natural environment: a comparison with obsessive–compulsive patients. *Beh. Res. and Ther.,* **14,** 19–24.

Boulougouris, J. L. and Bassiakos, L., 1973. Prolonged flooding in obsessive compulsive neurosis. *Beh. Res. and Ther.,* **11,** 227–231.

Bridger, W. H. and Mandel, I. J., 1964. A comparison of GSR fear responses produced by threat and electric shock. *J. Psychiat. Res.,* **2,** 31–40.

Broadhurst, A., 1976. It's never too late to learn. An application of conditioned inhibition to obsessional ruminations in an elderly patient. In Eysenck H. J. *Case Studies in Behaviour Therapy,* London, Routledge and Kegan Paul, pp. 173–184.

Brown, F. W., 1942. Heredity in the psychoneuroses. *Proc. Roy. Soc. Med.,* **35,** 785–90.

Bryant, B., Trower, P., Yardley, K., Urbeita, H. and Letemendia, F. J. J., 1976. A survey of social inadequacy among psychiatric outpatients. *Psychol. Med.,* **6,** 101–112.

Capstick, N., 1971. Anafranil in obsessional states—a follow-up study. *5th World Congress of Psychiatry, Mexico City.*

Capstick, N., 1975. Depressive reactions in the course of clomipramine therapy used in the treatment of obsessional conditions. *Scott. Med. J.,* **20,** Supplement 1, 47–50.

Carr, A. T., 1970. A psychological study of ritual behaviours and decision processes in compulsive neurosis. Unpublished PhD thesis, University of Birmingham.

Catts, S. and McConaghy, N., 1975. Ritual prevention in the treatment of obsessive compulsive neurosis. *Austr. N.Z. J. Psychiat.,* **9,** 37–41.

Cautela, J. R., 1967. Covert sensitization. *Psychol. Rep.,* **20,** 459–468.

Cautela, J. R., 1970. Covert reinforcement. *Beh. Ther.,* **1,** 33–50.

Cawley, R., 1974. Psychotherapy and obsessional disorders. In Beech, H. R. *Obsessional States,* London, Methuen, pp. 259–290.

Cooper, J. E., 1970. The Leyton Obsessional Inventory. *Psychol. Med.,* **1,** 48–64.

Cooper, J. E. and Kelleher, M., 1973. The Leyton Obsessional Inventory. A principal components analysis on normal subjects. *Psychol. Med.,* **3,** 204–208.

Cooper, J. E. and McNeill, J., 1968. A study of houseproud housewives and their interaction with their children. *J. Child Psychol. Psychiat.* **9,** 173–188.

Cooper, J. E., Gelder, M. G. and Marks, I. M., 1965. Results of behaviour therapy in 77 psychiatric patients. *Brit. Med. J.,* **1,** 1222–1225.

Dowson, J. H., 1977. The phenomenology of severe obsessive–compulsive neurosis. *Brit. J. Psychiat.,* **131,** 75–78.

Dunlap, K., 1932. *Habits, Their Making and Unmaking.* New York, Liveright.

Emmelkamp, P. M. G. and Kwee, K. G., 1977. Obsessional ruminations: a comparison between thought-stopping and prolonged exposure in imagination. *Beh. Res. and Ther.*, **15**, 441–444.

Eysenck, H. J., 1956. 'Warm-up' in pursuit rotor learning as a function of the extinction of conditioned inhibition. *Acta Psychol.*, **12**, 249–370.

Eysenck, H. J., 1960. *Behaviour Therapy and the Neuroses.* Oxford, Pergamon Press.

Eysenck, H. J. and Beech, H. R., 1971. Counter conditioning and related methods. In Bergin, A. E. and Garfield, S. L. (Eds.). *Handbook of Psychotherapy and Behaviour Change. An Empirical Analysis.* New York, John Wiley, pp. 543–611.

Eysenck, S. B. G. and Eysenck, H. J., 1969. Scores on three personality variables as a function of sex and social class. *Brit. J. Soc. Clin. Psychol.*, **8**, 69–76.

Franchina, J. J., Hauser, P. J. and Agee, C. M., 1975. Persistence of response prevention effects following retraining of escape behaviour. *Beh. Res. and Ther.*, **13**, 1–6.

Fransella, F., 1974. Thinking and the obsessional. In Beech, H. R. (Ed.). *Obsessional States.* London, Methuen, pp. 175–196.

Frederiksen, L. W., 1975. Treatment of ruminative thinking by self-monitoring. *J. Beh. Ther. and Exp. Psychiat.*, **6**, 258–259.

Furst, J. and Cooper, A., 1970. Failure of systematic desensitization in 2 cases of obsessive compulsive neurosis marked by fears of insecticide. *Beh. Res. and Ther.*, **8**, 203–206.

Gelder, M. G. and Marks, I. M., 1966. Severe agoraphobia: a controlled prospective trial of behaviour therapy. *Brit. J. Psychiat.*, **112**, 309–319.

Gelfand, D. M. and Hartmann, D. P., 1975. Child Behaviour: Analysis and Therapy. Oxford, Pergamon Press.

Gittleson, N. L., 1966. The effects of obsessions on depressive psychosis. *Brit. J. Psychiat.*, **112**, 253–258.

Gleitman, H., Nachmias, J. and Neisser, U., 1954. The S–R reinforcement theory of extinction. *Psychol. Rev.*, **61**, 23–33.

Gray, J. A., 1971. *The Psychology of Fear and Stress.* London, Weidenfeld and Nicolson.

Greer, H. S. and Cawley, R. H., 1966. *Some Observations on the Natural History of Neurotic Illness.* Mervyn Archdall Medical Monograph No 3. Australian Medical Association.

Groves, P. and Thompson, R. F., 1970. Habituation: A dual process theory. *Psychol. Rev.*, **77**, 419–450.

Gullick, E. L. and Blanchard, E. B., 1973. The use of psychotherapy and behaviour therapy in the treatment of an obsessive compulsive disorder: An experimental case study. *J. Nerv. Ment. Dis.*, **156**, 427–431.

Gurman, A. S., 1973. The effects and effectiveness of marital therapy: A review of outcome research. *Family Process.* **12**, 145–170.

Hackmann, A. and McLean, C., 1975. A comparison of flooding and thought-stopping in the treatment of obsessive compulsive neurosis. *Beh. Res. and Ther.*, **13**, 263–271.

Hall, R. and Goldberg, D. P., 1977. The role of social anxiety in social interaction difficulties. *Brit. J. Psychiat.*, **131**, 610–615.

Hallam, R. S., 1974. Extinction of ruminations: a case study. *Beh. Ther.*, **5**, 565–568.

Haslam, M. T., 1964. The treatment of an obsessional patient by reciprocal inhibition. *Beh. Res. and Ther.*, **2**, 213–216.

Henderson, D. K. and Gillespie, R. D., 1962. *Textbook of Psychiatry for Students and Practioners*, 9th edn. London, Oxford University Press.

Herrnstein, R. J., 1969. Method and theory in the study of avoidance. *Psychol. Rev.*, **76**, 49–69.

Hildreth, H. M., 1946. A battery of feeling and attitude scales for clinical use. *J. Clin. Psychol.*, **2**, 214–21.

Hodgson, R. J. and Rachman, S., 1972. The effects of contamination and washing in obsessional patients. *Beh. Res. and Ther.*, **10**, 111–117.

Hodgson, R. J. and Rachman, S., 1976. The modification of compulsive behaviour. In

Eysenck, H. J. (Ed.). *Case Studies in Behaviour Therapy* London, Routledge and Kegan Paul, pp. 17–41.

Hodgson, R. J and Rachman, S., 1977. Obsessional–compulsive complaints. *Beh. Res. and Ther.,* **15,** 389–396.

Hodgson, R. J., Rachman, S. and Marks, I. M., 1972. The treatment of chronic obsessive–compulsive neurosis; follow-up and further findings. *Beh. Res. and Ther.,* **10,** 181–189.

Hogan, R. A. and Kirchner, J. H., 1967. Preliminary report of the extinction of learned fears via short-term implosive therapy. *J. Abnorm. Psychol.,* **72,** 106–109.

Hull, C. L., 1943. *Principles of Behaviour.* New York, Appleton-Century.

Ingram, I. M., 1961. Obsessional illness in mental hospital patients. *J. Ment. Sci.,* **107,** 1035–1042.

Jacobson, E., 1938. *Progressive Relaxation.* Chicago, University of Chicago Press.

Janet, P., 1903. *Les Obsessions et al Psychoasthenie.* (2nd ed., 1908) Paris, Bailliere.

Jones, H. G., 1958. The status of inhibition in Hull's system: A theoretical revision. *Psychol. Rev.,* **65,** 179–182.

Jones, H. G., 1960. Continuation of Yates' treatment of a tiquer. In Eysenck, H. J., *Behaviour Therapy and the Neuroses.* Pergamon Press, pp. 250–258.

Kanfer, F. H., 1970. Self-monitoring: methodological limitations and clinical applications. *J. Cons. Clin. Psychol.,* **35,** 148–152.

Kanfer, F. H., 1971. The maintenance of behaviour by self-generated stimuli and reinforcement. In Jacobs, A. and Sachs, L. B. (Eds.). *The Psychology of Private Events.* New York, Academic Press.

Kanfer, F. H. and Karoly, P., 1972a. Self-regulation and its clinical application: some additional conceptualizations. In Johnson, R. C., Dokecki, P. R. and Mowler, O. H. *Socialization: Development of Character and Conscience,* New York, Holt, Rinehart and Winston.

Kanfer, F. H. and Karoly, P., 1972b. Self-control: A behavioristic excursion into the lion's den. *Beh. Ther.,* **3,** 398–416.

Kaplan, R. M. and Litrownik, A. J., 1977. Some statistical methods for the assessment of multiple outcome criteria in behavioural research. *Beh. Ther.,* **8,** 383–392.

Kelleher, M. J., 1972. Cross-national (Anglo-Irish) differences in obsessional symptoms and traits of personality. *Psychol. Med.,* **2,** 33–41.

Kendell, R. E., 1968. *The Classification of Depressive Illness.* Maudsley Monograph 18. London, Oxford University Press.

Kendell, R. E. and Discipio, W. J., 1970. Obsessional symotoms and obsessional personality traits in patients with depressive illness. *Psychol. Med.,* **1,** 65–72.

Kendrick, D. C., 1960. The theory of 'conditioned inhibition' as an explanation of negative practice effects: an experimental analysis. In Eysenck, H. J. (Ed.). *Behaviour Therapy and the Neuroses.* Oxford, Pergamon Press, pp. 221–235.

Kerlinger, F. N., 1964. *Foundations of Behavioural Research.* New York, Holt Rinehart and Winston.

Kringlen, E., 1965. Obsessional neurotics: A long term follow-up. *Brit. J. Psychiat.,* **111,** 709–722.

Kumar, K. and Wilkinson, J. C. M., 1971. Thought-stopping: a useful treatment in phobias of 'internal stimuli'. *Brit. J. Psychiat.,* **119,** 305–307.

Lader, M. H. and Mathews, A. M., 1968. A physiological model of phobic anxiety and desensitization. *Beh. Res. and Ther.,* **6,** 411–421.

Lambley, P., 1974. Differential effects of psychotherapy and behavioural techniques in a case of acute obsessive–compulsive disorder. *Brit. J. Psychiat.,* **125,** 181–183.

Lazarus, A. A., 1963. The results of behaviour therapy in 126 cases of severe neurosis. *Beh. Res. and Ther.,* **1,** 69–79.

Le Boeuf, A., 1974. An automated aversion device in the treatment of a compulsive handwashing ritual. *J. Beh. Ther. and Exp. Psychiat.,* **5,** 267–270.

Leger, L. 1975. Thought-stopping as a treatment for obsessional ruminations: an evaluation of a measure of clinical improvement. Unpublished M. Phil. thesis, University of London.

Lehner, F. J., 1960. Negative practice as a psychotherapeutic technique. In Eysenck, H. J. (Ed.). *Behaviour Therapy and the Neuroses.* Oxford, Pergamon Press, pp. 194–206.

Leitenberg, H., Agras, S., Edwards, J. A., Thomson, L. E. and Wince, J. P., 1970. Practice as a psychotherapeutic variable: An experimental analysis within single cases. *J. Psychiat. Res.,* **7,** 215–225.

Lewis, A. J., 1936. Problems of obsessional illness, *Proc. Roy. Soc. Med.,* **29,** 325–336.

Lewis, A. J., 1957. Obsessional illness. *Acte Neuropsiquiat Argent.,* **3,** 323–335.

Lewis, A. J. and Mapother, E., 1941. Obsessional disorder. In Price, (Ed.). *Textbook of the Practice of Medicine.* Oxford, Oxford University Press, pp. 1199–2001.

Levy, R. and Meyer, V., 1971. Ritual prevention in obsessional patients. *Proc. Roy. Soc. Med.,* **64,** 1115–1118.

Liddell, M. A., 1976. An investigation of psychological mechanisms in obsessional patients. Unpublished Ph.D. thesis, Institute of Psychiatry, University of London.

Lipper, S. and Feigenbaum, W. M., 1976. Obsessive–compulsive neurosis after viewing the fetus during therapeutic abortion. *Amer. J. Psychother.,* **30,** 666–674.

Lo, W. H., 1967. A follow-up study of obsessional neurotics in Hong Kong Chinese. *Brit. J. Psychiat.,* **113,** 823–832.

Logan, F. A., 1973. Self-control as habit, drive and incentive. *J. Abnorm. Psychol.,* **81,** 127–136.

Lomont, J. F., 1965. Reciprocal inhibition or extinction? *Beh. Res. and Ther.,* 3, 209–219.

Lorr, M. and Rubinstein, E. A., 1956. Personality patterns of neurotic adults in psychotherapy., *J. Consult. Psychol.,* **20,** 257–263.

Lorr, M., Rubinstein, E. A. and Jenkins, R. L., 1953. A factor analysis of personality ratings of out-patients in psychotherapy. *J. Abnorm. Soc. psychol.,* **48,** 511–514.

McFall, R. M. and Hammen, C. L., 1971. Motivation, structure and self-monitoring. Role of non-specific factors in smoking reduction. *J. Cons. Clin. Psychol.,* **37,** 80–86.

McGuire, R. J. and Vallance, M., 1964. Aversion therapy by electric shock—a simple technique. *Brit. Med. J.,* **1,** 151–152.

McReynolds, W. T. and Church, A., 1973. Self-control, study skills development and counseling approaches to the improvement of study behaviour. *Beh. Res. and Ther.,* 11, 233–235.

Mahoney, M., 1971. The self-management of covert behaviour: A case study. *Beh. Ther.,* **2,** 575–578.

Maier, N. R. F., 1949. Frustration: The study of behaviour without a goal. New York, McGraw-Hill.

Marks, I. M., 1977. Comparison of clomipramine and exposure in the treatment of ritualizing patients. Paper presented at British Association of Behavioural Psychotherapy Conference at Keele University.

Marks, I. M., 1975. Behavioural treatments of phobic and obsessive–compulsive disorders: A critical appraisal. In Herson, M., Eisler, R. M., and Miller, P. M. *Progress in Behaviour Modification,* Vol. 1. London, Academic Press, pp. 65–158.

Marks, I. M., Boulougouris, J. and Marset, P., 1971. Flooding versus desensitization in phobic disorders. *Brit. J. Psychiat.,* **119,** 353–375.

Marks, I. M., Connolly, J. and Hallam, R. S., 1973. The psychiatric nurse as therapist. *Brit. Med. J.,* **2,** 156–160.

Marks, I. M., Crowe, M., Drewe, E., Young, J. and Dewhurst, W. G., 1969. Obsesive–compulsive neurosis in identical twins. *Brit. J. Psychait.,* **115,** 991–998.

Marks, I. M., Hodgson, R. J. and Rachman, S., 1975. Treatemnt of chronic obsessive–compulsive neurosis by *in vivo* exposure: A two year follow-up and issues in treatment. *Brit. J. Psychiat.,* **127,** 349–364.

Marshall, W. K. and Micev, V., 1975. The role of intravenous clomipramine in the treatment of obsessional and phobic disorders. *Scott. Med. J.*, **20**, Supplement 1, 51–56.

Marston, A. R. and Cohen, N. J., 1966. The relationship of negative self-reinforcement to frustration and intropunitiveness. *J. Gen. Psychol.*, **74**, 237–243.

Marzillier, J. S., Lambert, C. and Kellet, J., 1976. A controlled evaluation of systematic desensitization and social skills training for socially inadequate psychiatric, patients. *Beh. Res. and Ther.*, **14**, 225–238.

Masters, W. H., and Johnson, V. E., 1970. *Human Sexual Inadequacy*. London, Churchill.

Mather, M. D., 1970. The treatment of an obsessive–compulsive patient by discrimination learning and reinforcement of decision making. *Beh. Res. and Ther.*, **8**, 315–318.

Mathews, A. M. and Gelder, M. G., 1969. Psychophysiological investigations of brief relaxation training. *J. Psychosom. Res.*, **13**, 1–18.

Mausner, B. and Platt, E. S., 1971. *Smoking: A Behavioural Analysis*. Oxford, Pergamon Press.

Mayer-Gross, W., Slater, E. and Roth, M., 1955. *Clinical Psychiatry* (2nd ed., 1960) London, Cassell.

Meichenbaum, D. H., Gilmore, J. B. and Fedoravicius, A. L. 1971. Group insight versus group desensitization in treating speech anxiety. *J. Cons. Clin. Psychol.*, **36**, 410–421.

Melamed, B. G. and Siegel, L. J., 1975. Self-directed *in vivo* treatment of an obsessive–compulsive checking ritual. *J. Beh. Ther. and Exp. Psychiat.*, **6**, 31–36.

Metzner, R., 1963. Some experimental analogues of obsession. *Beh. Res. and Ther.*, **1**, 231–236.

Meyer, V., 1966. Modification of expectations in cases with obsessional rituals. *Beh. Res. and Ther.*, **4**, 273–280.

Meyer, V. and Levy, R., 1970. Behavioural treatment of a homosexual with compulsive rituals. *Brit. J. Med. Psychol.*, **43**, 63–68.

Meyer, V. and Levy, R., 1973. Modification of behaviour in obsessive–compulsive disorders. In Adams, H. E. and Unikel, P. (Eds.). *Issues and Trends in Behaviour Therapy*. Springfield, Illinois, Thomas, pp. 77–139.

Meyer, V., Levy, R. and Schnurer, A., 1974. The behavioural treatment of obsessive–compulsive disorders. In Beech, H. R. (Ed.). *Obsessional States*. London, Methuen, pp. 233–258.

Meyer, V., Robertson, J. and Tatlow, A. 1975. Home treatment of an obsessive–compulsive disorder by response prevention. *J. Beh. Ther. and Exp. Psychiat.*, **6**, 37–39.

Mills, H. L., Agras, S., Barlow, D. H. and Mills, J. R., 1973. Compulsive rituals treated by response prevention. An experimental analysis. *Arch. Gen. Psychiat.*, **28**, 524–529.

Milner, A. D., Walker, V. and Beech, H. R., 1971. Decision processes and obsessional behaviour. *Brit. J. Soc. Clin. Psychol.*, **10**, 88–89.

Morel, M., 1866. Du delire emotif. *Arch. Gen. Med.*, **7**, 385, 530, 700.

Mowrer, O. H., 1951. Two-factor learning theory; summary and comment. *Psychol. Rev.*, **58**, 350–354.

Muller, C., 1953. Vorlaufige Mitteilung zur langen Katamnese der Swangskranken. *Nervenarzt.*, **24**, 112–115.

Murray, M. E., 1976. A dynamic synthesis of analytic and behavioural approaches to symptoms. *Amer. J. Psychother.*, **30**, 561–569.

O'Connor, J. P., 1953. A statistical test of psychoneurotic syndromes. *J. Abnorm. Soc. Psychol.*, **48**, 581–584.

Page, H. A., 1955. The facilitation of experimental extinction by response prevention as a function of the acquisition of a new response. *J. Comp. Physiol. Psychol.*, **48**, 14–16.

Perigault, J. A., 1974. An experimental investigation of obsessional behaviour with special reference to the Beech–Perigault Theory Unpublished Ph.D. thesis, Institute of Psychiatry, University of London.

Philpott, R., 1975. Recent advances in the behavioural measurement of obsessional illness. Difficulties common to these and other measures. *Scott. Med. J.*, **20**, Supplement 1, 35–42.

Pollitt, J., 1957. Natural history of obsessional states. *Brit. Med. J.*, **1**, 194–198.

Pollitt, J., 1960. Natural history studies in mental illness. *J. Ment. Sci.*, **106**, 93–112.

Pollitt, J., 1969. Obsessional states. *Brit. J. Hosp. Med.*, **2**, 1146–1150.

Powell, J. and Azrin, N. H., 1968. The effects of shock as a punisher for cigarette smoking. *J. App. Behav. Anal.*, **6**, 63–71.

Premack, D., 1970. Mechanisms of self control. In Hunt, W. (Ed.). *Learning Mechanisms in Smoking*. Chicago, Aldine Press, pp. 107–123.

Rabavilas, A. D. and Boulougouris, J. C., 1974. Physiological accompaniments of ruminations, flooding and thought stopping in obsessional patients. *Beh. Res. and Ther.*, **12**, 239–243.

Rabavilas, A. D., Boulougouris, J. C. and Stefanis, 1976. Duration of flooding sessions in the treatment of obsessive compulsive patients. *Beh. Res. and Ther.*, **14**, 349–357.

Rachman, S., 1969. Treatment by prolonged exposure to high intensity stimulation. *Beh. Res. and Ther.*, **7**, 295–302.

Rachman, S., 1971a. Obsessional ruminations. *Beh. Res. and Ther.*, **9**, 229–235.

Rachman, S., 1971b. *The Effects of Psychotherapy*. Oxford, Pergamon Press.

Rachman, S., 1973. Some similarities and differences between obsessional ruminations and morbid preoccupations. *Can. Psychiat. Ass. J.*, **18**, 71–74.

Rachman, S., 1974. Primary obsessional slowness. *Beh. Res. and Ther.*, **12**, 9–18.

Rachman, S., 1976. The modification of obsessions, a new formulation. *Beh. Res. and Ther.*, **14**, 437–443.

Rachman, S., De Silva, P. and Röper, G., 1976. The spontaneous decay of compulsive urges. *Beh. Res. and Ther.*, **14**, 445–453.

Rachman, S. and Hodgson, R. J., 1974. Synchrony and desynchrony in fear and avoidance. *Beh. Res. and Ther.*, **12**, 311–318.

Rachman, S., Hodgson, R. J. and Marks, I. M. , 1971. Treatment of chronic obsessive–compulsive neurosis. *Beh. Res. and Ther.*, **9**, 237–247.

Rachman, S., Hodgson, R. J. and Marzillier, J., 1970. Treatment of an obsessional–compulsive disorder by modelling. *Beh. Res. and Ther.*, **8**, 385–392.

Rachman, S., Marks, I. M. and Hodgson, R. J. 1973. The treament of obsessive–compulsive neurotics by modelling and flooding *in vivo*. *Beh. Res. and Ther.*, **11**, 463–471.

Rack, P. H., 1973. Clomipramine (Anafranil) in the treatment of obsessional states with specific reference to the Leyton Obsessional Inventory. *J. Int. Med. Res.*, **1**, 397–402.

Rainey, C. A., 1972. An obsessive–compulsive neurosis treated by flooding *in vivo*. *J. Beh. Ther. & Exp. Psychiat.*, **3**, 117–123.

Rescorla, R. H. and Solomon, R. L., 1967. Two-process learning theory: Relationships between Pavlovian conditioning and instrumental learning. *Psychol. Rev.*, **74**, 151–182.

Röper, G., 1977. The role of the patient in modelling/flooding. In Boulougouris, J. C. and Rabavilas, A. D. *The Treatment of Phobic and Obsessional States*. Oxford, Pergamon Press. pp. 65–71.

Röper, G. and Rachman, S., 1975. Obsessional–compulsive checking, replication and development. *Beh. Res. and Ther.*, **14**, 25–32.

Röper, G., Rachman, S. and Hodgson, R. J., 1973. An experiment in obsessional checking. *Beh. Res. and Ther.*, **11**, 271–277.

Röper, G., Rachman, S. and Marks, I. M., 1975. Passive and participant modelling in exposure treatment of obsessive compulsive neurotics. *Beh. Res. and Ther.*, **13**, 271–279.

Rubin, R. D., Merbaum, M. and Fried, R., 1971. Self-imposed punishment and de-sensitization. In Rubin, R. D., Fensterheim, H., Lazarus, A. and Franks, C. (Eds.).

Advances in Behaviour Therapy Academic Press, pp. 85–91.

Rüdin, E., 1953. Ein Beitrag zur Frage der Zwangskrank heit insobesondere ihrere hereditären Beziehungen. *Arch. Psychiat. Nervenk.*, **191**, 14–54.

Sakai, T., 1967. Clinico-genetic study on obsessive compulsive neurosis. *Bull. Osaka Med. Sch.*, Supplement XII, 323–331.

Sandler, J. and Hazari, A., 1960. The obsessional: On the psychological classification of obsessional character traits and symptoms. *Brit. J. Med. Psychol.*, **23**, 113–122.

Sargent, W. and Slater, E., 1950. Discussion on the treatment of obsessional nei *Proc. Roy. Soc. Med.*, **43**, 1007–1010.

Sherrington, C. S., 1947. *The Integrative Action of the Central Nervous System.* London, Cambridge University Press.

Siegel, S., 1956. Non-parametric Statistics for the Behavioral Sciences. New York, McGraw-Hill.

Skinner, B. F., 1953. Science and Human Behaviour. New York, Macmillan.

Slade, P. D., 1972. The effects of systematic desensitization on auditory hallucinations. *Beh. Res. and Ther.*, **10**, 85–91.

Slade, P. D., 1974. Psychometric studies of obsessional illness and obsessional personality. In Beech, H. R. (Ed.). *Obsessional States.* London, Methuen, pp. 95–112.

Slater, E. and Roth, M., 1969. In Mayer-Gross, W., Slater, E. and Roth, M. *Clinical Psychiatry*, 3rd ed. London: Baillière, Tindall and Cassell.

Solomon, R. L., Turner, L. H. and Lessec, M. S., 1968. Some effects of delay of punishment on resistance to temptation in dogs. *J. Pers. Soc. Psychol.*, **8**, 233–238.

Solyom, L., Garza-Perez, J., Lewidge, B. and Solyom, C., 1972. Paradoxical intention in the treatment of obsessive thoughts: A pilot study. *Comprehensive Psychiatry,* **13**, 291–297.

Solyom, L., Zamanzadeh, P., Lewidge, B., Kenny, F., 1971. Aversion relief treatment of obsessive neurosis. In Rubin, P., Fensterheim, M., Lazarus, A. and Franks, C. *Advances in Behaviour Therapy.* London, Academic Press, pp. 93–109.

Spielberger, C. D., Gorsuch, R. L., Lushene, R. E., 1970. *The 'State-Trait' Anxiety Inventory* Palo Alto, Consulting Psychologists Press.

Stampfl, T. G., 1967. Implosive therapy: the theory, the subhuman analogue, the strategy and the technique: Part 1. The theory. In Armitage, S. G. (Ed.). *Behavior Modification Techniques in the Treatment of Emotional Disorders.* Battle Creek, Mich., V A Publication, pp. 22–37.

Stern, R. S., 1970. Treatment of a case of obsessional neurosis using thoughts stopping technique. *Brit. J. Psychiat.*, **117**, 441–442.

Stern, R. S., Lipsedge, M. S., and Marks, I. M., 1973. Obsessive ruminations: a controlled trial of a thought stopping technique. *Beh. Res. and Ther.*, **7**, 659–662.

Stern, R. S. and Marks, I. M., 1973. Contract therapy in obsessive–compulsive neurosis with marital discord. *Brit. J. Psychiat.*, **123**, 681–684.

Sternberg, M., 1974. Physical treatments in obsessional disorders. In Beech, H.R. (Ed.). *Obsessional States.*, London, Methuen, pp. 291–306.

Tanner, B. A., 1971. Case report: use of relaxation and systematic desensitization to control multiple compulsive behaviour. *J. Beh. Ther. and Exp. Psychiat.*, **2**, 267–272.

Tayler, J. G. 1950. Reaction latency as a function of reaction potential and behaviour oscillation. *Psychol. Rev.*, **57**, 375–384.

Teasdale, J. D., 1974. Learning models of obsessional–compulsive disorder. In Beech, H. R. (Ed.). *Obsessional States.* London, Methuen, pp. 197–232.

Vaughan, M., 1975. An evaluation of self-control. Unpublished Ph.D. thesis, Institute of Psychiatry, University of London.

Vaughan, M., 1976. The relationships between obsessional personality, obsessions in depression and symptoms of depression. *Brit. J. Psychiat.*, **129**, 36–39.

Vila, J. and Beech, H. R., 1977. Vulnerability and conditioning in relation to the human menstrual cycle. *Brit. J. Soc. Clin. Psychol.*, **16**, 69–75.

Vila, J. and Beech, H. R., 1978. Vulnerability and defensive reactions in relation to the human menstrual cycle. *Brit. J. Soc. Clin. Psychol.*, 7, 93–100.

Walker, V. J., 1967. An investigation of ritualistic behaviour in obsessional patients. Unpublished Ph.D. thesis, Institute of Psychiatry, University of London.

Walker, V. J. and Beech, H. R., 1969. Mood state and the ritualistic behaviour of obsessional patients. *Brit. J. Psychiat.*, 115, 1261–1268.

Walton, D., 1960. The relevance of learning theory to the treatment of an obsessive–compulsive state. In Eysenck, H. J. (Ed.). *Behaviour Therapy and the Neuroses*. Oxford, Pergamon Press, pp. 153–164.

Walton, D. and Mather, M. D., 1963. Application of learning principles to the treatment of obsession–compulsive states in the acute and chronic phase of the illness. *Beh. Res. and Ther.*, 1, 163–175.

Walton, D. and Mather, M. D., 1967. In Eysenck, H. J. *Experiments in Behaviour Therapy*, Oxford, Pergamon Press, pp. 117–151.

Watson, J. P. and Marks, I. M., 1971. Relevant and irrelevant fear in flooding–a crossover study of phobic patients. *Beh. Ther.*, 2, 275–293.

Watts, F., 1971. Desensitization as an habituation phenomenon. 1 Stimulus intensity as a determinant of the effects of stimulus lengths. *Beh. Res. and Ther.*, 9, 209–217.

Waxman, D., 1975. An investigation into the use of Anafranil in phobic and obsessional disorders. *Scott. Med. J.*, 20, Supplement 1, 63–68.

Westphal, C., 1878. Zwangsvorstellungen. *Arch. Psychiat. Nervenk.*, 8, 734–750.

Whitman, T. L., 1972. Aversive control of smoking behaviour in a group context. *Beh. Res. and Ther.*, 10, 97–104.

Wisocki, P. A., 1970. Treatment of obsessive–compulsive behaviour by covert sensitization and covert reinforcement. A case report. *J. Beh. Ther. and Exp. Psychiat.*, 1, 233–239.

Wolpe, J., 1958. *Psychotherapy by Reciprocal Inhibition*. California, Stanford University Press.

Wolpe, J., 1964. Behaviour therapy in complex neurotic states. *Brit. J. Psychiat.*, 110, 28–34.

Wolpe, J., 1969. *The Practice of Behaviour Therapy*. New York, Pergamon Press.

Wolpe, J., 1973. *The Practice of Behaviour Therapy*, New York, 2nd Ed., Pergamon Press.

Wolpe, J., 1976. Malcontents—multimodel eclecticism, cognitive exclusivism and exposure empiricism. *J. Beh. Ther. and Exp. Psychiat.*, 7, 109–113.

Worsley, J. L., 1968. Behaviour therapy and obsessionality: theoretical considerations. In Freeman, H. (Ed.). *Progress in Behaviour Therapy—Proceedings of Symposium held in Postgraduate Medical Institute, University of Salford 1967*. Bristol, John Wright.

Worsley, J. L., 1970. The causation and treatment of obsessionality. In Burns, L. E. and Worsley, J. L. (Eds.). *Behaviour Therapy in the 1970s—Proceedings of a Symposium*. Bristol, John Wright, pp. 59–74.

Yamagami, T., 1971. The treatment of an obsession by thought-stopping. *J. Beh. Ther. and Exp. Psychiat.*, 2, 133–135.

Yates, A. J. 1958. The application of learning theory to the treatment of tics. *J. Abnorm. Soc. Psychol.*, 56, 158–182.

Author Index

Subject Index

188